Resource Management in Cloud Computing

Sakshi Patni • Deepika Saxena •
Ashutosh Kumar Singh

Resource Management in Cloud Computing

Concepts and Implementation

Sakshi Patni
Gachon University
Seongnam-si, Korea (Republic of)

Deepika Saxena
University of Aizu
Aizuwakamatsu, Japan

Ashutosh Kumar Singh
Indian Institute of Information Technology
Bhopal, Madhya Pradesh, India

ISBN 978-3-031-83052-5   ISBN 978-3-031-83053-2 (eBook)
https://doi.org/10.1007/978-3-031-83053-2

© The Editor(s) (if applicable) and The Author(s), under exclusive license to Springer Nature Switzerland AG 2025

This work is subject to copyright. All rights are solely and exclusively licensed by the Publisher, whether the whole or part of the material is concerned, specifically the rights of translation, reprinting, reuse of illustrations, recitation, broadcasting, reproduction on microfilms or in any other physical way, and transmission or information storage and retrieval, electronic adaptation, computer software, or by similar or dissimilar methodology now known or hereafter developed.
The use of general descriptive names, registered names, trademarks, service marks, etc. in this publication does not imply, even in the absence of a specific statement, that such names are exempt from the relevant protective laws and regulations and therefore free for general use.
The publisher, the authors and the editors are safe to assume that the advice and information in this book are believed to be true and accurate at the date of publication. Neither the publisher nor the authors or the editors give a warranty, expressed or implied, with respect to the material contained herein or for any errors or omissions that may have been made. The publisher remains neutral with regard to jurisdictional claims in published maps and institutional affiliations.

This Springer imprint is published by the registered company Springer Nature Switzerland AG
The registered company address is: Gewerbestrasse 11, 6330 Cham, Switzerland

If disposing of this product, please recycle the paper.

Dedicated to,

Nipun, Manik, and Parents
$\qquad\qquad\qquad\qquad\sim$ *Sakshi Patni*

Kuldeep, Ansh, Darsh, and Parents
$\qquad\qquad\qquad\qquad\sim$ *Deepika Saxena*

Anushka, Aakash, Akankshya, and Parents
$\qquad\qquad\qquad\qquad\sim$ *Ashutosh Kumar Singh*

Preface

Cloud computing has transformed the information technology environment by enabling unparalleled scale, flexibility, and cost-effectiveness. However, as cloud infrastructures become more sophisticated, successfully managing resources while maintaining security and energy efficiency has become more difficult. This book investigates creative methods for resolving these important problems in cloud computing settings. The fast popularity of cloud services has resulted in increased data center energy usage and security issues, especially in multi-tenant environments. Cloud service providers must optimize resource utilization and reduce energy consumption while adhering to tight security protocols and supporting a wide range of customer needs. Traditional techniques often fall short of reconciling these opposing goals in dynamic cloud systems. This book introduces fresh ideas and approaches for addressing the numerous difficulties of resource management, job scheduling, and security in cloud computing. The offered methods attempt to improve the efficiency, dependability, and security of cloud infrastructure by combining sophisticated algorithms, machine learning approaches, and unique architectural designs. The frameworks mentioned manage resource utilization, power consumption, and security when deploying workloads to servers. We present innovative models for optimizing virtual machine placements, enhancing traffic scalability, and improving energy efficiency in cloud environments. Additionally, we introduce frameworks designed to bolster security in multi-tenant scenarios while maintaining operational efficiency, addressing key challenges in modern cloud computing. In addition, we investigate sophisticated task scheduling algorithms and dynamic resource allocation approaches that respond to changing workloads and user needs. The book looks into heuristic models for optimum host selection as well as data security and leakage detection models, which are critical for ensuring data integrity in cloud settings. Throughout the book, we provide detailed mathematical models, algorithms, and experimental findings to illustrate the efficiency of the suggested methods. Real-world applications and case studies demonstrate how these frameworks can be used to address actual difficulties in cloud computing. This book is intended for academics, practitioners, and graduate students studying cloud computing, distributed systems, and cybersecurity. It provides useful information for cloud service providers, IT experts, and organizations trying to improve their cloud infrastructure and security procedures. The authors have included exercises at the end of each chapter to help reinforce important concepts and promote practical application of the ideas discussed. These exercises range from theoretical challenges to hands-on projects, allowing readers to gain a deeper grasp of cloud resource management and security, while also developing practical abilities.

The book is organized as follows Chapter 1 introduces fundamental concepts of cloud computing, including service models, deployment strategies, and the challenges of resource management in cloud environments. Chapter 2 explores various task scheduling algorithms, from traditional methods like First-Come-First-Serve to advanced heuristic and meta-heuristic approaches, discussing their impacts on system performance and resource utilization. Chapter 3 delves into static and dynamic resource allocation strategies, examining techniques for optimizing resource distribution among tasks and users while considering quality of service requirements. Chapter 4 presents adaptive resource allocation methods, including the Hierarchical Load balancer (HLB) and Application-aware Hierarchical Load Balancer (AHLB), demonstrating their effectiveness in improving resource utilization and system performance. Chapter 5 addresses security challenges in cloud environments, introducing models like the Robust Tenant Identification Framework (RTIF) for enhancing security in multi-tenant scenarios. Chapter 6 explores advanced heuristic models for selecting optimal hosts in cloud environments, presenting approaches like the Multi-Objective Virtual Machine Optimizer (MOVMO). Chapter 7 introduces innovative traffic management schemes such as the Adaptive Multi-Tier Traffic Distributor (AMultiTD) and Secure Resource Distribution Framework (SRDF), addressing both security and energy efficiency in cloud networks. Chapter 8 focuses on data protection in cloud environments, presenting models for secure secret sharing and data leakage detection. Finally, Chapter 9 summarizes the work discussed in the book.

Seongnam-si, Korea (Republic of)	Sakshi Patni
Aizuwakamatsu, Japan	Deepika Saxena
Bhopal, Madhya Pradesh, India	Ashutosh Kumar Singh
September 2024	

Acknowledgments

From the Authors

We are grateful to the editorial staff at Springer Nature for their professionalism, patience, and important advice throughout the publishing process. Their experience was critical in bringing this work to its final form. We are thankful to our universities for providing the resources and atmosphere necessary for our study. We sincerely appreciate our colleagues for their collaborative attitude and excellent efforts. The authors also thank the technical reviewers for painstakingly reviewing the text and providing important suggestions for improvement. Finally, we express our heartfelt gratitude to our friends and family for their continuous support, understanding, and encouragement. Your faith in us has been a constant source of inspiration and strength during this journey. We express our heartfelt gratitude to everyone who has contributed to this effort, either directly or indirectly.

Seongnam-si, Korea (Republic of)	Sakshi Patni
Aizuwakamatsu, Japan	Deepika Saxena
Bhopal, Madhya Pradesh, India	Ashutosh Kumar Singh
September 2024	

From Sakshi Patni

Above all, I want to thank God from the bottom of my heart for leading me on this path. I owe my parents a great deal for their steadfast encouragement and support throughout my life. My achievement has been based on their love and sacrifices. I am so grateful to my in-laws for their support and understanding, which have been so invaluable to me. My sincere gratitude is extended to my husband, Nipun Patni, for his unwavering support, tolerance, and affection. Throughout this journey, my strength has been your support. Thank you for being my delight and inspiration, Manik, our son. With particular thanks to the Ministry of Electronics and Information Technology (MeitY), Government of India, I was able to complete my study under the Visvesvaraya PhD Scheme for Electronics & IT. My academic goals have been greatly aided by this help. All of the instructors from high school and college who have influenced my academic career deserve my sincere thanks. My development as a scholar has been greatly aided by your commitment and knowledge. I wish to express sincerest thanks to my Ph.D. supervisor, Prof. Ashutosh Kumar Singh, for his invaluable guidance, sage advice, constant motivation, and continuous support. Your mentorship has been pivotal in shaping my research and this book. I would especially want to express my gratitude to Prof. Joohyung Lee, my postdoctoral mentor, for his invaluable advice on research. Your knowledge and assistance has greatly improved my academic experience. I would want to express my sincere gratitude to everyone who has helped with this effort, whether directly or indirectly. This book is a tribute to the wisdom and combined support of everyone listed above.

Seongnam-si, Korea (Republic of)   Sakshi Patni
September 2024

From Deepika Saxena

First and foremost, I express my deepest gratitude to the Almighty for his endless blessings, guidance, and strength that have been the foundation of my journey. I extend my heartfelt thanks to my loving parents, whose unwavering support and encouragement have always inspired me to pursue my dreams. I am equally grateful to my siblings, Shilpi, Disha, and Ankit, for their constant love and belief in me. To my dearest husband, Kuldeep, and my wonderful sons, Ansh and Darsh, your love, patience, and understanding have been my greatest source of strength and motivation. I am also deeply thankful to my parents-in-law for their support and kindness throughout this journey. I owe a special debt of gratitude to my primary and secondary school teachers, and to my university teachers, for shaping the foundation of my education. I am sincerely thankful to my Ph.D. supervisor, Prof. Ashutosh Kumar Singh, for his invaluable mentorship, and to my Post-Doctoral supervisor, Prof. Volker Lindenstruth, for his guidance and support. I also want to acknowledge all my friends and colleagues, whose encouragement and collaboration have played a pivotal role in strengthening my capabilities and keeping my spirit high. To each and every one of you, I am eternally grateful.

Aizuwakamatsu, Japan   Deepika Saxena
September 2024

Declarations

Competing Interests

The authors declare the following competing interests:

- Sakshi Patni, the first author, received a scholarship under the Ministry of Electronics and Information Technology (MeitY), Government of India, to complete her study under the Visvesvaraya PhD Scheme for Electronics & IT. This support has greatly aided her academic goals and contributed to the research presented in this book.
- The remaining authors, Deepika Saxena and Ashutosh Kumar Singh, declare that they have no competing financial interests or personal relationships that could have appeared to influence the work reported in this book.

Ethics Approval

The authors declare that the research and content presented in this book did not involve any animal or human subjects. As such, no specific ethical approval was required for this work. The book is based on theoretical research, analysis of publicly available data, and the author's expertise in the field. All sources used have been properly cited and credited throughout the book. The authors affirm that they have adhered to all applicable ethical guidelines for academic publishing, including but not limited to:

- Maintaining academic integrity and avoiding plagiarism
- Providing accurate and truthful representation of research findings
- Ensuring fair representation of previous work in the field

Seongnam-si, Korea (Republic of)   Sakshi Patni
Aizuwakamatsu, Japan   Deepika Saxena
Bhopal, Madhya Pradesh, India   Ashutosh Kumar Singh
September 2024

Contents

1	**Introduction**	1
1.1	Background	1
1.2	Cloud Computing	3
1.3	Features of Cloud Computing	6
1.4	Deployment Models	7
1.5	Service Models	8
1.6	Challenges of Cloud Computing	9
1.7	Applications of Cloud Computing	12
1.8	Resource Management	13
	1.8.1 Resource Utilization	15
	1.8.2 Load Balancing	16
	1.8.3 Resource Scheduling Techniques	19
1.9	Evaluation Metrics	20
	1.9.1 Makespan	20
	1.9.2 Resource Utilization	21
	1.9.3 Energy Efficiency	21
	1.9.4 Secure VM Allocation	21
	1.9.5 Failure Number of Processing Events	22
	1.9.6 Throughput Performance	22
	1.9.7 SLA Violation Rate	22
1.10	Summary	23
1.11	Exercises	23
	References	25
2	**Task Scheduling**	27
2.1	Introduction	27
	2.1.1 Task Scheduling System	28
	2.1.2 Fundamental Considerations	29
2.2	Task Scheduling Algorithms	31
	2.2.1 Static Scheduling Algorithms	32
	2.2.2 Dynamic Scheduling Algorithms	39

	2.3	Heuristics and Metaheuristics in Cloud Task Scheduling	41
		2.3.1 Heuristics	41
		2.3.2 Metaheuristics	42
		2.3.3 Comparison and Application	43
		2.3.4 Adaptive Scheduling Algorithm	43
	2.4	Summary	45
	2.5	Exercises	45
	References		46
3	**Resource Allocation Methods**		**49**
	3.1	Introduction	49
	3.2	Resource Allocation Methods	52
		3.2.1 Static Allocation	53
		3.2.2 Dynamic Allocation	54
	3.3	Allocation Policies or Techniques	59
		3.3.1 Priority-based Allocation	60
		3.3.2 Agent-oriented Allocation	60
		3.3.3 SLA-based Allocation	61
		3.3.4 Energy-usage-based Allocation	62
		3.3.5 Action-based Allocation	62
		3.3.6 Cost-based Allocation	63
	3.4	Summary	64
	3.5	Exercises	64
	References		66
4	**Dynamic Resource Allocation Models**		**67**
	4.1	Introduction	67
	4.2	Hierarchical Load Balancer for Cloud Data Centers	68
		4.2.1 System Model	69
		4.2.2 Resource Constraints	70
		4.2.3 Load Balancing Performance	71
		4.2.4 Resource Allocation	71
		4.2.5 Algorithm	73
	4.3	Performance Evaluation	74
	4.4	Application-aware Hierarchical Load Balancing	76
		4.4.1 Design of AHLB	77
		4.4.2 Optimal Resource Allocation in AHLB	79
	4.5	Results and Analysis	81
	4.6	Summary	83
	4.7	Exercises	84
	References		86
5	**Secure Cloud Resource Management**		**89**
	5.1	Introduction	89
	5.2	Cloud Security Fundamentals	90
		5.2.1 Cloud Security Types	90

		5.2.2 Fundamental Equations and Concepts of Cloud Security	92
		5.2.3 Cloud Security Difficulties	93
	5.3	Cloud Security Essentials: Multi-tenancy Attacks and Safe Load Balancing	93
		5.3.1 Multi-tenancy Attacks	93
		5.3.2 Secure Load Balancing	95
	5.4	Robust Tenant Identification Framework for Shared Cloud Environments	97
		5.4.1 Security Assumptions for Cloud Load Balancing	98
		5.4.2 RTIF	99
		5.4.3 Performance Evaluation and Analysis	104
	5.5	Summary	108
	5.6	Exercises	108
	References		109

6 Heuristic Models for Optimal Host Selection ... 111
6.1	Introduction	111
6.2	Adaptive Resource Allocation with Predictive Modeling	113
	6.2.1 Problem Formulation	114
	6.2.2 Architecture of ARAPM	116
	6.2.3 Performance Evaluation	119
6.3	Multi-Objective Virtual Machine Optimizer	122
	6.3.1 Advanced Maximum Likelihood Estimation in MOVMO	123
	6.3.2 Results and Analysis for MOVMO	127
6.4	Summary	131
6.5	Exercises	132
References		133

7 Secure and Energy-Efficient Cloud Traffic Management Schemes ... 135
7.1	Introduction	135
7.2	Secure Resource Distribution for Mitigating Colocation Risks	136
	7.2.1 Probabilistic Model	137
	7.2.2 Attacker's Approach for VM Allocation Policies	140
	7.2.3 Results and Analysis	141
7.3	Adaptive Multi-tier Traffic Distributor for Security and Energy Optimization	145
	7.3.1 AMultiTD Design	146
	7.3.2 Problem Illustration	149
	7.3.3 Experimental Setup	150
	7.3.4 Results and Analysis	152
7.4	Summary	154
7.5	Exercises	155
References		156

8 Data Security and Leakage Detection Models ... 159
- 8.1 Introduction ... 159
- 8.2 Distributed Encryption Key Management ... 160
  - 8.2.1 Mathematical Model ... 161
  - 8.2.2 Authorized Structure ... 161
  - 8.2.3 Key Management ... 162
  - 8.2.4 DEKM Components and Processes ... 164
- 8.3 DEKM: Secure Communication and Participant Evaluation ... 166
  - 8.3.1 Secure Communication in DEKM ... 166
  - 8.3.2 Integrity Verifier Analysis ... 166
  - 8.3.3 Algorithms ... 169
- 8.4 Performance Evaluation and Analysis ... 169
  - 8.4.1 DEKM Evaluation ... 170
- 8.5 Insider Threat Detection and Attribution (ITDA) ... 177
  - 8.5.1 ITDA Architecture ... 177
  - 8.5.2 Distributed Computation and Threat Analysis ... 177
  - 8.5.3 Threat Attribution ... 178
  - 8.5.4 Distributed Computation Model in ITDA ... 178
  - 8.5.5 Secure Map Reduce Computations ... 182
  - 8.5.6 Secure Computation and Threat Detection in ITDA ... 182
  - 8.5.7 ITDA Performance Evaluation ... 184
- 8.6 Summary ... 186
- 8.7 Exercises ... 187
- References ... 188

9 Conclusion and Future Trends ... 191
- 9.1 Summary ... 191
- 9.2 Applications of Cloud Computing Technologies ... 193
  - 9.2.1 Enterprise and Business ... 194
  - 9.2.2 Healthcare and Life Sciences ... 194
  - 9.2.3 Financial Services ... 194
  - 9.2.4 Education and Research ... 194
  - 9.2.5 Government and Public Services ... 194
  - 9.2.6 Media and Entertainment ... 195
  - 9.2.7 IoT and Edge Computing ... 195
  - 9.2.8 Retail and E-commerce ... 195
  - 9.2.9 Energy and Utilities ... 195
- 9.3 Future Trends ... 196
- 9.4 Exercises ... 197
- References ... 198

A Solutions of Exercises ... 201
- A.1 Chapter 1 ... 201
- A.2 Chapter 2 ... 204
- A.3 Chapter 3 ... 208

A.4	Chapter 4	209
A.5	Chapter 5	210
A.6	Chapter 6	212
A.7	Chapter 7	213
A.8	Chapter 8	213
A.9	Chapter 9	214

Glossary 217

Index 219

Acronyms

ACO	Ant Colony Optimization
AHLB	Application-Aware Hierarchical Load Balancing
AMultiTD	Adaptive Multi-tier Traffic Distributor
CPU	Central Processing Unit
CRM	Customer Relationship Management
CSP	Cloud Service Provider
DEKM	Distributed Encryption Key Management
GA	Genetic Algorithm
GDPR	General Data Protection Regulation
EHR	Electronic Health Record
ERP	Enterprise Resource Planning
FCFS	First-Come-First-Serve
HLB	Hierarchical Load Balancing
IaaS	Infrastructure as a Service
IoT	Internet of Things
IT	Information Technology
ITDA	Insider Threat Detection and Attribution
KO	Key Orchestrator
MOOC	Massive Open Online Course
PaaS	Platform as a Service
PSO	Particle Swarm Optimization
QoS	Quality of Service
RD	Random Deployment
RRS	Round-Robin Scheduling
RTIF	Robust Tenant Identification Framework
SaaS	Software as a Service
SAP	Systems, Applications & Products in Data Processing
SCA	Side Channel Attack

SJF	Shortest Job First
SLA	Service Level Agreement
SRDF	Secure Resource Distribution Framework
VM	Virtual Machine

Chapter 1
Introduction

Abstract This chapter provides a thorough overview of cloud computing, including its core ideas, service models, deployment techniques, and difficulties with resource management. It follows the development of cloud computing and looks at public, private, hybrid, and community cloud deployments in addition to the Infrastructure as a Service (IaaS), Platform as a Service (PaaS), and Software as a Service (SaaS) models. The chapter explores the main barriers to cloud adoption, such as resource optimization, cost management, and data security. Resource management receives a lot of attention, and load balancing, resource scaling, and job scheduling strategies are being explored. In addition to introducing important performance measures like makespan, resource utilization, energy efficiency, and security in VM allocation. The chapter presents a comprehensive taxonomy of resource management techniques while connecting fundamental cloud computing concepts with advanced strategies to illuminate both current capabilities and future directions.

Keywords Cloud computing · Virtualization · Service models · Deployment models · Resource management · Load balancing · Quality of service (QoS) · Performance metrics

1.1 Background

Computing in the cloud may be traced back to the development of a number of fundamental technologies and ideas that have played a significant role in shaping the current computing environment [1]. The history of cloud computing may be traced back to the following advancements in the cloud computing industry:

- **Time-sharing systems:** In the 1960s, time-sharing systems made it possible for numerous users to use mainframe computers at the same time. This was the beginning of the concept of shared computing resources.
- **Grid computing:** It is a computer system that was developed in the 1990s with the purpose of using dispersed computing capacity to tackle complicated problems. Grid computing is often used in academic and scientific environments.

- **Utility computing**: It is an idea that gained popularity in the early 2000s. It offered the provision of computer resources in the form of a metered service, comparable to the use of existing utilities such as electricity or water systems.
- **Virtualization:** The development of virtualization technology in the late 1990s and early 2000s made it possible to make more effective use of hardware resources, which is an essential component of cloud architecture.
- **Maturity of the Internet:** The widespread use of high-speed Internet made it possible to access distant computer resources in an efficient manner.
- **Web 2.0:** The advent of interactive, user-centric online applications in the middle of the 2000s highlighted the potential for providing sophisticated services via the Internet. This phenomenon is now referred to as Online 2.0.
- **Service-Oriented Architecture:** This method of designing software, which became popular in the early 2000s, was known as Service-Oriented Architecture (SOA). It placed an emphasis on the creation of services that were loosely connected and reusable, which is a philosophy that is fundamental to cloud computing.
- **Cloud Services:** Companies such as Salesforce.com (1999) and Amazon Web Services (2002) were among the pioneers in the cloud service industry. These companies demonstrated the feasibility of the business by delivering early kinds of cloud services.
- **Smart Phone Revolution:** During the latter part of the 2000s, the proliferation of smartphones led to a rise in the need for cloud-based services that could enable mobile apps and data storage.
- **Big Data and Analytics:** The proliferation of data and the need for scalable analytics capabilities in the 2010s were further factors that boosted consumer adoption of cloud computing.
- **Open-Source Technologies:** The creation of open-source cloud platforms such as OpenStack (2010) has made cloud computing more accessible to the general public.
- **Containerization:** The proliferation of container technologies such as Docker (2013) has improved the mobility and efficiency of cloud applications since their introduction.

This technical progression, in conjunction with shifting corporate requirements and IT strategy, laid the groundwork for the broad adoption of cloud computing in its current form which we are familiar with today. The cloud model was developed as a reaction to the need for computing resources that were more flexible, scalable, and cost-effective. This resulted in a fundamental shift in the way that organizations approach the delivery of services and the architecture of information technology [2].

Cloud computing has rapidly evolved from a nascent concept to a transformative force in the technology landscape, fundamentally reshaping the computing industry. This paradigm shift has captivated businesses, developers, and IT professionals alike, becoming a cornerstone of modern digital infrastructure. Far from being merely a passing trend, cloud computing has established itself as a critical driver of innovation, efficiency, and scalability across diverse sectors. Its pervasive influence extends beyond simple data storage, encompassing a wide array of services that are revolutionizing how organizations approach their IT strategies and operations. As cloud technologies continue to mature and expand, they are not just meeting current computational needs but are also paving the way for future advancements in areas such as artificial intelligence, big data analytics, and the Internet of Things. This evolution underscores cloud computing's position not just as a buzzword, but as a foundational element of the contemporary digital ecosystem.

1.2 Cloud Computing

Cloud computing has lately emerged as one of the most popular terms in the computer industry. It represents the most recent advancement in computation, in which information technology resources are provided as services. Users are offered on-demand, scalable, device-independent, and dependable services through cloud computing. Cloud computing is currently in high demand, as it enables the provision of computation and storage capacity to a wide range of end users. Clouds are distributed technology platforms that utilize advanced technological advancements to create environments that are both highly scalable and resilient. These environments can be remotely accessed by organizations in a variety of potent ways. Cloud computing is distinct from client-server, grid computing, virtualization, peer-to-peer, and its various levels. In recent years, the need for high-performance computing has driven tremendous advances in computing technologies. This has led to new computational models like cluster computing, grid computing, and most notably, cloud computing. Cloud computing provides on-demand access to computing resources over the Internet. There are three main types of cloud computing deployments: public cloud, private cloud, and hybrid cloud. Cloud providers offer different kinds of services that fall into three broad categories: SaaS, IaaS, and PaaS [3]. Cloud computing has been developed in a phased approach as a result of the evolution of technologies over time:

- **Utility computing**: In this model, the service provider owns, operates, and manages the computing and other infrastructure, and enterprise subscribers access it as needed on a rental or metered basis or through an on-demand pay-per-use invoicing model.
- **Computer Cluster:** A computer cluster is a collection of interconnected computers that operate in a closely coupled environment, giving the impression that they are a singular entity in many ways.
- **Grid computing:** It is a network of computer resources that operate in tandem, much like a supercomputer, to process and implement resource-intensive applications. It is a hardware architecture that combines a variety of computer resources to achieve a primary goal. A grid is capable of performing a variety of scientific or technical tasks that are too complex for a supercomputer and necessitate a significant number of computers to process or access a large volume of data [4].

Fig. 1.1 Cloud computing architecture

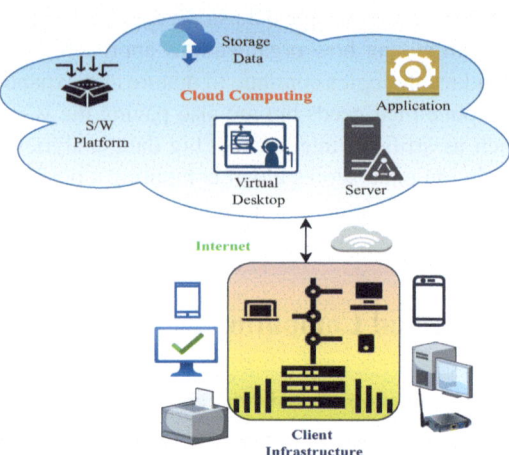

- **Cloud computing:** It is based on the sharing of computing resources, rather than the use of dedicated local servers or personal devices to manage applications. It enables the provision of dynamically scalable and frequently virtualized resources as a server over the Internet.

Figure 1.1 illustrates the core concept of cloud computing. At the center is a cloud shape labeled "Cloud Computing", connected to various components through the Internet. The cloud encompasses key elements of IT infrastructure, including storage, data, applications, software, platforms, servers, and virtual desktops. On the opposite side, a client device is shown, representing end users accessing these cloud services. This visual effectively conveys how cloud computing centralizes diverse computing resources and services, making them accessible to users over the Internet, and demonstrates the broad scope of capabilities offered by cloud platforms. Cloud computing provides IT services by enabling the use of Web-based tools and applications to access resources from the Internet, rather than requiring a direct connection to a server. Cloud-based storage enables the saving of files to a remote database over the Internet, as opposed to a proprietary hard drive or local storage device. Cloud computing is fundamentally dependent on an Internet connection, and devices that have access to the Internet can access the data and software programs necessary to run it. The term cloud computing is derived from the fact that the information being accessed is located in a virtual space. The cloud enables its users to work remotely and access its services regardless of their location. Companies that extend cloud services enable users to store files and applications on remote servers and then access all data via the Internet [5]. The Internet is transformed into the cloud, and your data, work, and applications are accessible from any device that can connect to the Internet, regardless of its location. Cloud-based services are accessible from any location in the world, provided that an Internet connection is available.

1.2 Cloud Computing

Cloud computing infrastructure is composed of services that have been proven to be highly reliable and have been tested over time. These services are constructed on servers that may contain differing degrees of virtualization technology. Commercial offerings have developed to satisfy the quality of service (QoS) needs of consumers and typically offer a service level agreement to their clients. Typically, customers do not possess the infrastructure utilized in a cloud computing environment, they may abandon capital expenditure and utilize resources as a service by paying for the resources they ingest. In the end, cloud computing is expected to provide supercomputing capabilities to the general public at a minimal capital cost. Multi-tenancy is facilitated by cloud computing, which in turn allows for the sharing of resources and costs among a large number of users. The cost of infrastructure is reduced, and efficacy is enhanced in cloud computing environments through the dynamic allocation of CPU, storage, and network bandwidth through resource centralization. The utilization of numerous redundant sites in cloud computing leads to enhanced dynamic scalabilities and increased reliability that adapt to the evolving requirements. The sustainability issues of cloud computing, which are a result of the increased energy consumption at the resource site, are resolved by implementing more energy-efficient systems and improving resource utilization. The term "Cloud" is frequently employed as a metaphor for the Internet and can be defined as a novel form of utility computing that primarily employs virtual servers that have been made accessible to third parties via the Internet. The world has been significantly diminished by the cloud, which perceives no boundaries. In spite of its global reach, the Internet adheres exclusively to establish communication channels. The cloud's most significant contribution to date may be the globalization of computing assets. Due to this, the cloud is the focus of numerous intricate geopolitical discussions [6].

The fundamental concept of cloud computing is easily comprehensible when one considers the objectives of contemporary IT environments, which may include the dynamic expansion of capacity or the addition of enhanced capabilities to their existing infrastructure. This is accomplished without the need to invest in the procurement of new infrastructure, the training of personnel, or the upgrading of software licenses. A service that can be utilized over the Internet and extend the extant capabilities of an IT company is provided by cloud computing models that incorporate a subscription-based or pay-per-use paradigm.

Cloud computing is a distributed computing paradigm that operates on a large scale and involves numerous hosts and application queries. It is a potential and foreseeable method of optimizing resource utilization and providing a variety of computing IT services. It is primarily admired in the academic and IT sectors. It is widely acknowledged as utility-based systems with the assistance of virtualization. Users only pay for the resources that they use. The traffic rate in data center networks has increased exponentially as a result of the accelerated growth of cloud computing.

1.3 Features of Cloud Computing

Because of its unique properties, cloud computing is currently one of the fastest-growing industries. Cloud service deployment has accelerated across industries due to the flexibility that cloud services give in the form of an increasing assortment of tools and technologies. This blog will teach you the fundamentals of cloud computing. Because of its unique properties, cloud computing is currently one of the fastest-growing industries. Cloud service's flexibility and increasing array of tools and technologies have accelerated their application across industries [7]. Some of the features of cloud computing are as follows:

- **Shared Resources**: Resource pooling is a key feature of the cloud computing concept. A cloud service provider may share resources with several clients via resource pooling, allowing them to benefit from a unique set of services suited to their personal needs. It is a multiclient approach that may be used to store, process, and provide bandwidth-based services. When it comes to administration, real-time resource allocation does not contradict with the customer's viewpoint.
- **Service is available on demand**: It is regarded as one of the most important components of cloud computing. As a result, the client may routinely monitor the server's uptime, capabilities, and allocated network storage. This essential characteristic distinguishes cloud computing, and a customer may also control computing capacities based on their needs.
- **Simple maintenance:** This is one of the most enticing features of the cloud. Servers are straightforward to administer, and downtime is minimal or even nonexistent at times. These cloud-powered resources are often upgraded to optimize their capabilities and potential. The upgrades are more device compatible and faster than previous versions.
- **Capability for Scalability and Rapid Elasticity:** Cloud computing's rapid scalability is a key feature and advantage. This feature of the cloud allows it to manage workloads that need a large number of servers for a short period of time in an efficient and cost-effective way. Because of cloud computing's rapid scalability, many customers have workloads that can be completed at a low cost. This is achievable because to cloud computing.
- **Cost-effective:** This cloud capacity helps to reduce the amount of money that companies spend on information technology. In the case of cloud computing, clients must pay the administration for the space they utilize. There are no additional or cover-up costs, and thus no payment is required. Administration is inexpensive, and in most cases, some space is offered for free with no limits.
- **Measured Services:** Reporting Services is only one of the many services that cloud computing provides, giving it an edge over other choices for enterprises. The measuring and reporting solution benefits both cloud providers and their customers. Furthermore, this allows both the service provider and the client to monitor and report on which services were utilized and for what reasons. It makes it easier to check invoices and ensure that resources are used efficiently.

1.4 Deployment Models

Figure 1.2 depicts the four cloud deployment models: public, private, hybrid, and community. Public cloud services are accessible to the entire public over the Internet. Amazon Elastic Compute Cloud, Google AppEngine, Windows Azure Service Platform, and other public clouds provide services on a pay-per-use or free basis. Private clouds are used for personal usage or to give services to a single organization. Eucalyptus, OpenNebula, and OpenStack are examples of private clouds that provide comparable benefits to public clouds. A hybrid cloud is a mix of two or more public and private clouds tied by service level agreements [8]:

- **Public Cloud**: Public cloud model is meant to support the accessibility to its users independent of their geographic location, association to institutions, etc. In this model, the cloud service providers are responsible to render requested services to its consumers. The key benefits of a public cloud model are reliability, scalability, cost efficiency, flexibility, and others. However, these models are less secure and limited customization is allowed.
- **Private Cloud**: As the name suggests, a cloud infrastructure that is dedicated to serve individual organizations is referred as private cloud that can be managed by the organization itself or a third party. These systems are more expensive due to the fact that a huge amount of capital investments are required to acquire and maintain them. A private cloud system offers high security and privacy along with control on its behavior. However, these systems are unable to scale effectively and the cost of ownership is high.
- **Hybrid Cloud**: Hybrid cloud is a combination of both public and private deployment models. These systems offer the benefits of both models including scalability, security, privacy, low cost, and others. A hybrid model uses public

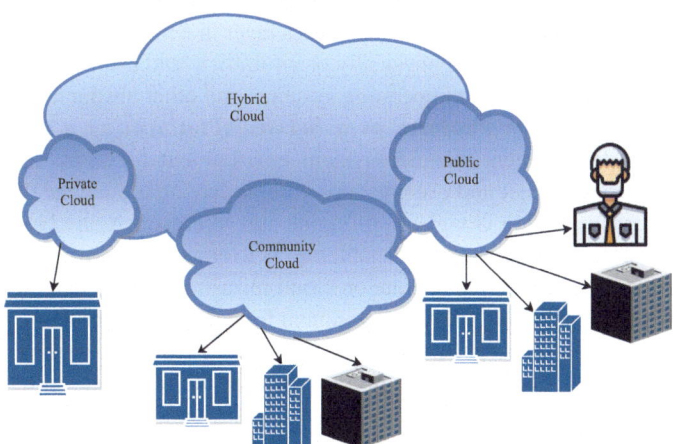

Fig. 1.2 Deployment models

cloud infrastructure to perform the noncritical tasks and private servers for security intensive tasks. These systems need a complex networking to operate effectively.
- **Community Cloud**: These are cloud infrastructures that several organizations share with similar goals or concerns (such as mission, security requirements, policy, or compliance issues). The collaborating organizations may administer them internally, or a third-party service may handle them. Community clouds offer a compromise between the financial advantages of public clouds and the security and privacy of private clouds.

1.5 Service Models

Virtualization has brought about a significant shift in the world; it helps to decrease the overhead costs associated with server maintenance and offers a free method for resource utilization that is dependent on the computing needs. System administrators and trusted authority agents are responsible for managing the cloud environment, and virtualization is a significant step toward achieving this goal. Wide-ranging network access is made possible by the technology via the use of resource pooling, on-demand self-service, and quick flexibility. High availability, dynamic scalability, controlled computing power, and ease of capital investment are all impacted by this factor [9]. This cloud stack provides services beginning with the lowest layer and progressing all the way up to the highest layer; each layer represents a different service model as shown in Fig. 1.3:

- At the foundation is **Infrastructure as a Service (IaaS)**, which provides virtualized computing resources over the Internet. IaaS allows users to manage and control operating systems, storage, and deployed applications while abstracting the underlying hardware infrastructure. Examples include Amazon Elastic Compute Cloud and Rackspace Cloud. It is a layer in which computing resources are aggregated and managed physically or virtually to end users. These users can deploy and run the software, operating systems, and other abstracted hardware.
- Building upon this is **Platform as a Service (Platform as a service)**, this provides a development and deployment environment for apps. PaaS allows developers to construct and execute apps without having to manage the underlying infrastructure, with Google App Engine and Microsoft Azure being popular examples. It is a middle layer that enables users to create API-driven apps that can be configured remotely and operate on cloud infrastructure. Google App Engine and Microsoft Azure provide an environment for developing software executions.
- At the top of the stack is **Software as a Service (SaaS)**, delivering ready-to-use applications directly to end users over the Internet. SaaS eliminates the need for local installation and maintenance of software, with applications like Google Apps and Salesforce CRM exemplifying this model. Each of these service models offers unique benefits and implementation options, allowing

1.6 Challenges of Cloud Computing

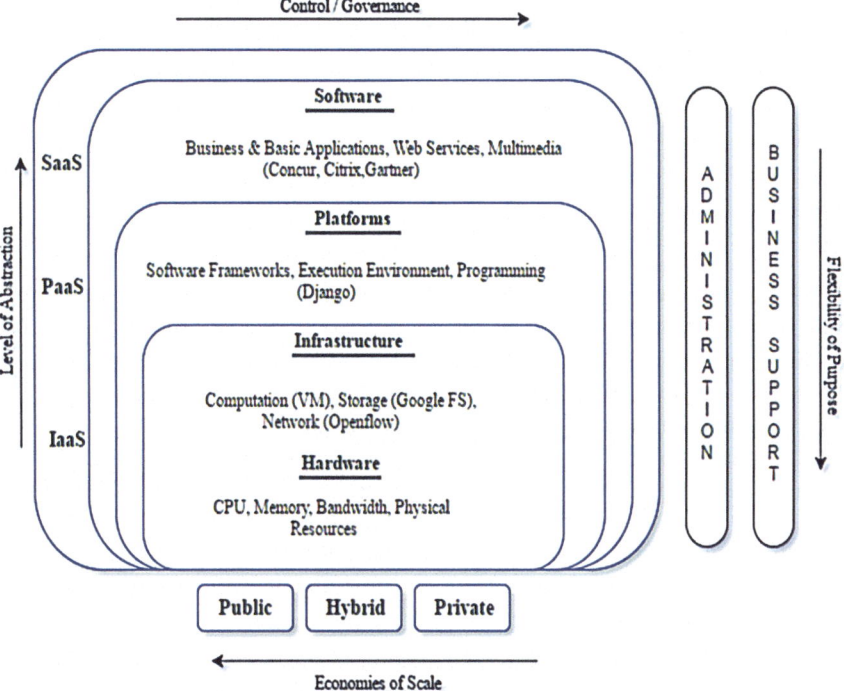

Fig. 1.3 Service model view of cloud computing

organizations to choose the level of control and management that best suits their specific requirements and capabilities in the cloud environment.

Figure 1.3 illustrates the layered architecture of cloud computing services and their relationship to control, governance, and economies of scale. It depicts the three main service models: IaaS, PaaS, and SaaS, each building upon the layer below. The diagram also shows the progression from hardware resources at the bottom to business applications at the top, indicating increasing levels of abstraction. On the sides, it highlights the administrative and business support aspects, as well as the deployment models (public, hybrid, private) at the bottom, demonstrating the comprehensive nature of cloud computing ecosystems.

1.6 Challenges of Cloud Computing

- **Privacy and Security of Data:** A variety of critical issues are involved in the realm of data security and privacy in cloud computing. Organizations encounter difficulties in safeguarding the confidentiality and integrity of information that is not under their direct control when they entrust their data to cloud providers. This encompasses safeguarding against data breaches and unauthorized access, which can have severe repercussions for both the organization and its clients. Compliance with data protection regulations, such as GDPR, introduces an additional layer of complexity, particularly when data is transferred across international borders. It is of the utmost importance to ensure privacy and prevent data leakage among users who share the same infrastructure in multi-tenant environments. Robust encryption and security protocols are necessary to ensure the security of data both during transfer and at repose.

- **Resource Provisioning:** Optimizing cloud efficacy and cost-effectiveness necessitates efficient resource provisioning. In order to prevent over-provisioning, which can result in excessive costs, or under-provisioning, which can contribute to performance issues, cloud providers and consumers must accurately predict resource requirements. The difficulty is in dynamically scaling resources up or down in response to real-time demand, particularly when encountered with unanticipated surges in usage. This necessitates the implementation of sophisticated algorithms and monitoring systems to analyze utilization patterns and make intelligent allocation decisions. Additionally, the complexity of this challenge is exacerbated by the optimization of resource allocation across a variety of duties with variable required resources.
- **Load Balancing:** In cloud environments, load balancing is indispensable for guaranteeing reliability and performance. It involves the equitable distribution of the incoming network traffic across multiple servers to prevent any single resource from becoming overloaded. The difficulty is in real-time adaptation to changing traffic patterns, maintaining tolerance to defects and ensuring high availability. In order to make the most optimal routing decisions, effective load balancing must also take into account factors such as server capacity, current traffic, and response times. Load balancing across various geographic regions and hybrid cloud environments adds an additional element of complexity as cloud applications become more intricate and distributed.
- **Secure Virtual Machine Allocation:** In multi-tenant cloud environments, the allocation of secure virtual machines is a critical challenge. The primary objective is to ensure that unauthorized access or data leakage is prevented by maintaining robust isolation between VMs. This encompasses the prevention of VM escape assaults, in which an adversary may attempt to exit a VM to obtain access to the underlying host system or other VMs. It is also essential to secure VM-to-VM communication, as vulnerabilities in this area could result in lateral movement by adversaries within the cloud infrastructure. Another substantial obstacle is the expeditious patching of virtual machines without disrupting services and the management of VM vulnerabilities. Additionally, it is imperative that cloud providers and users remain vigilant against side-channel attacks, which involve the observation of shared resource utilization patterns by one VM in an attempt to extract information from another [9].
- **Cost Control**: The dynamic and intricate character of cloud services presents distinctive challenges in the context of cost management in cloud computing.

1.6 Challenges of Cloud Computing

Organizations are required to traverse complex pricing models that can differ considerably between providers and services. While the pay-as-you-go model is adaptable, it necessitates meticulous oversight to prevent unforeseen expenses resulting from resource overuse or inefficient utilization. Balancing budget constraints with performance requirements is a perpetual challenge, particularly as business needs and duties change. Organizations must also evaluate the expenses associated with data transfer, storage, and supplementary services that fall outside the scope of fundamental compute resources. To use effective cost-cutting strategies, you need to fully understand the cloud platform and your company's specific needs. For example, you could use reserved instances for predictable workloads or spot instances for tasks that are not critical.

- **Performance Obstacles:** The shared and distributed character of resources in cloud environments makes it difficult to maintain consistent performance. Ensuring minimal latency for time-sensitive applications, particularly when dealing with geographically dispersed users and resources, is a significant challenge. Another substantial concern is the performance variability that results from multi-tenancy, as the actions of one user may potentially affect others who share the same underlying infrastructure. The optimization of application performance in virtualized environments necessitates a meticulous assessment of potential constraints and resource allocation. Users of cloud services must also consider the prospect of performance degradation during periods of high resource contention. Additional complication is introduced by the necessity of ensuring consistent performance in hybrid cloud configurations or across various cloud regions, necessitating sophisticated monitoring and management tools [10].

- **Significant Reliance on the Network:** Cloud computing's fundamental aspect and challenge is its dependence on Internet connectivity. The availability and efficacy of cloud services can be substantially influenced by network-related issues. User experience can be significantly impacted by bandwidth and latency constraints, particularly in applications that necessitate real-time interactions or substantial data transfers. It is imperative to maintain business continuity in the event of network disruptions, which frequently requires the implementation of hybrid configurations or redundant connections. Another critical concern is the security of data in transit across networks, necessitating the implementation of secure protocols and robust encryption. In order to reduce network burden and associated costs, which can be substantial for data-intensive applications, organizations must also optimize their data transfer strategies. It is becoming increasingly crucial to manage and mitigate the risks associated with network dependence as cloud services become more pervasive in business operations.

These challenges are interconnected, and addressing them often requires a holistic approach to cloud architecture, management, and security. As cloud technologies evolve, new solutions are continually being developed to mitigate these challenges, but they remain key considerations for organizations adopting or expanding their use of cloud computing [11].

1.7 Applications of Cloud Computing

Cloud computing has revolutionized numerous sectors. Here are six key areas where cloud technology has made significant impacts:

1. **Business and Enterprise Solutions**: Through scalable ERP platforms like SAP S/4HANA Cloud, CRM systems like Salesforce, and collaboration tools like Microsoft 365, cloud computing revolutionizes corporate processes. These solutions facilitate more productive teamwork, better customer interactions, and effective administration of key procedures. Because of the cloud's scalability, these solutions can expand with enterprises and provide real-time data access and smooth remote communication [12].
2. **Healthcare and Telemedicine**: Epic and other cloud-based EHR solutions enhance patient outcomes and care coordination. Telemedicine solutions, like Teladoc, provide remote patient-provider consultations and diagnosis. Because of its enormous processing capacity, cloud computing also drives cutting-edge medical imaging analysis and research, allowing AI-driven diagnoses and speeding up medication development.
3. **Financial Services and FinTech**: Cloud computing is used by the financial industry to provide new products, better consumer experiences, and more security. Online banking systems provide real-time transactions and round-the-clock assistance. Transaction management is revolutionized by cloud-based payment processors such as Square and Stripe. Cloud technology is used by FinTech businesses like Robinhood to provide services like commission-free stock trading with real-time market data.
4. **E-commerce and Retail**: With tools like Shopify, cloud computing revolutionizes e-commerce by making it possible for companies to launch online shopfronts rapidly. A large portion of the e-commerce infrastructure on the Internet is powered by Amazon Web Services, which offers scalability for traffic surges. Systems for managing inventories in the cloud, such as NetSuite, allow for real-time monitoring across sites, maximizing stock levels and enhancing the effectiveness of the supply chain.
5. **Media and Entertainment Streaming**: Cloud infrastructure is necessary for streaming services like Netflix and Spotify to distribute material to millions of users at once. Smooth streaming, tailored suggestions, and quick market development are all made possible by the cloud. High-quality gaming is becoming more accessible thanks to cloud gaming services like PlayStation becoming, which let players stream games without the need for powerful local gear.
6. **Internet of Things (IoT) and Smart Technologies**: From industrial IoT platforms like GE Predix to smart household appliances like Amazon Alexa, cloud computing is driving the Internet of Things revolution. Through data analysis, it improves industrial processes and makes advanced features in consumer gadgets possible. Cloud computing is being used by smart city programs to gather and manage garbage and traffic efficiently, demonstrating the technology's potential to create sustainable urban settings.

These applications demonstrate the versatility and transformative power of cloud computing across multiple sectors. They highlight key advantages such as scalability, cost-effectiveness, improved accessibility, enhanced data analytics capabilities, and the enablement of new business models.

1.8 Resource Management

Resource management stands as a cornerstone in cloud computing systems, playing a pivotal role in orchestrating the complex dance of computing resources. At its core, the objective of a resource management model is to efficiently handle the acquisition, allocation, and release of computing resources, ensuring that they are utilized in a manner that optimizes various critical metrics [13]. The effectiveness of resource management is gauged through multiple criteria, each representing a crucial aspect of cloud system performance and user satisfaction as shown in Fig. 1.4. These criteria include:

- **Resource Utilization**: Maximizing the use of available resources to ensure cost-effectiveness
- **Power Consumption:** Minimizing energy usage to reduce operational costs and environmental impact
- **Operational Cost:** Optimizing expenses associated with running and maintaining cloud services
- **Quality of Service (QoS)**: Ensuring that services meet or exceed predefined performance standards
- **Service Level Agreements (SLAs)**: Adhering to contractual obligations between service providers and users
- **User Response Time:** Minimizing the time taken for users to receive responses to their requests

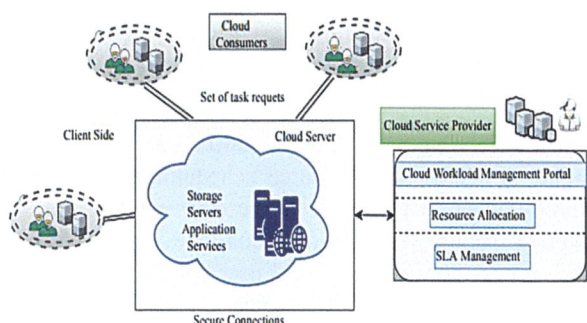

Fig. 1.4 Resource management with Cloud Computing Architecture

Cloud resource provisioning, a key component of resource management, is the process of allocating virtualized resources to users based on their demands. This process involves several steps:

- Request Acceptance: Cloud service providers receive and process resource requests from users.
- Virtual Machine Creation: Based on user requirements, an appropriate number of virtual machines are instantiated.
- Resource Allocation: These VMs are then allocated to users, matching their specific needs.
- QoS and SLA Compliance: The provisioning process ensures that allocated resources meet quality of service parameters and comply with SLA negotiations.
- Workload Matching: Resources are matched to anticipated workloads to optimize performance.

The primary goal of resource provisioning is to identify and select the most suitable resources for incoming requests. This optimization aims to provide applications with the minimum necessary resources while maintaining a desirable level of service quality. Key performance indicators in this context include minimizing execution time and maximizing throughput. From a business perspective, resource provisioning seeks to strike a balance between user satisfaction and provider profitability. It aims to map incoming requests to running virtual machines in a way that minimizes costs and response times for users while maximizing profit for the service provider [14]. To achieve effective resource management, three key approaches are typically employed:

- Load Balancing: This technique involves distributing workloads across multiple computing resources to prevent any single resource from becoming overwhelmed. It enhances overall system performance and reliability.
- Resource Scaling and Provisioning: This approach dynamically adjusts the number of allocated resources based on demand fluctuations. It includes both scaling up (adding resources) and scaling down (removing resources) as needed.
- Resource Scheduling: This involves planning and organizing the execution of tasks across available resources. Effective scheduling algorithms aim to optimize resource utilization while meeting performance requirements.

These three approaches work in concert to create a comprehensive resource management strategy. Load balancing ensures even distribution of work, resource scaling adapts to changing demands, and resource scheduling optimizes the execution order and resource allocation for tasks. In the ever-evolving landscape of cloud computing, effective resource management continues to be a critical challenge. As applications become more complex and user expectations grow, the need for sophisticated, adaptive, and intelligent resource management systems becomes increasingly paramount. Future developments in this area are likely to incorporate advanced machine learning techniques, predictive analytics, and even more granular control over resource allocation to meet the growing demands of cloud-based services [15]. Figure 1.5 presents a comprehensive overview of Resource

1.8 Resource Management

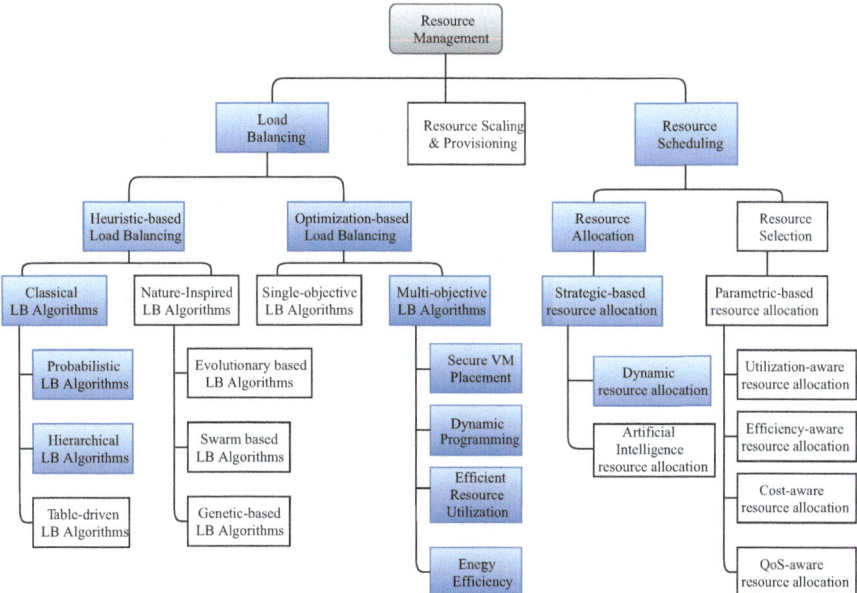

Fig. 1.5 Cloud resource management taxonomy

Management in cloud computing, divided into three main categories: Resource Scheduling, Resource Scaling and Provisioning, and Load Balancing. Each category is further broken down into various subcategories and approaches, illustrating the complexity and depth of resource management strategies in cloud environments. The blue-highlighted elements—Secure VM Placement, Energy Efficiency, and Efficient Resource Utilization—represent the key challenges that will be the focus of upcoming chapters in the book. These challenges are critical aspects of cloud computing that require innovative solutions to enhance security, reduce energy consumption, and optimize resource usage. By addressing these specific areas, the book aims to provide in-depth insights and strategies for tackling some of the most pressing issues in modern cloud resource management.

1.8.1 Resource Utilization

Resources form the foundation of cloud computing. In a multi-tenant model, resources are pooled and dynamically allocated to serve multiple consumers based on their demands. The primary objective of a resource management model is to efficiently handle the allocation and deallocation of computing resources. Effective resource management aims to optimize various criteria, including resource utilization, energy consumption, operational expenses, Quality of Service (QoS),

Service Level Agreement (SLA) compliance, and user response times. To achieve these objectives, optimal task scheduling is crucial for identifying the most suitable resources for deployment. Cloud resource scheduling can be defined as finding an "optimal" mapping $M : T \times R \rightarrow A$ that assigns N required tasks (or virtual resources) $T = \{T_1, T_2, \ldots, T_N\}$ to K available cloud (or physical) resources $R = \{R_1, R_2, \ldots, R_K\}$. Figure 2.1 illustrates a scenario where two incoming tasks share a single resource in cloud resource scheduling. The utilization of each resource type is calculated based on its available capacity and usage [16]. For the jth resource type of cloud provider i, the resource utilization is expressed as

$$U_{i,j} = \frac{1}{cl_{i,j}} \sum_{k=1}^{L} (D_k \cdot R_{k,j}) \qquad (1.1)$$

where:

- $U_{i,j}$ is the utilization of resource type j for provider i.
- $cl_{i,j}$ is the capacity of resource type j for provider i.
- L is the total number of tasks.
- D_k is the duration of task k.
- $R_{k,j}$ is the amount of resource type j required by task k.

The total utilization of resources for all types of resources for the cloud provider i is calculated as

$$U_i = \frac{1}{RT} \sum_{j=1}^{RT} U_{i,j} \qquad (1.2)$$

where:

- U_i is the overall utilization for provider i.
- RT is the total number of resource types.

The success of cloud computing services is fundamentally based on the efficient utilization of cloud resources. However, cloud providers face the challenge of maximizing the utilization of their finite resources to meet growing demands and optimize their operations.

1.8.2 Load Balancing

Load balancing is a critical component in the virtualized landscape of cloud computing, acting as a virtual traffic director to efficiently distribute incoming workloads across multiple processors or servers. This process is fundamental to enhancing the concurrent user capacity and overall reliability of applications in

1.8 Resource Management

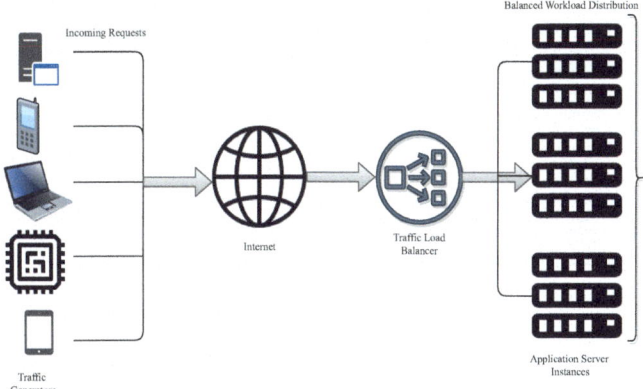

Fig. 1.6 Load balancing

cloud environments. The primary function of a load balancer is to uniformly distribute workloads among available servers, ensuring that no single server becomes a bottleneck. Load balancers employ sophisticated algorithms to identify the most suitable servers or computing resources that can meet specific application requirements. This intelligent distribution prevents high volumes of network traffic from overwhelming individual servers, thereby maintaining system stability and performance. Figure 1.6 provides a schematic representation of load balancing in a distributed computing environment. In this scenario, user requests originate from various traffic generators via the Internet and are intercepted by the traffic load balancer. The load balancer then distributes these requests uniformly among accessible and eligible application server instances. This distribution extends beyond mere website traffic, encompassing CPU load, network load, and memory capacity utilization of each server [17]. The concept of load in this context is multifaceted. It includes:

- **Website traffic**: The volume and frequency of user requests
- **CPU load**: The computational demands on server processors
- **Network load**: The bandwidth consumption and data transfer requirements
- **Memory capacity**: The utilization of server RAM and storage resources

An effective load balancing technique ensures that each system within the network handles an equitable amount of work at any given moment. This equilibrium prevents scenarios where some servers are overburdened, while others remain underutilized. The ultimate goals are to achieve optimal response times, maximize resource utilization, and maintain system stability. Load balancing methods can be broadly categorized into two main types, as illustrated in Fig. 1.7:

- **Static Load Balancing:**
  - Requires prior knowledge of the system.

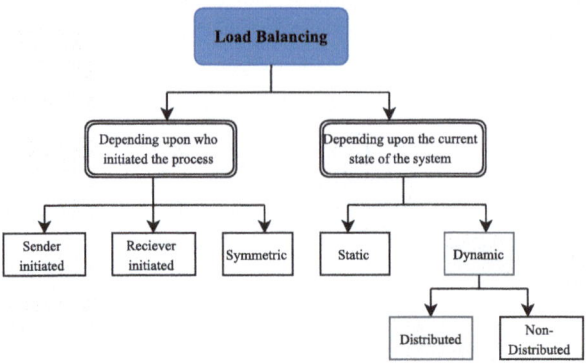

Fig. 1.7 Load balancing categorization

- Task assignment to processors is predetermined before program execution.
- Suitable for stable and predictable environments.
- Less adaptive to real-time changes in system load.

- **Dynamic Load Balancing:**

  - Based on the current system state.
  - Offers superior performance compared to static algorithms.
  - Deals with real-time network conditions.
  - Continuously identifies the least loaded server in the system.
  - Preferred for balancing load in volatile environments.
  - Utilizes the present state of the system to make load distribution decisions.

Dynamic load balancing algorithms are particularly adept at handling the fluctuating demands typical in cloud environments. They perform real-time redistribution by transferring tasks from heavily loaded processors to lightly loaded ones. This adaptive approach aims to optimize application performance and resource utilization continuously. The implementation of dynamic load balancing involves several key components:

- Real-time monitoring of system resources
- Rapid decision-making algorithms to determine optimal task distribution
- Efficient task migration mechanisms
- Predictive analysis to anticipate upcoming load changes

As cloud computing environments become increasingly complex, load balancing strategies continue to evolve. Advanced techniques now incorporate machine learning algorithms to predict traffic patterns and preemptively adjust resource allocation. Additionally, geo-distributed load balancing has gained prominence, allowing for the distribution of traffic across multiple data centers to minimize latency and improve fault tolerance.

1.8.3 Resource Scheduling Techniques

Resource scheduling in cloud computing is a critical process that determines the allocation of activities based on specified Quality of Service (QoS) parameters. This process is responsible for selecting optimal VMs for task execution, utilizing either heuristic or metaheuristic algorithms, while ensuring that QoS constraints are met. The primary objective of Resource Provisioning with Scheduling (RPS) is to allocate VMs to users without violating Service Level Agreements (SLAs) and to fulfill user demands effectively. This process begins with understanding user expectations and requirements based on anticipated workloads. SLA commitments are established between users and service providers after thorough workload analysis. Before task allocation, the system monitors cloud resources running and calculates the load on each resource. Overutilized VMs are avoided for task allocation. The system then maps incoming workloads to available resources, assessing whether the current running VMs are sufficient for execution. If resources are insufficient, horizontal scalability is implemented to increase capacity; otherwise, the workload is allocated to existing resources, and the required QoS parameters are evaluated. Resource scheduling schemes can be categorized into five hybrid categories:

- **Efficiency-Aware Resource Scheduling:** Focuses on optimizing resource consumption to enhance overall efficiency, improving metrics such as response time, execution time, makespan, bandwidth/speed, and task priority.
- **Energy-Aware Resource Scheduling:** Addresses the challenges of high energy consumption in data centers, aiming to reduce power usage while maintaining performance.
- **Load Balancing-Aware Resource Scheduling:** Aims to distribute workloads evenly across VMs and data center infrastructure, preventing overload and ensuring efficient system performance.
- **QoS-Aware Resource Scheduling:** Emphasizes scheduling tasks according to QoS requirements, focusing on availability, reliability, throughput, recovery time, fault tolerance, and SLA compliance for both providers and users.
- **Utilization-Aware Resource Scheduling:** Concentrates on maximizing resource utilization across cloud infrastructure.

Figure 1.8 illustrates these categories, with oval shapes representing the performance metrics used to evaluate proposed scheduling methods. This classification provides a comprehensive framework for understanding and developing resource scheduling strategies in cloud environments. Effective resource scheduling is crucial for optimizing cloud performance, ensuring efficient resource utilization, maintaining energy efficiency, balancing loads across the infrastructure, and meeting QoS requirements. As cloud computing continues to evolve, developing sophisticated scheduling algorithms that can address these multiple objectives simultaneously remains a key area of research and development in the field.

Fig. 1.8 Classification of resource scheduling

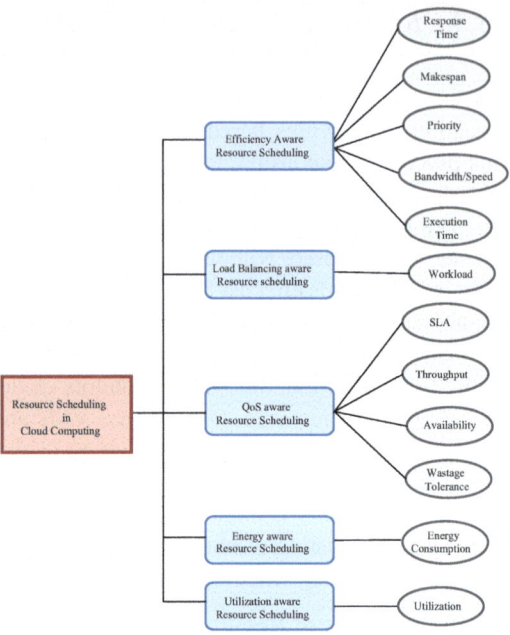

1.9 Evaluation Metrics

The performances of the proposed frameworks in the upcoming chapters are comprehensively assessed using the following metrics:

1.9.1 Makespan

Makespan represents the total time required to process all tasks from start to finish. It is a crucial metric in scheduling contexts, particularly when assigning job requests to physical hosts. The processing time typically increases with the number of requested tasks. Cloud Service Providers (CSPs) seek an optimal mapping of virtual machines and servers to maximize their economic gain. The completion time of the last task on VM j is calculated as

$$TC_j^M = \sum_{k=1}^{r-1} p_j + (k-1) * m, \quad \forall j = \{1, 2, \ldots, m\} \quad (1.3)$$

The optimal makespan is then determined by

$$MS_{opt} = \max_{k=1,2,\ldots,m} \sum_{l=1}^{k} TC_l^M + p_{n-l+1}/k \quad (1.4)$$

1.9.2 Resource Utilization

Resource utilization is a critical parameter for measuring the efficiency of any scheduling algorithm. The experiments focus on finding the optimal VM that utilizes the least amount of resources for efficient cloudlet deployment. The average resource utilization of a data center Φ_δ that needs to be maximized is calculated as

$$\Phi_\delta = \frac{\sum_{i=1}^{t} \Phi_{i=1}^{C} + \sum_{i=1}^{t} \Phi_{i=1}^{M} + \sum_{i=1}^{t} \Phi_{i=1}^{B}}{|N| \times \sum_{i=1}^{t} \Theta_i} \quad (1.5)$$

where $|N|$ represents the number of resources considered (typically $|N| = 3$ for CPU, memory, and bandwidth), and $\Phi_{i=1}^{C}$, $\Phi_{i=1}^{M}$, and $\Phi_{i=1}^{B}$ represent the utilization of CPU, memory, and bandwidth, respectively. The utilization of each resource type for a single physical host is computed as

$$\Phi_i^R = \frac{\sum_{i=1}^{n} \Theta_i \times VM_j^R}{\uplus_i^R}, \quad R \in \{C, M, B\} \quad (1.6)$$

1.9.3 Energy Efficiency

Energy consumption in cloud data centers has increased dramatically in recent years. This study aims to maximize resource utilization while minimizing energy consumption. Research has shown that energy consumption has a linear relationship with processor utilization, with CPU consumption being the primary contributor to energy use. The energy consumption model assumes three server states: active, idle, and sleep. The energy consumption of a single host k is calculated as

$$\beth_k = \begin{cases} \Im \times [\Phi_i^R \times \eth_k^{active} + (1 - \Phi_i^R) \times \eth_k^{idle}], & \text{Host state: on} \\ \Im \times \eth_k^{sleep}, & \text{Host state: off} \end{cases} \quad (1.7)$$

The total energy consumption of a cloud data center is then defined as

$$\beth = \sum_{k=0}^{n} \beth_k \quad (1.8)$$

1.9.4 Secure VM Allocation

This metric addresses the prevention of side-channel attacks through optimized VM management policies. The study focuses on minimizing the chances of ordinary

VMs being coresident with malicious VMs. The reliability of the grouping Ξ_{tk} is calculated to assess the security of the VM placements:

$$\Xi_{tk} = \sum_{i=1}^{|SM|} R_{SM_i}, tk \left(\sum_{v=1}^{VM} f_{uj} tk.|VM_{uj}.h_i| \right) \quad (1.9)$$

where R_{SM_i} is the credibility marking the security levels of hosts, tk represents time, $f_{uj}tk$ means the members of the same family, and $|VM_{uj}.h_i|$ are VMs belonging to the same user uj placed on the same host h_i.

1.9.5 Failure Number of Processing Events

This metric counts the number of tasks that fail during scheduling and deployment, particularly when chosen physical machines cannot meet task demands. The number of failures tends to increase with the number of requested tasks as the system's ability to handle tasks gradually weakens.

1.9.6 Throughput Performance

This measure evaluates the load balancing effectiveness, considering factors such as:

- Task handling ability
- Response time to calculate a task request
- Number of completed services per unit time

These parameters are used to calculate the throughput rate and evaluate the external service performance with respect to increasing time.

1.9.7 SLA Violation Rate

The SLA violation rate is calculated to measure service availability for customers. An SLA ensures a minimum level of service is maintained, guaranteeing reliability, availability, and responsiveness of systems and applications. The SLA violation rate is computed as

$$SLA_{Vrate} = \frac{Number\ of\ Requests\ Violated}{Number\ of\ Total\ Requests} \quad (1.10)$$

These comprehensive metrics provide a holistic evaluation of the proposed cloud computing frameworks, encompassing efficiency, security, energy consumption, and service quality aspects. By analyzing these metrics, researchers can gain valuable insights into the performance and effectiveness of their proposed scheduling and resource management strategies in cloud environments.

1.10 Summary

This chapter has given a thorough introduction to cloud computing, covering everything from its basic ideas and service models to the complex problems with resource management. It builds a solid basis for comprehending the revolutionary effect of cloud computing on contemporary IT infrastructure by examining the development of cloud technologies, different deployment tactics, and service models. The thorough analysis of resource management demonstrates how important it is to maximizing cloud performance, affordability, and user happiness. The chapter's examination of load balancing, resource scaling, and job scheduling strategies highlights the complexity of resource management in dynamic cloud systems. Along with important assessment indicators, a whole taxonomy of resource management techniques has been introduced, providing insightful information for practitioners and scholars alike. Resource management systems that are complex, flexible, and intelligent are becoming more and more essential as cloud computing develops. More precise control over resource allocation, predictive analytics, and sophisticated machine learning methods are probably in store for future advances. The incorporation of security measures, such as avoiding side-channel attacks through improved virtual machine management, will have a significant impact on the future of cloud resource management. In summary, even though cloud computing provides never-before-seen scale and flexibility, efficient resource management is still a major obstacle. To satisfy the increasing needs of sophisticated applications and user expectations, further research and innovation in this field will be necessary to ensure cloud technologies continue to improve.

1.11 Exercises

1. Consider a scenario where a company needs to migrate its application to the cloud. The company has the following options:
   - IaaS: $0.04 per hour for a single virtual machine.
   - PaaS: $500 flat fee per month, including platform maintenance.
   - SaaS: $10 per user per month. The company has 50 users.

a. Calculate the total cost of each cloud service model (IaaS, PaaS, and SaaS) for one month assuming the application will run for 24 hours daily on IaaS and will be accessed by all 50 users on SaaS.
b. Discuss which service model is the most cost-effective for the company, considering both cost and other nonfinancial factors (e.g., maintenance, scalability).

2. Compare and contrast the four cloud deployment models (public, private, hybrid, and community clouds). Discuss the suitability of each model for different types of organizations (e.g., small businesses, government agencies, large enterprises).

   a. For each cloud deployment model, provide one real-world example of an organization or industry that commonly uses that model.
   b. Write a short essay (500–700 words) discussing the key advantages and limitations of each deployment model.

3. Develop a small project where you demonstrate the use of virtualization and distributed computing in setting up a cloud environment.

   a. Set up a small virtualized environment on your local machine using a tool like VirtualBox or VMware. Create at least two virtual machines (VMs).
   b. Install a distributed computing framework like Hadoop or Apache Spark on these VMs.
   c. Perform a simple distributed task (e.g., word count on a large dataset) across your virtual machines and explain how the distributed task is managed by the framework.

4. Analyze a real-world case where a large organization faced challenges in cloud adoption, particularly in areas such as data security, load balancing, or cost management.

   a. Choose a company that experienced issues with cloud migration (e.g., Dropbox, Target, or any large enterprise with a public cloud failure or difficulty).
   b. Write a case study (800–1000 words) discussing the specific challenges the company faced during cloud adoption, how they mitigated these challenges, and what lessons can be drawn for future cloud migrations.

5. Consider a cloud data center with 10 Virtual Machines (VMs) and a set of 15 tasks. Each VM has different computing capacities (in MIPS) as shown in the table below. The tasks have different computational requirements. Apply the Longest Job First (LJF) scheduling algorithm to allocate the tasks to the VMs.

VM capacities (MIPS)	[1500, 2000, 1800, 1600, 2200, 2400, 2100, 1700, 1900, 2300]
Task requirements (MIPS)	[1000, 1800, 2200, 900, 2400, 1100, 1300, 1500, 2100, 2000, 1700, 1600, 1400, 2300, 2500]

6. Perform a comparative analysis of at least two scheduling algorithms:
   a. Round Robin
   b. Min-Min

   Provide the evaluation in terms of response time, makespan, and energy consumption for the allocation of VMs to tasks in a simulated cloud environment.
7. Consider a cloud resource management scenario where 5 VMs process 10 tasks of varying sizes. The makespan (total time to complete all tasks) for each task using Round Robin scheduling is given as follows (in seconds): [120, 150, 180, 90, 110, 95, 200, 160, 130, 140]. Calculate the following metrics:

   a. Average completion time
   b. Throughput (the number of tasks completed per unit time)
   c. Utilization of the VMs

[Hint]: Students will calculate these metrics using the provided makespan data, ensuring they understand how to evaluate scheduling performance quantitatively.

References

1. Buyya, R., Broberg, J., Goscinski, A.M. (eds.): Cloud computing: Principles and paradigms. John Wiley & Sons, London (2010)
2. Comer, D.: The Cloud Computing Book: The Future of Computing Explained, 1st edn. Chapman and Hall/CRC (2021). https://doi.org/10.1201/9781003147503
3. Marinescu, D.C.: Cloud Computing: Theory and Practice. Morgan Kaufmann, Los Altos (2022)
4. Rittinghouse, J.W., Ransome, J.F.: Cloud Computing: Implementation, Management, and Security, 1st edn. CRC Press, Boca Raton (2009). https://doi.org/10.1201/9781439806814
5. Dalbom, S., Willners, V., Sonntag, D.: Value assessment of cloud manufacturing for large-scale manufacturing organizations (2023)
6. Wang, W., Zhang, Y., Huang, R., Ren, J., Lyu, F., Zhang, Y.: Efficient resource management and expansion scheme for collaborative edge-cloud computing. IEEE Trans. Mobile Comput. **23**(4), 2731–2747 (2024). https://doi.org/10.1109/TMC.2023.3267497
7. Edington Alexa, M., Kishore, R.: Forensics framework for cloud computing. Comput. Electr. Eng. **60**, 193–205 (2017)
8. Gong, S., Zhu, X., Zhang, R., Zhao, H., Guo, C.: An intelligent resource management solution for hospital information system based on cloud computing platform. IEEE Trans. Reliab. **72**(1), 329–342 (2023). https://doi.org/10.1109/TR.2022.3161359
9. Chiappa, S., Videla, E., Viana-Céspedes, V., Piñeyro, P., Rossit, D.A.: Cloud manufacturing architectures: State-of-art, research challenges and platforms description. J. Ind. Inform. Integr. **34**, 100472 (2023)
10. Chhabra, S., Singh, A.K.: Beyond lightning: a systematic review of information security in the age of cloud computing using key management. Int. J. Comput. Eng. Appl. **11**(12), 299–315
11. Sharif, Z., Jung, L.T., Razzak, I., Alazab, M.: Adaptive and priority-based resource allocation for efficient resources utilization in mobile-edge computing. IEEE Internet Things J. **10**(4), 3079–3093 (2023). https://doi.org/10.1109/JIOT.2021.3111838
12. Wang, J., Li, J., Gao, Z., Han, Z., Qiu, C., Wang, X.: Resource management and pricing for cloud computing based mobile blockchain with pooling. IEEE Trans. Cloud Comput. **11**(1), 128–138 (2023). https://doi.org/10.1109/TCC.2021.3081580

13. Chhabra, S., Singh, A.K.: Dynamic data leakage detection model based approach for MapReduce computational security in cloud. In: 2016 Fifth International Conference on Eco-Friendly Computing and Communication Systems (ICECCS), pp. 13–19. IEEE, Piscataway (2016)
14. Han, Y., Chan, J., Alpcan, T., Leckie, C.: Using virtual machine allocation policies to defend against co-resident attacks in cloud computing. IEEE Trans. Depend. Secure Comput. **14**(1), 95–108 (2017)
15. Duan, J., Yang, Y.: A load balancing and multi-tenancy oriented data center virtualization framework. IEEE Trans. Parallel Distrib. Syst. **28**(8), 2131–2144 (2017)
16. Wang, Z., Hayat, M.M., Ghani, N., Shaban, K.B.: Optimizing cloud-service performance: efficient resource provisioning via optimal workload allocation. IEEE Trans. Parallel Distrib. Syst. **28**(6), 1689–1702 (2017)
17. Khan, A.U.R., Othman, M., Madani, S.A., Khan, S.U.: A survey of mobile cloud computing application models. IEEE Commun. Surv. Tutorials **16**(1), 393–413 (2014). https://doi.org/10.1109/SURV.2013.062613.00160

Chapter 2
Task Scheduling

Abstract This chapter explores the critical role of task scheduling in cloud computing environments, examining various algorithms designed to optimize resource allocation and system performance. It presents an overview of both static and dynamic scheduling approaches, highlighting their respective strengths and limitations in addressing the complex, multifaceted challenges of cloud task management. The discussion encompasses traditional methods such as First Come First Serve (FCFS) and Shortest Job First (SJF), as well as more advanced techniques including Round Robin, Adaptive Scheduling, and heuristic-based algorithms like Genetic Algorithms and Ant Colony Optimization. The chapter analyzes these algorithms in terms of their impact on key performance metrics such as execution time, resource utilization, and load balancing. Additionally, it considers the growing importance of adaptability and multi-objective optimization in response to the dynamic nature of cloud workloads. By comparing different scheduling strategies and their applications, this chapter provides insights into selecting and implementing effective task scheduling solutions for diverse cloud computing scenarios.

Keywords Task scheduling · Scheduling algorithms · Static scheduling · Dynamic scheduling · First come first serve (FCFS) · Round robin · Heuristics · Metaheuristics · Load distribution

2.1 Introduction

In the ever-evolving landscape of modern computing, task scheduling has emerged as a critical component in optimizing system performance, particularly within the realm of cloud computing. At its core, task scheduling is the process of assigning a set of tasks or processes to available computing resources, with the goal of maximizing efficiency and minimizing execution time [1]. The advent of cloud computing has revolutionized the way we approach distributed systems and resource allocation. This paradigm shift has brought forth new challenges and opportunities in task scheduling, as it must now account for the dynamic, scalable, and multi-tenant nature of cloud environments. In a cloud computing context, task scheduling algorithms aim to achieve optimal performance by considering various factors:

- **Resource utilization**: Efficiently distribute workloads across available processors and nodes to maximize resource usage.
- **Makespan minimization**: Reducing the total time required to complete a set of tasks, often referred to as the makespan.
- **Load balancing**: Ensure that no single resource becomes a bottleneck by evenly distributing tasks across the available infrastructure.
- **Quality of service (QoS)**: Meeting user-defined requirements and SLAs for task execution.
- **Energy efficiency**: Optimize resource allocation to minimize power consumption without compromising performance.

The complexity of task scheduling in cloud environments is due to the heterogeneous nature of both tasks and the available resources. Some applications may require intensive CPU processing, while others might be more memory or I/O bound. Similarly, the distributed resources in a cloud system may vary in their capabilities and availability. Dynamic load balancing mechanisms play a crucial role in adapting to the ever-changing demands of cloud-based applications. These mechanisms must be capable of reallocating tasks on-the-fly as new requests arrive or as the system state changes. This adaptability is essential for maintaining optimal performance and ensuring fair resource distribution among multiple users and applications [2].

2.1.1 Task Scheduling System

There are three stages in the cloud computing work scheduling system:

- A collection of tasks (Cloudlets) issued by cloud users that must be completed make up the first task level.
- The second scheduling level is responsible for assigning tasks to the appropriate resources to maximize resource use while minimizing makespan. The total time needed to complete all jobs from start to finish is known as the makespan.
- The third level of VMs consists of a group of VMs that carry out the duties shown in Fig. 2.1.

The task scheduling process in cloud computing environments involves two critical steps, each playing a vital role in optimizing resource allocation and performance. Initially, the system undertakes a comprehensive survey of its virtual landscape. This crucial first step employs a data center broker, which acts as an intelligent intermediary between user requests and available resources. The broker's primary function is to discover and catalog all VMs currently active within the cloud infrastructure. However, its role extends beyond mere identification. The broker meticulously collects and analyzes a wide array of status information for

2.1 Introduction

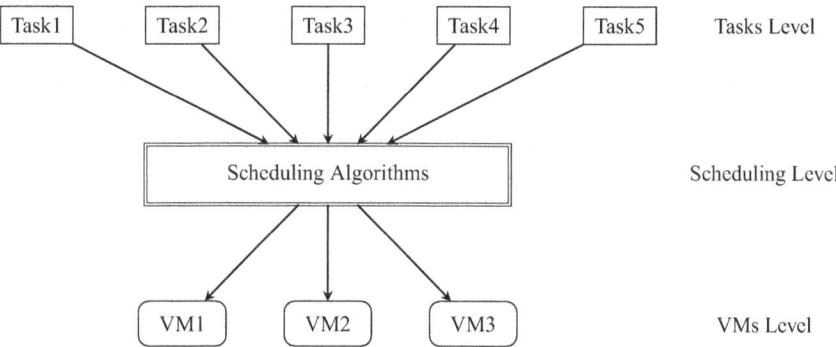

Fig. 2.1 Task scheduling system

each VM. This data may include current workload levels, processing capabilities, available memory and storage, network performance metrics, and even energy consumption rates. By gathering this detailed information, the broker creates a comprehensive, real-time map of the cloud's resource landscape, providing a solid foundation for informed decision-making in the subsequent steps of the scheduling process. Following this thorough resource assessment, the system progresses to the pivotal second step: VM selection. This phase involves a sophisticated matching process where the specific properties and requirements of each incoming task are carefully evaluated against the capabilities and current status of the available VMs. The scheduler, armed with the detailed resource information gathered by the broker, employs advanced algorithms to determine the most suitable VM for each task. This selection process considers multiple factors, such as the computational demands of the task, its memory and storage requirements, any specific software dependencies, deadline constraints, and even data locality concerns. The goal is not just to find an available VM, but to identify the one that offers the optimal balance of performance, efficiency, and cost-effectiveness for the particular task at hand [3]. This two-step approach ensures that tasks are allocated to resources in a manner that maximizes overall system performance while meeting the specific needs of individual workloads. By first establishing a clear picture of available resources and then making informed, task-specific allocation decisions, cloud systems can achieve high levels of efficiency, flexibility, and user satisfaction.

2.1.2 Fundamental Considerations

One important aspect of cloud computing is task scheduling. It has a significant impact on user satisfaction, resource use, and system performance. Task scheduling is more difficult in cloud systems due to the dispersed resources, hardware variability, and frequent workload changes:

- **Managing several objectives**: In cloud computing, task scheduling requires careful goal balancing. Schedulers have to manage many goals at once, often with competing demands. They strive to preserve energy across the system and decrease the total time to do all jobs (makespan). To prevent any one user from controlling the system, they must simultaneously preserve user fairness and make sure that all resources are used effectively. Another important consideration is cost control, as schedulers aim to minimize the total cost of completing activities. Schedulers utilize smart algorithms and complex mathematical models to find the best combination of these different aims in order to meet the demands of different users and system specifications [4].
- **Working with VMs**: These are fundamental to cloud computing, require task schedulers that possess comprehensive knowledge of their management and operational processes for optimal performance. This entails managing VMs throughout their whole lives, from creation to disposal. Moving VMs between physical servers with the least amount of interruption to ongoing operations is a significant problem. In order to get the best performance, schedulers must also carefully consider where to put each VM, deciding which real server to use for each one. Another crucial component is resource sharing, which requires schedulers to control how virtual machines on the same physical server divide up CPU, memory, and network resources. They also have to take care of VM size, making sure that each VM is given the appropriate number of resources according to its present responsibilities and any future requirements.
- **Fulfilling Quality Promises**: Service Level Agreements (SLAs), which are legal agreements between cloud service providers and their clients, include precise pledges about the quality of their services. Organizers of tasks are essential to fulfilling these commitments. They have to keep an eye on system performance all the time to make sure SLAs are being fulfilled. This often entails putting in place priority management systems, which provide resources preferred access to jobs that are more important or time sensitive. Another tactic is resource reserve, in which certain resources are held back for urgent or high-priority activities. In addition, schedulers must use admission control, carefully considering whether to take on new assignments in light of the system's present workload and unfulfilled promises. Together, these strategies maximize system performance while preserving the desired level of service quality.
- **Changing with the Times**: Cloud environments are dynamic by nature, with demand changing quickly. Due to these shifting circumstances, task schedulers need to be very flexible. Auto-scaling techniques, which automatically add or remove resources as demand ebbs and flows, are often used to accomplish this flexibility. Additionally, load prediction algorithms may be used by schedulers to try to anticipate future demand and allocate resources ahead of time. Another important component is dynamic resource allocation, which enables the system to modify resource distribution in real time in response to shifting demands. Schedulers can efficiently balance the load by redistributing ongoing jobs across machines thanks to task migration features. Furthermore, in order to ensure uninterrupted operation even during unforeseen spikes in activity, schedulers

need to be capable of managing abrupt spikes in demand (burst management) without interfering with existing services.
- **Managing Various Hardware Types**: Cloud infrastructures often consist of a wide range of hardware, and efficient task scheduling requires a thorough understanding of this heterogeneity. Resource profiling is a necessary activity for schedulers to do in order to have a thorough grasp of the capabilities and constraints of every piece of hardware in the system. In order for each activity to be completed effectively, they must also examine the requirements. Schedulers may match jobs to the best hardware using this information, resulting in optimum performance. This might include using specialized hardware, such as GPUs or FPGAs, to certain jobs that can capitalize on their distinct characteristics. To get the greatest outcomes, schedulers may also need to optimize performance, which involves adjusting how jobs operate on various kinds of hardware.
- **Energy-aware and cost-aware scheduling**: Energy-aware and cost-aware scheduling has grown in significance as worries about the environmental effects of data centers and the need of cost-effective operations have intensified. Schedulers may use strategies like dynamic voltage and frequency scaling (DVFS) to save energy and server consolidation, which concentrates workloads on a smaller number of servers so that others can be turned down. Schedulers in public cloud systems have to weigh the costs of their choices and strike a balance between budgetary restraints and performance needs. This might include employing reserved instances for predictable, long-term workloads or using less expensive resources, such as spot instances, for less important operations in order to save expenses.
- **Data Locality and Network Awareness**: In applications that use a lot of data, task execution time and overall system performance may be greatly impacted by the location of data. In cloud contexts, task schedulers have to take data locality into account, trying to schedule jobs on or close to the nodes that have the necessary data. This lessens network congestion and the overhead associated with data transport. In addition, schedulers need to be cognizant of the network's structure and bandwidth when determining where to put things. This is especially crucial in geographically dispersed cloud systems, since application performance may be greatly impacted by inter-data center connectivity.

2.2 Task Scheduling Algorithms

Task scheduling is a critical component in cloud computing environments, responsible for allocating resources to tasks in a way that optimizes system performance, resource utilization, and user satisfaction. The complexity of this process stems from the heterogeneous nature of both tasks and resources, as well as the dynamic and often unpredictable workload patterns in cloud environments [5].

Scheduling algorithms in cloud computing can be broadly categorized into two main types: static and dynamic. Static scheduling algorithms make decisions based on information available before execution begins. These algorithms are typically simpler to implement and are often suitable for small- to medium-scale cloud environments where workloads and resource availability are relatively predictable. Examples of static scheduling algorithms include FCFS, SJF, and MAX-MIN. On the other hand, dynamic scheduling algorithms make decisions in real time based on the current state of the system. These algorithms are more adaptable and are better suited for large-scale cloud environments where workloads and resource availability can change rapidly. Dynamic algorithms include Round Robin (RR), Min-Min, and more complex approaches like Genetic Algorithms (GA), Ant Colony Optimization (ACO), and Particle Swarm Optimization (PSO).

2.2.1 Static Scheduling Algorithms

Static scheduling algorithms are characterized by their deterministic nature, where decisions about task allocation are made before the actual execution begins. These algorithms rely on preexisting knowledge about the tasks and resources, such as estimated execution times, resource capabilities, and task dependencies. While they may lack the adaptability of dynamic algorithms, static schedulers often provide predictable performance and are easier to implement and analyze.

The key characteristics of static algorithms are:

- Pre-execution planning
- Reliance on a priori information
- Typically lower runtime overhead
- Predictable scheduling decisions
- Suitable for stable and predictable environments

Let us explore some of the most common static scheduling algorithms in more detail:

2.2.1.1 First Come First Serve:

FCFS is perhaps the simplest static scheduling algorithm. Tasks are executed in the order they arrive in the queue, without any prioritization or reordering.

Advantages:

- Simple to implement and understand
- Fair in the sense that no task is prioritized over others based on any criteria
- Low scheduling overhead

Disadvantages:

- Can lead to poor resource utilization if long tasks block shorter ones
- May result in high average waiting times

2.2 Task Scheduling Algorithms

- Not optimal for systems with varying task lengths

- **Assumptions and Constraints:**
  In the context of task scheduling within cloud computing environments, several key assumptions and constraints guide the allocation process [6]:
  - The number of tasks invariably exceeds the number of available VMs, necessitating multiple task executions per VM.
  - Each task is exclusively assigned to a single VM, precluding task distribution across multiple resources.
  - Task lengths exhibit diversity, ranging from small to medium to large computational requirements.
  - Once initiated, task execution proceeds without interruption, ensuring continuity of processing.
  - VMs operate independently, maintaining autonomy in resource management and control.
  - VMs are dedicated resources, incapable of concurrent task processing. A VM remains committed to its current task until completion before considering subsequent assignments.

- **Task Characteristics:**
  For illustrative purposes, consider a scenario with 15 tasks, each characterized by varying computational demands. Table 2.1 presents a hypothetical set of tasks with their respective lengths, ordered by arrival time.
  Virtual Machine Properties: To accommodate the diverse task requirements, we consider a heterogeneous set of six VMs, each with distinct processing capabilities. The VMs are categorized based on their Million Instructions Per Second (MIPS) ratings, as follows:
  - VM Set = {VM1, VM2, VM3, VM4, VM5, VM6}
  - Corresponding MIPS = {500, 500, 1500, 1500, 2500, 2500}

This deliberate selection of VMs with varied processing powers aims to enhance load balancing across the system. By providing VMs tailored to different task categories (small, medium, large), we can more effectively match task requirements to appropriate resources. This approach mitigates the risk of load imbalance that might occur if VMs with uniform capabilities were used across all task categories, given the inherent variability in task lengths and computational demands [7].

Table 2.1 Task Set with Diverse Computational Requirements

Task ID	Length	Task ID	Length	Task ID	Length
T1	1000	T6	2000	T11	1500
T2	500	T7	2500	T12	1000
T3	1500	T8	1000	T13	2000
T4	2000	T9	500	T14	1500
T5	1000	T10	1500	T15	500

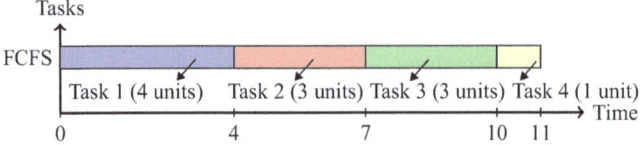

Fig. 2.2 FCFS scheduling

2.2.1.2 First Come First Serve Scheduling

FCFS is one of the simplest scheduling algorithms used in cloud computing environments. In FCFS, tasks are executed in the order they arrive, regardless of their length or priority. This approach is straightforward to implement but may lead to inefficiencies, especially when short tasks are queued behind longer ones.

Figure 2.2 illustrates the FCFS scheduling process for a sample set of tasks:

In this example, we can observe that shorter tasks (like Task 4) may experience significant waiting times if they arrive after longer tasks. This can lead to increased average waiting times and potentially poor resource utilization, especially in scenarios with a mix of short and long tasks. Despite these drawbacks, FCFS remains useful as a baseline for comparison with more sophisticated scheduling algorithms in cloud environments:

- **FCFS Scheduling Algorithm in Cloud Computing:** The FCFS scheduling algorithm in cloud computing environments operates on a simple principle: Tasks are executed in the order of their arrival. While straightforward, this approach can lead to inefficiencies, particularly when dealing with tasks of varying sizes. Figure 2.3 illustrates the working mechanism of the FCFS algorithm, demonstrating how tasks are allocated to VMs based on their arrival sequence.

In Fig. 2.3, arrows represent the first set of task assignments, dashed arrows indicate the second set, and solid arrows denote the third set. This visual representation highlights a key inefficiency of the FCFS approach: Larger tasks, such as t1, can significantly delay the execution of smaller, subsequent tasks like t7 and t12. This delay cascades through the system, leading to increased Total Waiting Time (TWT), Execution Time (ET), and Total Finish Time (TFT), while simultaneously reducing overall fairness in task execution. The allocation of tasks to VMs under the FCFS algorithm can be summarized as follows:

- VM1: t1 → t7 → t12
- VM2: t2 → t8 → t14
- VM3: t3 → t9 → t15
- VM4: t4 → t10
- VM5: t5 → t11
- VM6: t6 → t13

2.2 Task Scheduling Algorithms

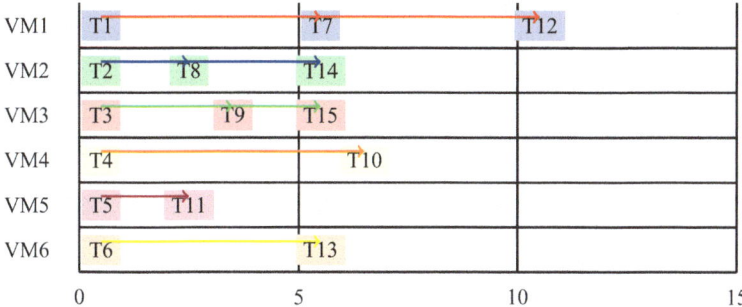

Fig. 2.3 FCFS task scheduling algorithm working mechanism

Table 2.2 Impact of FCFS on task waiting times

Task ID	Arrival time	Burst time	Start time	Finish time	Waiting time
T1	0	10	0	10	0
T2	1	5	10	15	9
T3	3	8	15	23	12
T4	5	12	23	35	18
T5	6	4	35	39	29

Table 2.2 demonstrates how the FCFS scheduling algorithm impacts the waiting time for each task. This table clearly illustrates the cumulative effect of task sequencing on overall system performance. This FCFS implementation, while simple to implement, clearly demonstrates the potential for inefficiency in task scheduling, particularly in environments with diverse task sizes and arrival patterns. The delay of smaller tasks behind larger ones not only increases overall waiting and execution times but also impacts system responsiveness and user satisfaction. These observations underscore the need for more sophisticated scheduling algorithms in cloud computing environments that can better handle task diversity and optimize resource utilization [8].

2.2.1.3 SJF Scheduling in Cloud Computing

The SJF algorithm is a task scheduling approach in cloud computing that prioritizes tasks based on their execution time. In this paradigm, tasks with shorter execution times are given higher priority and are scheduled to run before longer tasks. This method aims to optimize overall system performance and reduce average waiting times:

- **Operational mechanism:**
  In a cloud environment implementing SJF:
  1. Tasks are initially sorted based on their estimated execution lengths.

2. The task list is organized in ascending order of execution time.
3. Tasks are then sequentially assigned to available Virtual Machines (VMs).

For instance, consider a scenario with 15 tasks and 6 VMs. The task allocation might proceed as follows:

- VM1: T4 → T6 → T7
- VM2: T10 → T9 → T1
- VM3: T11 → T13 → T8
- VM4: T5 → T14
- VM5: T12 → T2
- VM6: T3 → T15

- **Advantages:**
  The SJF algorithm offers several benefits in cloud task scheduling:

  - **Reduced waiting times:** Compared to algorithms like FCFS, SJF typically results in lower average waiting times for tasks.
  - **Optimal average waiting time:** Among task scheduling algorithms, SJF is known to achieve the minimum average waiting time, enhancing overall system efficiency.
  - **Improved throughput:** By prioritizing shorter tasks, the system can complete a larger number of tasks in a given time frame.

- **Disadvantages:**
  Despite its advantages, SJF has some notable drawbacks:

  - **Potential unfairness:** Longer tasks may experience extended waiting times as shorter tasks are consistently prioritized. This can lead to task starvation in extreme cases.
  - **Execution time estimation:** The effectiveness of SJF heavily relies on accurate estimations of task execution times, which can be challenging in dynamic cloud environments.
  - **Total finish time (TFT):** While individual short tasks complete quickly, the overall TFT for all tasks may be prolonged due to the delayed execution of longer tasks.

  Figure 2.4 illustrates the SJF scheduling algorithm in a cloud computing environment. It shows five Virtual Machines (VM1 to VM5) executing tasks of varying lengths over time. Shorter tasks (represented by smaller colored rectangles) are prioritized and scheduled earlier, while longer tasks are allocated later. This visual representation demonstrates how SJF minimizes average waiting time by prioritizing quicker tasks but also highlights potential delays for longer tasks in the queue.

- **Considerations for Cloud Environments:**
  In cloud computing scenarios, several factors influence the effectiveness of SJF:

2.2 Task Scheduling Algorithms

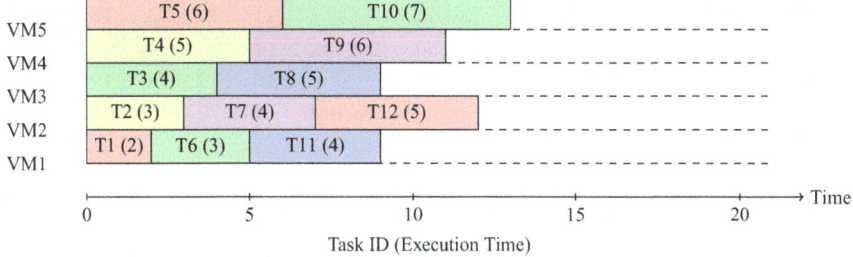

Fig. 2.4 SJF task scheduling in cloud environment

- **Task heterogeneity:** Cloud workloads often consist of tasks with varying resource requirements and execution times, making accurate scheduling crucial.
- **Resource elasticity:** The ability to dynamically allocate and deallocate resources in cloud environments can complement SJF's efficiency [9].
- **Quality of service (QoS):** While SJF optimizes average waiting time, it may not always align with specific QoS requirements of all cloud services.
- **Scalability:** As the number of tasks and VMs increases, the computational overhead of sorting and scheduling tasks may become significant.

The SJF algorithm presents a compelling approach to task scheduling in cloud computing environments, offering significant improvements in average waiting times and system throughput. However, its implementation requires careful consideration of potential fairness issues and the challenges of accurately estimating task execution times in dynamic cloud settings. As cloud computing continues to evolve, hybrid or adaptive scheduling approaches that incorporate SJF principles alongside other methodologies may offer more balanced solutions to the complex task scheduling requirements of modern cloud systems.

2.2.1.4 Max-Min Algorithm

The MAX-MIN algorithm represents a sophisticated approach to task scheduling in cloud computing environments. This method prioritizes tasks based on their completion time, giving precedence to longer tasks that require more execution time. The algorithm then assigns these tasks to VMs that offer the minimum overall execution time, aiming to optimize resource utilization and system throughput:

- **Operational Mechanism:**
  The MAX-MIN algorithm operates as follows:

  1. Tasks are sorted in descending order based on their estimated completion time.
  2. Each task is then assigned to the VM that provides the minimum overall execution time.

Table 2.3 Example task set for MAX-MIN scheduling

Task ID	T1	T2	T3	T4	T5
Execution time (ms)	180	90	120	60	150
Task ID	T6	T7	T8	T9	T10
Execution time (ms)	100	70	200	110	130

To illustrate this process, consider the following example with 10 tasks and four VMs:

After sorting and allocation of Table 2.3, the task distribution might look like this:

- VM1: T8 → T5 → T7
- VM2: T1 → T6
- VM3: T3 → T9 → T4
- VM4: T10 → T2

- **Advantages:** The MAX-MIN algorithm offers several benefits in cloud task scheduling:

  - **Efficient resource utilization:** By prioritizing longer tasks, MAX-MIN aims to keep powerful resources consistently engaged, potentially improving overall system utilization [10].
  - **Reduced makespan:** In scenarios with a mix of long and short tasks, MAX-MIN can reduce the total completion time (makespan) of the entire task set.
  - **Load balancing:** The algorithm attempts to distribute lengthy tasks across available resources, which can lead to better load balancing in heterogeneous cloud environments.

- **Disadvantages:**
  Despite its advantages, MAX-MIN has some notable limitations:

  - **Increased waiting time for shorter tasks:** Small- and medium-sized tasks may experience significant delays as longer tasks monopolize available resources.
  - **Potential for resource underutilization:** If the workload consists primarily of long tasks, some VMs may remain idle while waiting for these tasks to complete.
  - **Fairness concerns:** The prioritization of longer tasks can lead to unfair treatment of shorter, potentially more urgent tasks.

- **Performance analysis:**
  To evaluate the performance of MAX-MIN compared to other algorithms like FCFS and SJF, we can consider metrics such as Total Waiting Time (TWT) and Total Finish Time (TFT).

  This comparison reveals in Table 2.4 that while MAX-MIN may not always provide the lowest waiting times or finish times, it can offer a balance between

2.2 Task Scheduling Algorithms

Table 2.4 Comparison of scheduling algorithms

Metric	FCFS	SJF	MAX-MIN
Total waiting time (ms)	2850	1620	2100
Total finish time (ms)	4260	3030	3510

the extremes of FCFS and SJF, particularly in environments with diverse task lengths.

- **Considerations for cloud environments:** When implementing MAX-MIN in cloud computing scenarios, several factors warrant consideration:
  - **Workload characteristics:** MAX-MIN tends to perform well in environments with a significant disparity between task execution times.
  - **Resource heterogeneity:** The algorithm can leverage the diverse capabilities of cloud resources by matching long-running tasks to high-performance VMs.
  - **Dynamic task arrival:** In real-world cloud environments, the continuous arrival of new tasks may require periodic re-evaluation of the scheduling decisions.
  - **Quality of service (QoS) requirements:** While MAX-MIN optimizes for long tasks, it may need to be balanced with other scheduling criteria to meet diverse QoS needs.

The MAX-MIN algorithm presents a unique approach to task scheduling in cloud computing, offering potential benefits in resource utilization and overall system throughput, particularly for workloads dominated by longer tasks. However, its implementation requires careful consideration of the trade-offs between prioritizing long-running tasks and ensuring fair, responsive service for shorter tasks. As cloud computing environments continue to evolve, hybrid approaches that combine the strengths of MAX-MIN with other scheduling paradigms may offer more balanced solutions to the complex task scheduling challenges in modern cloud systems.

2.2.2 Dynamic Scheduling Algorithms

2.2.2.1 Round Robin Algorithm

The Round Robin algorithm is a dynamic, time-sharing scheduling approach that is frequently employed in cloud computing environments. It is based on the principle of equitable distribution of processing time among VMs or duties:

- **Primary characteristics:**
  - Time slicing: The algorithm divides the available processing time into equal-sized time quanta or slices.
  - Cyclic allocation: To guarantee equitable distribution of CPU time, each task or VM is assigned a time segment in a circular order.

- Preemption: When the time quantum of a task expires, it is preempted and directed to the end of the ready queue.
- Context switching: Following each time segment, the system executes a context transition to the subsequent task in the queue.

- **Operational Mechanism:**
  - Tasks are organized in a circular sequence.
  - Each task is sequentially assigned a predetermined time allotment by the scheduler.
  - Tasks are eliminated from the queue when they are completed within their designated time frame.
  - If a task is not completed, it is preempted and relegated to the end of the backlog.

- **Benefits:**
  - Fairness: Guarantees that all tasks are assigned equally, thereby preventing deprivation.
  - Simplicity: Simple to comprehend and execute.
  - Time-sharing systems and interactive environments are well-suited for responsiveness.
  - Load balancing: Effortlessly distributes the burden among the available resources.

- **List of disadvantages:**
  - Performance overhead: The frequency of context transitioning can result in an increase in overhead.
  - Quantum size dilemma: The selection of the most suitable time quantum is a difficult task that has an impact on performance.
  - Not priority aware: Does not take into account the urgency or priorities of tasks.

Round Robin scheduling is widely used in cloud computing for three key purposes: First, it efficiently distributes VMs across physical hosts, ensuring balanced usage of hardware resources. Second, it allocates tasks among available virtual machines, promoting fair access to computational power. Third, it manages network protocol scheduling in cloud data centers, evenly distributing bandwidth to maintain consistent performance. This versatile algorithm's simplicity and fairness make it a fundamental tool in cloud resource management, providing a balanced approach to handling diverse workloads and resource demands in complex cloud environments [11].

Figure 2.5 illustrates Round Robin scheduling in a cloud environment with four VMs. It shows how four tasks (T1–T4) are allocated equal time quanta in a cyclic manner across the VMs. The circular arrow at the bottom represents the Round Robin cycle, demonstrating the algorithm's fair and rotational nature in distributing processing time among tasks. The Round Robin algorithm is a popular choice in

2.3 Heuristics and Metaheuristics in Cloud Task Scheduling

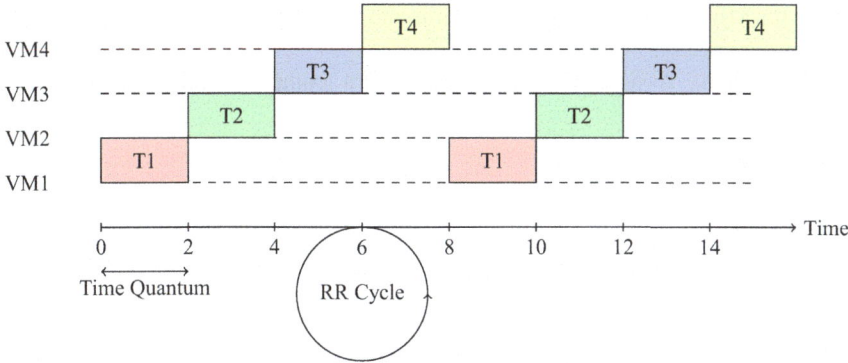

Fig. 2.5 Round Robin scheduling in cloud environment

cloud computing due to its impartiality and simplicity, particularly in scenarios that necessitate responsiveness and balanced resource utilization. Nevertheless, its efficacy may fluctuate contingent upon the workload's characteristics and the cloud environment's particular needs.

2.3 Heuristics and Metaheuristics in Cloud Task Scheduling

In complex environments such as cloud computing, both heuristics and metaheuristics play crucial roles in solving optimization problems, particularly in task scheduling. Let us explore these two categories of problem-solving approaches [12]:

2.3.1 Heuristics

Heuristics are problem-specific techniques designed to find good solutions quickly when classic methods are too slow or fail to find exact solutions. In the context of cloud task scheduling:

- **Characteristics:**
  - Tailored to specific problems or problem types
  - Often based on intuition, common sense, or domain knowledge
  - Generally faster but may not guarantee optimal solutions
  - Useful for reducing the search space in complex problems
- **Examples in cloud task scheduling:**
  - **Shortest job first (SJF):** Prioritizes tasks with the shortest execution time.
  - **Longest job first (LJF):** Prioritizes tasks with the longest execution time.

- **Min-Min:** Assigns tasks with minimum completion time to available resources.
- **Max-Min:** Assigns tasks with maximum completion time to available resources.

- **Advantages:**
    - Quick decision-making in resource allocation
    - Simplicity in implementation
    - Effective for specific, well-defined problem scenarios
- **Limitations:**
    - May lead to suboptimal solutions in complex scenarios
    - Limited adaptability to changing conditions
    - Often not suitable for multi-objective optimization

2.3.2 Metaheuristics

Metaheuristics are higher-level procedures designed to find, generate, or select a heuristic that may provide a sufficiently good solution to an optimization problem. In cloud task scheduling [13]:

- **Characteristics:**
    - Problem-independent strategies
    - Applicable to a wide range of optimization problems
    - Often inspired by natural phenomena or processes
    - Capable of balancing exploration and exploitation in the search space
- **Examples in Cloud Task Scheduling:**
    - **Genetic Algorithms (GA):** Inspired by principles of natural selection:
        - Represents tasks as "chromosomes".
        - Develops a population of potential scheduling solutions.
        - Uses crossover and mutation to generate new solutions.
        - Selects fittest solutions for survival and reproduction.
    - **Ant Colony Optimization (ACO):** Based on foraging behavior of ants:
        - Represents tasks as nodes in a graph.
        - Uses virtual ants to traverse the graph, leaving pheromone trails.
        - Stronger pheromone trails indicate better scheduling decisions.
        - Iteratively updates pheromones to converge on good solutions.
    - **Particle Swarm Optimization (PSO):** Inspired by social behavior of bird flocking or fish schooling:

- Each particle represents a potential scheduling solution.
- Particles move through solution space, updating positions based on global and personal best solutions.
- Swarm converges toward optimal regions of the solution space.

- **Advantages:**
  - Flexibility in handling changing conditions
  - Ability to manage multiple, often conflicting, optimization criteria
  - Scalability for large-scale scheduling problems
  - Potential to avoid local optima and find global or near-global optimal solutions
- **Limitations:**
  - Stochastic nature can lead to variability in solution quality between runs.
  - May require careful parameter tuning for optimal performance.
  - Need to balance solution quality against computational overhead.

2.3.3 Comparison and Application

While both heuristics and metaheuristics aim to solve complex optimization problems, their approaches and applications differ [14]:

- Heuristics are more suitable for specific, well-defined problems where quick decisions are crucial. They excel in scenarios where the problem structure is well-understood and can be exploited directly.
- Metaheuristics are preferred for more complex, multi-objective problems or when the problem space is less understood. They are particularly useful in dynamic cloud environments where adaptability is key.
- In practice, cloud task scheduling often employs a combination of both approaches. For instance, a metaheuristic like GA or ACO might use problem-specific heuristics to initialize solutions or guide local search procedures.

Understanding the distinction between heuristics and metaheuristics is crucial for effective algorithm selection and implementation in cloud task scheduling, allowing for optimized resource utilization, reduced energy consumption, and minimized execution time in diverse and dynamic cloud computing environments.

2.3.4 Adaptive Scheduling Algorithm

Adaptive scheduling algorithms are dynamic task allocation strategies that continuously adjust their decisions based on the current state of the cloud system and real-time performance metrics. These algorithms are designed to respond to the

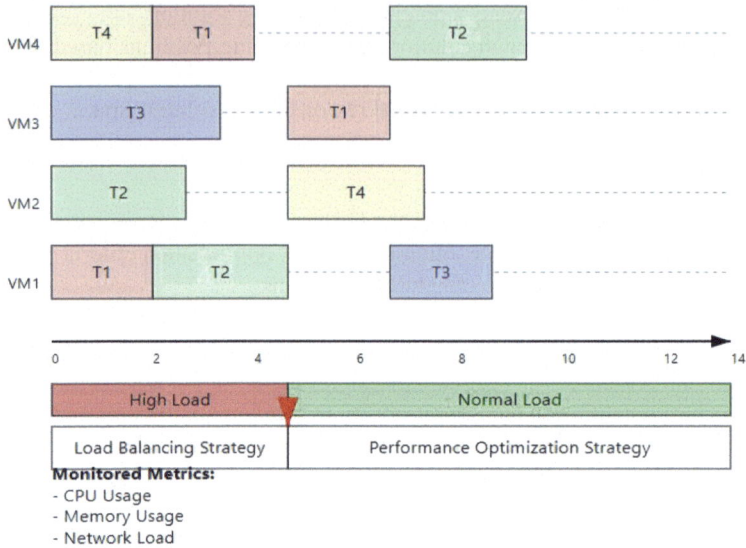

Fig. 2.6 Adaptive scheduling algorithm with dynamic strategy adaptation

ever-changing conditions in cloud environments, such as fluctuating workloads, varying resource availability, and diverse task requirements [7, 13]:

- **Features of Adaptive Scheduling Algorithm include:**
    - Real-time monitoring of system performance and resource utilization
    - Dynamic adjustment of scheduling parameters
    - Ability to switch between different scheduling strategies
    - Continuous optimization based on predefined performance goals

    An adaptive scheduling algorithm in a cloud environment is depicted in Fig. 2.6.
- **Primary elements are as follows:**
    - Task allocation: The upper portion illustrates the distribution of tasks (T1–T4) across four VMs over time. The allocation pattern is contingent upon the current state of the system.
    - System state indicator: The bar at the bottom of the screen denotes the changing system state, transitioning from "High Load" to "Normal Load" at the midpoint.
    - Strategy adaptation: The vertical arrow denotes the point at which the algorithm modifies its strategy in response to the alteration in system state.
    - Diverse approaches: The algorithm's transition from a "Load Balancing Strategy" during high load to a "Performance Optimization Strategy" during normal load is illustrated by the labels at the bottom [15, 16].

- **In this adaptive scheduling scenario:**
  - Tasks are distributed more equitably across VMs to mitigate the burden during the heavy demand period (left side).
  - The algorithm transitions to a strategy that may prioritize performance, potentially clustering tasks differently, as the burden normalizes (right side).
  - The algorithm modifies its scheduling decisions in real time by perpetually monitoring system metrics.

Flexible, context-aware scheduling that can adapt to evolving conditions in the cloud environment is enabled by this methodology. The algorithm can ensure optimal performance and resource utilization in a variety of burden conditions by adjusting its strategy in accordance with the current system state.

2.4 Summary

In cloud computing environments, task scheduling is a complex and critical challenge that has a substantial impact on user satisfaction, resource utilization, and system performance. This chapter has examined a variety of scheduling algorithms, including classical static methods such as FCFS and SJF, as well as more advanced dynamic methods like Round Robin, Adaptive Scheduling, and heuristic-based algorithms like Ant Colony Optimization and Genetic Algorithms. Each algorithm addresses distinct aspects of the scheduling problem, offering varying advantages and trade-offs. Static algorithms offer predictability and simplicity; however, they may encounter difficulties in cloud environments due to their dynamic nature. Conversely, dynamic and adaptive algorithms provide adaptability and responsiveness to evolving system states, albeit at the cost of increased complexity. The capacity to manage multi-objective optimization in large-scale environments is facilitated by heuristic-based approaches. The selection of a scheduling algorithm is contingent upon the performance objectives, workload patterns, and characteristics of the cloud environment. As cloud computing continues to develop, the potential of hybrid approaches to address the diverse and evolving requirements of modern cloud systems is evident. These approaches incorporate the assets of multiple algorithms. Ultimately, the potential of cloud computing is maximized by effective task scheduling, which is essential for the optimization of performance, the optimization of resource efficiency, and the deliverance of high-quality services.

2.5 Exercises

1. A cloud system receives five tasks with burst times of 10, 4, 6, 3, and 8 milliseconds, respectively. Calculate the average waiting time and turnaround time using both the First Come First Serve (FCFS) and Shortest Job First (SJF) scheduling algorithms.

2. Given five tasks arriving at the same time with burst times of 12, 5, 8, 6, and 10 milliseconds, simulate a Round Robin scheduling process with a time quantum of 4 ms. Calculate the average waiting time and turnaround time.
3. Develop a simple Genetic Algorithm (GA) to optimize task scheduling in a cloud environment. The tasks have different execution times and priorities. Write a pseudocode for the GA, and explain how fitness is calculated based on execution time and priority.
4. Compare the performance of static scheduling (FCFS) and dynamic scheduling (Round Robin) in a cloud environment where the load varies significantly over time. Discuss which algorithm performs better in terms of load balancing and resource utilization.
5. Implement Ant Colony Optimization (ACO) to solve the task scheduling problem in a simulated cloud environment. Outline the key parameters (e.g., pheromone evaporation rate, initial pheromone level) and describe how the algorithm evolves over time to optimize scheduling decisions.
6. In the context of multi-objective optimization, discuss how Adaptive Scheduling can be used to balance competing objectives such as minimizing execution time and maximizing resource utilization. Provide a practical example of how these objectives can be weighted and optimized.
7. Choose two scheduling algorithms, for example, Genetic Algorithm (GA) and Round Robin (RR), and compare their performance in cloud computing. Your task includes:

    a. Explaining how each algorithm works
    b. Simulating or describing their performance in terms of execution time, resource usage, and task distribution (load balancing)
    c. Identifying when each algorithm is more effective based on different workloads (e.g., similar or different task sizes)
    d. Presenting your findings using charts or tables

8. Implement an Ant Colony Optimization (ACO) algorithm for task scheduling in a cloud system. Your task includes:

    a. Coding an ACO algorithm to assign tasks
    b. Adjusting ACO parameters (e.g., pheromone levels) to improve scheduling
    c. Comparing ACO results with a simple algorithm like Shortest Job First (SJF) based on execution time, total time (makespan), and resource usage
    d. Writing a short report to explain your work and comparison

References

1. Singh, R.M., Paul, S., Kumar, A.: Task scheduling in cloud computing. Int. J. Comput. Sci. Inf. Technol. **5**(6), 7940–7944 (2014)
2. Arunarani, A.R., Manjula, D., Sugumaran, V.: Task scheduling techniques in cloud computing: a literature survey. Future Gener. Comput. Syst. **91**, 407–415 (2019)

References

3. Gawali, M.B., Shinde, S.K.: Task scheduling and resource allocation in cloud computing using a heuristic approach. J. Cloud Comput. **7**, 1–16 (2018)
4. Lin, X., Wang, Y., Xie, Q., Pedram, M.: Task scheduling with dynamic voltage and frequency scaling for energy minimization in the mobile cloud computing environment. IEEE Trans. Serv. Comput. **8**(2), 175–186 (2015). https://doi.org/10.1109/TSC.2014.2381227
5. Li, K., Jia, L., Shi, X.: Research on cloud computing task scheduling based on PSOMC. J. Web Eng. **21**(6), 1749–1766 (2022). https://doi.org/10.13052/jwe1540-9589.2161
6. Prity, F.S., Gazi, M.H., Uddin, K.A.: A review of task scheduling in cloud computing based on nature-inspired optimization algorithm. Cluster Comput. **26**(5), 3037–3067 (2023)
7. Lipsa, S., Dash, R.K., Ivković, N., Cengiz, K.: Task scheduling in cloud computing: a priority-based heuristic approach. IEEE Access **11**, 27111–27126 (2023). https://doi.org/10.1109/ACCESS.2023.3255781
8. Gad, A.G., Houssein, E.H., Zhou, M., Suganthan, P.N., Wazery, Y.M.: Damping-assisted evolutionary swarm intelligence for industrial IoT task scheduling in cloud computing. IEEE Internet Things J. **11**, 1698–1710 (2024)
9. Nabi, S., Ibrahim, M., Jimenez, J.M.: DRALBA: dynamic and resource aware load balanced scheduling approach for cloud computing. IEEE Access **9**, 61283–61297 (2021). https://doi.org/10.1109/ACCESS.2021.3074145
10. Marahatta, A., Pirbhulal, S., Zhang, F., Parizi, R.M., Choo, K.-K.R., Liu, Z.: Classification-based and energy-efficient dynamic task scheduling scheme for virtualized cloud data center. IEEE Trans. Cloud Comput. **9**(4), 1376–1390 (2021). https://doi.org/10.1109/TCC.2019.2918226
11. Sabat, N.R., Sahoo, R.R., Pradhan, M.R., Acharya, B.: Hybrid technique for optimal task scheduling in cloud computing environments. TELKOMNIKA (Telecommunication Computing Electronics and Control) **22**(2), 380–392 (2024)
12. Al-Maytami, B.A., Fan, P., Hussain, A., Baker, T., Liatsis, P.: A task scheduling algorithm with improved makespan based on prediction of tasks computation time algorithm for cloud computing. IEEE Access **7**, 160916–160926 (2019). https://doi.org/10.1109/ACCESS.2019.2948704
13. Chhabra, S., Saxena, D., Rekha, S.: A review on secure cloud resource management. Authorea Preprints (2023)
14. Pang, S., Li, W., He, H., Shan, Z., Wang, X.: An EDA-GA hybrid algorithm for multi-objective task scheduling in cloud computing. IEEE Access **7**, 146379–146389 (2019). https://doi.org/10.1109/ACCESS.2019.2946216
15. Mangalampalli, S., Karri, G.R., Kumar, M., Khalaf, O.I., Romero, C.A.T., Sahib, G.A.: DRLBTSA: deep reinforcement learning based task-scheduling algorithm in cloud computing. Multimed. Tools Appl. **83**(3), 8359–8387 (2024)
16. Kruekaew, B., Kimpan, W.: Multi-objective task scheduling optimization for load balancing in cloud computing environment using hybrid artificial bee colony algorithm with reinforcement learning. IEEE Access **10**, 17803–17818 (2022). https://doi.org/10.1109/ACCESS.2022.3149955

Chapter 3
Resource Allocation Methods

Abstract This chapter explores various methods of resource allocation in cloud computing, focusing on their efficiency, scalability, and adaptability to changing user demands. The crucial significance that resource allocation plays in cloud computing settings is examined. It presents dynamic resource allocation as a crucial tactic for maximizing system efficiency, cutting expenses, and guaranteeing user happiness. The chapter covers a variety of resource allocation strategies, such as auction-based tactics, heuristic-based methods, optimization-based approaches, and static and dynamic allocation. It explores various strategies for allocation, including those that are cost-based, action-based, energy-usage-based, priority-based, agent-oriented, SLA-based, and so on. The chapter talks about the challenges of implementing dynamic resource allocation well, like predicting demand accurately and making sure that schedules work well across multiple infrastructures. It also stresses how important virtualization technology is for enabling flexible resource management. In order to improve the efficacy and economics of cloud computing environments, the chapter offers a thorough review of resource allocation strategies, which helps users and cloud service providers gain important insights.

Keywords Resource provisioning · Static allocation · Dynamic allocation · Priority-based allocation · SLA-based allocation · Energy-aware Allocation · Cost-based allocation · Resource utilization

3.1 Introduction

In recent years, cloud computing has emerged as a transformative technology that has revolutionized the way resources are allocated and managed in computing environments. Cloud computing offers a paradigm shift from traditional computing models, providing businesses and users with the ability to access and utilize computing resources on-demand, without the need for significant upfront investments in hardware and infrastructure. The elasticity and scalability offered by cloud computing have made it an attractive option for organizations seeking to optimize their resource utilization and adapt to changing business requirements

[1]. One of the key challenges in cloud computing is the efficient allocation of resources to meet the dynamic demands of users. As the number of users and applications hosted in cloud environments continues to grow, the complexity of resource allocation becomes increasingly significant. Cloud service providers must ensure that resources are allocated in a way that maximizes system performance, minimizes costs, and guarantees user satisfaction. This is where dynamic resource allocation comes into play. Dynamic resource allocation refers to the process of automatically adjusting the allocation of computing resources based on real-time system load and user demands. Unlike static resource allocation, where resources are pre-allocated and remain fixed, dynamic resource allocation allows for the flexible and adaptive management of resources in response to changing requirements. By dynamically allocating resources, cloud systems can optimize resource utilization, prevent resource wastage, and ensure that user requests are serviced effectively. The concept of dynamic resource allocation is closely tied to the use of virtualization technology in cloud computing. Virtualization enables the creation of VMs that can be dynamically provisioned and deprovisioned based on user demands. Each VM represents a self-contained computing environment with its own operating system, applications, and resources. By leveraging virtualization, cloud systems can allocate resources at a fine-grained level, allowing for the efficient sharing of physical resources among multiple users and applications [2].

Dynamic resource allocation brings several benefits to cloud computing environments. Firstly, it enables cloud service providers to optimize resource utilization by allocating resources only when they are needed. This leads to improved system efficiency and cost savings, as idle resources can be reallocated to other tasks or users. Secondly, dynamic resource allocation enhances the scalability and elasticity of cloud systems. As user demands fluctuate, resources can be automatically scaled up or down to meet the changing requirements, ensuring that applications have access to the necessary resources to maintain optimal performance. Moreover, dynamic resource allocation plays a crucial role in ensuring QoS in cloud computing environments. By prioritizing resource allocation based on user requirements and SLAs, cloud service providers can guarantee that critical applications and high-priority tasks receive the necessary resources to meet their performance objectives. This is particularly important in scenarios where different users have varying levels of service requirements, such as in multi-tenant cloud environments [3]. However, implementing effective dynamic resource allocation in cloud computing presents several challenges. One of the primary challenges is the accurate prediction of resource demands. Cloud service providers must employ sophisticated techniques to forecast future resource requirements based on historical data, user behavior patterns, and application characteristics. Inaccurate predictions can lead to over-provisioning or under-provisioning of resources, resulting in suboptimal performance and increased costs. Another challenge lies in the efficient scheduling and placement of resources across distributed cloud infrastructures. Cloud systems often consist of multiple data centers and server clusters, each with its own set of resources and constraints. Dynamically allocating resources across these distributed environments requires advanced scheduling algorithms and resource management

3.1 Introduction

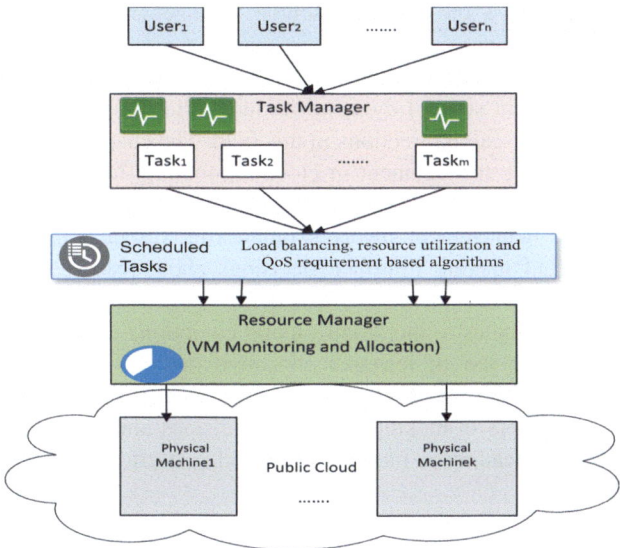

Fig. 3.1 Resource scheduling architecture

frameworks that can take into account factors such as network latency, data locality, and resource heterogeneity.

Figure 3.1 illustrates the task scheduling process in a cloud computing environment. The task scheduler receives scheduled tasks and employs various algorithms based on load balancing, resource utilization, and QoS requirements to optimize task execution. These algorithms ensure efficient allocation of resources and maximize system performance while meeting user expectations [4]. Furthermore, ensuring the security and isolation of dynamically allocated resources is crucial in cloud computing environments. As resources are shared among multiple users and applications, adequate security measures must be in place to prevent unauthorized access, data breaches, and performance interference. This involves implementing secure virtualization techniques, network isolation mechanisms, and access control policies to maintain the confidentiality, integrity, and availability of allocated resources. Despite these challenges, the benefits of dynamic resource allocation in cloud computing far outweigh the complexities involved. By enabling efficient resource utilization, improved scalability, and enhanced QoS, dynamic resource allocation contributes to the overall success and adoption of cloud computing. As cloud technologies continue to evolve, research efforts are focused on developing advanced resource allocation techniques, such as machine learning-based approaches, to further optimize resource management in cloud environments [5].

In the following sections of this chapter, we will delve deeper into the various methods and techniques used for dynamic resource allocation in cloud computing. We will explore the use of virtualization technology, priority-based allocation algorithms, load balancing mechanisms, and resource reservation strategies. Additionally, we will discuss the role of resource management frameworks and the importance of monitoring and analytics in enabling effective dynamic resource allocation. Through this comprehensive analysis, we aim to provide valuable insights into the current state of dynamic resource allocation in cloud computing and highlight future research directions in this field. The chapter also discusses the importance of resource management in cloud computing, highlighting its role in optimizing resource utilization, reducing costs, and improving system performance. Effective resource management involves monitoring resource usage, predicting future demands, and making informed decisions about resource allocation and scheduling.

This chapter contributes to the field of cloud computing concepts by providing a comprehensive overview of resource allocation methods and their impact on system performance. The insights gained from this chapter can assist cloud service providers and users in making informed decisions about resource allocation strategies, ultimately leading to more efficient and cost-effective cloud computing environments.

3.2 Resource Allocation Methods

Resource allocation is a fundamental aspect of cloud computing that deals with the efficient distribution and assignment of computing resources to tasks or applications. In cloud environments, resources such as CPU, memory, storage, and network bandwidth are dynamically allocated to meet the varying demands of users and applications. Effective resource allocation is crucial for optimizing system performance, minimizing costs, and ensuring user satisfaction. Resource provisioning in cloud computing, also known as cloud provisioning, involves allocating services and resources from a cloud provider to a customer. It encompasses the selection, deployment, and management of software (like load balancers and database systems) and hardware resources (such as CPU, storage, and networks) to ensure optimal application performance. Effective resource provisioning involves two key strategies: Static Provisioning/Dynamic Provisioning and Static/Dynamic Allocation of resources, tailored to application needs. The goal is to avoid over-provisioning (unnecessary costs) and under-provisioning (performance issues) [6, 7]. Power management is also vital, with measures to reduce consumption, heat, and optimize VM placement. Both cloud users and providers seek cost-effectiveness while ensuring resource efficiency. The cloud users aim for cost-effective resource rental, while providers aim to maximize profitability through efficient resource distribution. Resource allocation methods in cloud computing as shown in Fig. 3.2 determine how resources are assigned to tasks or users. These methods include static allocation, dynamic allocation, heuristic-based allocation, optimization-based allocation, and auction-based allocation.

3.2 Resource Allocation Methods

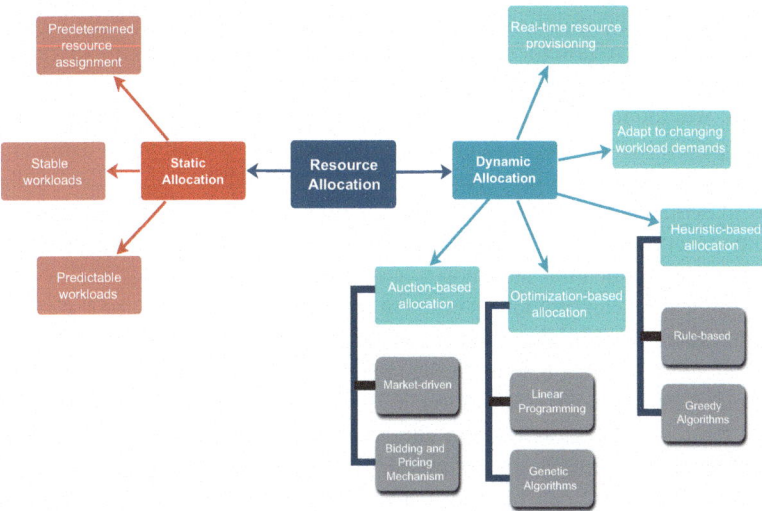

Fig. 3.2 Resource allocation methods

3.2.1 Static Allocation

Static provisioning is a resource allocation method in cloud computing that is well-suited for applications with predictable and consistent resource requirements. In this approach, the cloud provider allocates a fixed set of resources to the customer, who is then responsible for managing and utilizing these resources effectively without exceeding the allocated capacity. This method is particularly useful for applications with stable workloads, such as a database server requiring a specific amount of CPU, RAM, and storage. Under static provisioning, the cloud service provider prepares the necessary resources before the service commences, and the customer is charged either a one-time fee or a recurring monthly cost. However, this pre-allocation of resources can lead to potential issues of over-provisioning or under-provisioning, as the customer must estimate their resource needs in advance, which may not always align with the actual demand. The total resources allocated to all customers should not exceed the total available resources.

$$\sum_{i=1}^{N} A_i \leq R \tag{3.1}$$

where R is the total resources available, N is number of customers, and A_i is amount of resources allocated to customer i. There are three types of static allocation:

1. **Predetermined resource assignment**: In perpetual allocation, resources are allocated to customers for an indefinite period. Once the resources are assigned, they remain with the customer until they explicitly release them or terminate the

service. This type of allocation is suitable for customers who have long-term, stable resource requirements and want to ensure the availability of resources without the need for frequent adjustments [8].
2. **Stable workloads**: Stable workloads are characterized by consistent resource usage patterns over time, with minimal fluctuations or variations in demand. The resource usage remains relatively steady over time, without significant spikes or dips in demand. This consistency enables efficient resource allocation and helps avoid over-provisioning or under-provisioning of resources. When the resource needs of an application are known in advance and remain relatively constant, static allocation can provide an efficient and cost-effective solution.
3. **Predictable Workloads**: Predictable workloads are characterized by well-defined and consistent resource usage patterns, allowing for accurate estimation and planning of resource allocation. When the resource needs of an application can be reliably forecasted, static allocation offers several benefits. Predictable workloads often have predictable scaling requirements. The growth or changes in resource demand can be anticipated based on factors such as user growth, data volume increase, or planned application enhancements. This predictability enables proactive capacity planning and resource allocation adjustments to accommodate future needs.

3.2.2 Dynamic Allocation

Dynamic provisioning is a flexible and cost-effective resource allocation method in cloud computing that adjusts the allocated resources based on the varying demands of applications. In this approach, the cloud service provider dynamically adds or removes resources as needed, allowing customers to scale their resource usage up or down in real time. This elasticity enables efficient resource utilization and helps avoid the issues of over-provisioning or under-provisioning associated with static provisioning. One of the key advantages of dynamic provisioning is its pay-per-use model, also known as the pay-as-you-go model. Under this pricing scheme, customers are billed only for the actual resources they consume, rather than paying for a fixed amount of pre-allocated resources. This model provides financial benefits to customers, as they can optimize their resource usage and costs based on their changing requirements [9]. Dynamic provisioning is particularly suitable for applications with unpredictable or fluctuating workloads, such as web servers or data processing tasks. For example, an e-commerce website may experience varying traffic loads throughout the day, requiring different levels of CPU, memory, and storage resources. With dynamic provisioning, the customer can automatically scale the resources based on the incoming traffic, ensuring optimal performance and user experience. To facilitate dynamic provisioning, cloud service providers often employ virtualization technologies and sophisticated resource management systems. These systems monitor the resource utilization of each customer and dynamically allocate or deallocate resources based on predefined policies and

3.2 Resource Allocation Methods

thresholds [10]. This process is typically transparent to the customer, who can focus on their application logic, while the cloud platform handles the resource management aspects. The total resources allocated to all customers should not exceed the total available resources at any given time t.

$$\sum_{i=1}^{N(t)} A_i(t) \leq R(t) \tag{3.2}$$

The actual resource utilization by a customer should not exceed the allocated resources at time t.

$$D_i(t) \leq A_i(t), \text{ for each customer } i \tag{3.3}$$

The total cost incurred by a customer over a period of time (from t_1 to t_2) is the sum of the costs at each time point.

$$\text{Total Cost for customer } i = \int_{t_1}^{t_2} C_i(t), dt \tag{3.4}$$

where $C_i(t)$ is the cost charged to customer i at time t. These equations capture the dynamic nature of resource allocation and billing in dynamic provisioning. The resource allocation $A_i(t)$ adapts to the actual demand $D_i(t)$ at each time point, ensuring optimal utilization. The cost calculation is based on the actual resource usage, providing a pay-per-use model. The total cost for a customer is determined by integrating the costs over a specific time period. Dynamic provisioning offers flexibility, cost optimization, and efficient resource utilization for applications with varying resource requirements. However, it also requires careful monitoring and management to ensure that resources are not oversubscribed, which could lead to performance degradation or unexpected costs:

1. **Real-time resource provisioning**: Real-time resource provisioning is a dynamic allocation technique used in cloud computing environments. It allows for automatic and immediate allocation or deallocation of resources based on the fluctuating demands of applications or workloads. This method empowers the cloud system to dynamically scale resources, such as CPU, memory, or storage, up or down in real time, adapting to the changing resource needs of users. In real-time resource provisioning, the cloud provider constantly monitors the resource usage and performance indicators of the applications hosted on the cloud infrastructure. When there is an increased demand for resources, the system automatically provisions additional resources to handle the increased workload. On the other hand, when the demand decreases, the system releases the surplus resources, optimizing resource utilization and cost-effectiveness [11]. Real-time resource provisioning offers numerous advantages, including flexibility, agility, and cost efficiency.

2. **Adapt to changing workloads**: Dynamic allocation methods in cloud computing are designed to adapt to the changing workloads of applications and services by automatically adjusting resource allocation based on real-time demands and requirements. These methods rely on real-time monitoring, workload analysis, and prediction to understand workload characteristics and anticipate future resource needs. Through automatic scaling, elastic resource allocation, load balancing, and threshold-based scaling, dynamic allocation methods enable applications to seamlessly handle sudden spikes in traffic or user activity without experiencing performance degradation. The cloud system continuously optimizes resource allocation based on changing workload patterns, maximizing resource utilization (U), minimizing costs (C), and maintaining desired performance levels (P). Mathematical models, such as time series analysis and machine learning algorithms, are employed to predict future resource requirements (R) based on historical data (H), i.e., $R = f(H)$. Scaling policies are defined using threshold-based rules, where resources are provisioned or released when certain metrics (M), such as CPU utilization or response time, exceed or fall below predefined thresholds (T), i.e., if $M > T$, then scale up; if $M < T$, then scale down. By using these methods and mathematical foundations, dynamic allocation methods can respond well to how workloads change, making sure that performance is at its best and costs are kept low in the cloud.
3. **Heuristic-based allocation**: Heuristic-based allocation in cloud computing is a resource allocation approach that relies on predefined rules, policies, or algorithms to make allocation decisions. The methods use heuristics, which are practical and often experience-based techniques, to determine the optimal allocation of resources to applications or workloads. Mathematically, let $A = a_1, a_2, \ldots, a_n$ be the set of applications or workloads, and $R = r_1, r_2, \ldots, r_m$ be the set of available resources.

Figure 3.3 shows the working of heuristic algorithms. It illustrates how to find the best optimal solution for deployment. This thesis works on the heuristic models for task scheduling that is based on finding the optimal host that not only minimizes the makespan time of tasks but also increases the resource utilization. It meets the resources and fulfills the objectives for better deployment of tasks in the cloud environment.

The allocation problem can be formulated as a mapping function $f : A \rightarrow R$, where each application a_i is mapped to a resource r_j based on the heuristic rules or policies. The heuristic rules can be represented as a set of conditions and actions:

$$\text{if } condition_1 \text{ then } action_1$$

$$\text{if } condition_2 \text{ then } action_2$$

$$\vdots$$

$$\text{if } condition_k \text{ then } action_k$$

3.2 Resource Allocation Methods

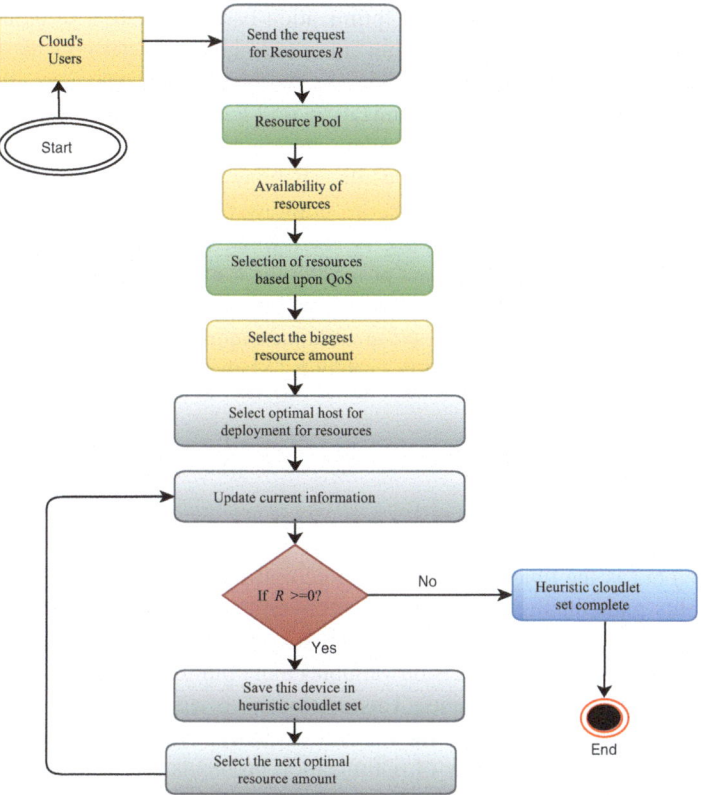

Fig. 3.3 Working of heuristic algorithm

These conditions are evaluated based on the current system state, and the corresponding actions determine the resource allocation decisions. Heuristic-based allocation methods, such as rule-based allocation, priority-based allocation, and greedy algorithms, have the advantage of being simple to implement and can provide fast allocation decisions, but they may not always produce the best possible allocation in dynamic or complex cloud environments:

a. **Rule-based allocation**: Rule-based allocation algorithms in heuristic-based allocation use a set of predefined if-then rules to determine resource allocation decisions. These rules are evaluated based on the current system state, and the corresponding actions are taken to allocate resources to applications or workloads.

b. **Greedy algorithm**: Greedy algorithms in heuristic-based allocation make locally optimal decisions at each step, aiming to find a globally optimal solution. They allocate resources to applications based on their immediate resource requirements, without considering the long-term impact on overall system performance.

4. **Optimization-based allocation**: Optimization-based allocation in cloud computing leverages mathematical optimization techniques to determine the optimal allocation of resources to applications or workloads. The resource allocation problem is formulated as an optimization problem, where the objective is to maximize or minimize a specific goal, such as minimizing cost, maximizing performance, or ensuring fairness, while satisfying a set of defined constraints.

   Various optimization techniques are employed depending on the nature of the problem. Linear programming is used when the objective function and constraints are linear, while integer programming is used when decision variables are required to be integers. Heuristic optimization techniques, such as genetic algorithms and particle swarm optimization, are applied to solve complex, nonlinear, or large-scale optimization problems. Mathematically, the optimization problem is represented as

   $$\text{max/min} \quad f(x) \text{ subject to} \qquad g_i(x) \leq 0, \quad i = 1, 2, \ldots, m$$
   $$h_j(x) = 0, \quad j = 1, 2, \ldots, p \qquad x \in \mathbb{R}^n \text{ or } x \in \mathbb{Z}^n$$

   where $f(x)$ is the objective function to be optimized, $g_i(x)$ and $h_j(x)$ are the inequality and equality constraints, respectively, and x is the vector of decision variables representing the resource allocation. Optimization-based allocation aims to find the values of decision variables that optimize the objective function while satisfying the constraints. This approach provides theoretically optimal solutions, taking into account the defined objectives and constraints. However, the computational complexity of optimization problems can be high, especially for large-scale cloud environments, requiring efficient solvers and heuristic techniques to obtain near-optimal solutions in a practical time frame:

   - **Linear programming**: It is an optimization method employed when the objective function and constraints can be expressed as linear equations or inequalities. It seeks to determine the optimal values of decision variables that optimize a linear objective function while satisfying a set of linear constraints. LP problems are efficiently solved using algorithms such as the simplex method or interior-point methods.
   - **Genetic algorithms**: It is a heuristic optimization technique that draws inspiration from the principles of natural selection and genetics. They involve encoding potential solutions as chromosomes, assessing their fitness based on the objective function, and applying genetic operators like selection, crossover, and mutation to evolve the population iteratively. GA is effective for tackling complex, nonlinear, or large-scale optimization problems and can provide near-optimal solutions within a practical computational time [12].

5. **Auction-based allocation**: Auction-based allocation is a market-driven approach to resource allocation in cloud computing, where resources are allocated to users based on their willingness to pay. In this method, users bid for resources, and the allocation is determined by the auction mechanism, with the goal of maximizing

the overall utility or revenue while ensuring fair and efficient allocation. Cloud providers act as auctioneers, and users act as bidders, submitting their bids indicating their resource requirements and maximum price. The auction-based allocation problem can be formulated as an optimization problem. Let N be the set of users and R be the set of resources. Each user $i \in N$ has a valuation function $v_i(r)$ that represents their willingness to pay for a resource $r \in R$. The objective is to allocate resources to users in a way that maximizes the total utility or revenue.

The optimization problem can be expressed as

$$\max \sum_{i \in N} \sum_{r \in R} v_i(r) \cdot x_{i,r}$$

$$\text{subject to} \quad \sum_{i \in N} x_{i,r} \leq 1, \quad \forall r \in R$$

$$x_{i,r} \in {0, 1}, \quad \forall i \in N, \forall r \in R$$

where $x_{i,r}$ is a binary decision variable indicating whether resource r is allocated to user i. The first constraint ensures that each resource is allocated to at most one user, and the second constraint enforces binary allocation:

- **Market-driven**: This resource allocation in cloud computing involves allocating resources based on supply and demand principles, allowing users to bid for resources according to their willingness to pay. This approach promotes efficient allocation, fair competition, and dynamic pricing.
- **Billing and pricing mechanisms**: Pay-as-you-go, spot pricing, and reserved pricing are crucial components of market-driven allocation, determining how users are charged for resource usage. These pricing mechanisms offer flexibility and cost optimization opportunities for users while enabling providers to maximize revenue and efficiently utilize resources.

3.3 Allocation Policies or Techniques

Figure 3.4 presents an overview of various resource allocation techniques used in cloud computing environments. These techniques include priority-based allocation, agent-oriented allocation, SLA-based allocation, energy-usage-based allocation, action-based allocation, and cost-based allocation. Each of these techniques focuses on different aspects and criteria to optimize resource allocation, ensuring efficient utilization of resources while meeting the specific requirements of tasks, applications, and users in the cloud [13].

Fig. 3.4 Resource allocation techniques

3.3.1 Priority-based Allocation

Priority-based allocation assigns resources to tasks or applications based on their relative importance or priority. Each task is assigned a priority value, and resources are allocated according to the priority order. The allocation can be represented mathematically as

$$\text{Allocation}(i) = \frac{P_i}{\sum_{j=1}^{n} P_j} \tag{3.5}$$

where P_i is the priority of task i, and n is the total number of tasks. This equation calculates the proportion of resources allocated to task i based on its priority relative to the sum of all task priorities. In practice, priority-based allocation can be implemented using different priority assignment schemes, such as static priorities, dynamic priorities based on task characteristics, or user-defined priorities. The priority values can be determined based on factors like task urgency, criticality, or SLA requirements. Priority-based allocation ensures that high-priority tasks receive resources before low-priority tasks, allowing for the prioritization of critical or time-sensitive workloads. However, it may lead to the starvation of low-priority tasks if high-priority tasks consume most of the resources. To mitigate this, techniques like priority inheritance or priority aging can be employed to prevent indefinite starvation.

3.3.2 Agent-oriented Allocation

Agent-oriented allocation involves the use of intelligent agents to manage and allocate resources in a distributed manner. Each agent is responsible for a specific set

3.3 Allocation Policies or Techniques

of resources and communicates with other agents to coordinate allocation decisions. The objective of agent-oriented allocation is to maximize the overall utility, which can be represented as

$$\max \sum_{i=1}^{m} U_i(A_i) \quad (3.6)$$

where A_i is the allocation decision made by agent i, U_i is the utility function of agent i, and m is the total number of agents. The utility function represents the satisfaction or benefit achieved by an agent based on its allocation decision. Agent-oriented allocation enables decentralized and collaborative resource management, allowing agents to adapt to dynamic changes in the system. Agents can employ various negotiation and coordination mechanisms, such as auction-based approaches or consensus algorithms, to reach optimal allocation decisions. The main advantage of agent-oriented allocation is its ability to handle complex and dynamic resource allocation scenarios. Agents can consider multiple factors, such as resource availability, task requirements, and system load, to make informed allocation decisions. However, the effectiveness of agent-oriented allocation depends on the design and coordination mechanisms of the agents, as well as the communication overhead among them.

3.3.3 SLA-based Allocation

SLA-based allocation focuses on meeting the agreed-upon service levels between the cloud provider and the users. The allocation aims to minimize the SLA violations, which can be expressed as

$$\min \sum_{i=1}^{n} \max(0, S_i - R_i) \quad (3.7)$$

where S_i is the SLA requirement for task i, R_i is the resources allocated to task i, and n is the total number of tasks. This equation minimizes the sum of SLA violations, where a violation occurs when the allocated resources R_i are less than the SLA requirement S_i. SLA-based allocation prioritizes tasks or applications based on their SLA commitments and dynamically adjusts resource allocation to maintain the desired service quality. It involves monitoring the performance metrics specified in the SLAs, such as response time, throughput, or availability, and taking corrective actions when SLA violations are detected. To implement SLA-based allocation, techniques like resource reservation, performance prediction, and dynamic resource scaling can be employed. Resource reservation ensures that the necessary resources are allocated to meet the SLA requirements, while performance prediction helps in proactively identifying potential SLA violations. Dynamic resource scaling allows for the adjustment of resource allocation based on the actual performance measurements and SLA conformance.

3.3.4 Energy-usage-based Allocation

Energy-usage-based allocation aims to optimize resource allocation while minimizing energy consumption in the cloud environment. It takes into account the energy efficiency of resources and allocates tasks to resources that consume less energy. The objective of energy-usage-based allocation can be represented as

$$\min \sum_{i=1}^{m} E_i \cdot x_i \tag{3.8}$$

where E_i is the energy consumption of resource i, x_i is a binary variable indicating whether resource i is used, and m is the total number of resources. This equation minimizes the total energy consumption, subject to the resource capacity and task performance constraints. Energy-usage-based allocation involves monitoring energy consumption patterns, consolidating workloads onto fewer resources during low-demand periods, and leveraging power-saving features of hardware components. It may also consider the thermal characteristics of resources and optimize the placement of tasks to minimize cooling energy consumption. To implement energy-usage-based allocation, techniques like dynamic voltage and frequency scaling (DVFS), resource consolidation, and power-aware scheduling can be employed. DVFS allows for the adjustment of CPU voltage and frequency to reduce energy consumption, while resource consolidation involves migrating tasks to a smaller number of active resources to minimize idle energy waste. Power-aware scheduling considers the energy profiles of resources and assigns tasks to the most energy-efficient resources available [14].

3.3.5 Action-based Allocation

Action-based allocation considers the specific actions or operations performed by tasks or applications when allocating resources. It analyzes the resource requirements of different actions and allocates resources accordingly. The allocation can be represented as

$$\text{Allocation}(i) = \frac{r_i}{\sum_{j=1}^{n} r_j} \tag{3.9}$$

3.3 Allocation Policies or Techniques

where r_i is the resources required for action a_i of task i, and n is the total number of tasks. This equation calculates the proportion of resources allocated to task i based on the resource requirements of its action relative to the total resource requirements of all tasks. Action-based allocation considers the specific characteristics and demands of individual tasks or applications. For example, tasks involving CPU-intensive computations would be allocated more CPU resources, while tasks requiring high I/O operations would be allocated more storage and network resources. To implement action-based allocation, techniques like profiling and resource usage prediction can be employed. Profiling involves analyzing the resource usage patterns of tasks or applications to identify their resource requirements for different actions. Resource usage prediction helps in estimating the future resource demands based on historical data and machine learning models.

3.3.6 Cost-based Allocation

Cost-based allocation focuses on minimizing the overall operational costs while meeting the resource requirements of tasks or applications. It considers factors such as the pricing models of cloud resources, the duration of resource usage, and the performance requirements of tasks. The objective of cost-based allocation can be represented as

$$\min \sum_{i=1}^{m} C_i \cdot x_i \qquad (3.10)$$

where C_i is the cost of using resource i, x_i is a binary variable indicating whether resource i is used, and m is the total number of resources. This equation minimizes the total cost, subject to the resource capacity and task performance constraints. Cost-based allocation employs optimization algorithms to determine the most cost-effective combination of resources for each task or application. It considers the pricing models of different resource types, such as on-demand instances, reserved instances, or spot instances, and selects the optimal mix of resources based on the workload requirements and budget constraints. To implement cost-based allocation, techniques like linear programming, integer programming, or heuristic algorithms can be used [15]. These techniques solve the optimization problem and determine the optimal resource allocation that minimizes the total cost while satisfying the performance requirements. Cost-based allocation helps organizations optimize their cloud spending and make informed decisions about resource allocation based on budget constraints. It enables them to balance cost and performance objectives and utilize the most cost-effective resources available in the cloud environment. These resource allocation techniques offer different approaches to optimize resource utilization, meet performance requirements, and achieve specific objectives in cloud computing environments. The choice of technique depends on the specific requirements, constraints, and characteristics of the workloads and the cloud infrastructure.

3.4 Summary

This chapter presents a detailed review of resource allocation strategies in cloud computing, emphasizing its importance in improving system performance, cost efficiency, and user happiness. The chapter examines the transition from static to dynamic resource allocation, emphasizing the need of flexibility and adaptability in addressing changing user demands. The key resource allocation methods explored include static and dynamic allocation, heuristic-based approaches, optimization-based techniques, and auction-based tactics. The chapter looks into several allocation strategies such as priority-based, agent-oriented, SLA-based, energy-usage-based, action-based, and cost-based allocations, each of which provides distinct benefits for particular circumstances. The relevance of virtualization technology in allowing efficient resource management is highlighted, as are the limitations of implementing effective dynamic resource allocation. These problems include accurate demand forecast, effective scheduling across dispersed infrastructures, and balancing numerous goals including performance, affordability, and energy economy. The chapter emphasizes the need of advanced algorithms and frameworks for managing the complexity of resource allocation in cloud systems. It emphasizes the potential of future technology, such as machine learning, to improve resource allocation tactics. Overall, this chapter offers useful insights for cloud service providers and consumers, assisting in the creation of more efficient, cost-effective, and user-centered cloud computing environments. It paves the way for more study and innovation in cloud resource management.

3.5 Exercises

1. Compare the following resource allocation strategies in cloud computing:

    a. VM technology
    b. Dynamic resource provisioning
    c. Load balancing

    Your comparison should focus on the following factors:

    - Scalability
    - Adaptability to changing user demands
    - Efficiency in terms of resource utilization

2. A cloud service provider uses a modified priority algorithm to allocate resources for different tasks. Assume the following tasks arrive:

    - Task A (Priority 1): 1000 units of computation, costs $0.05 per unit
    - Task B (Priority 2): 800 units of computation, costs $0.03 per unit
    - Task C (Priority 3): 600 units of computation, costs $0.02 per unit

3.5 Exercises

Use a modified priority scheduling algorithm to calculate:

a. The total cost of processing these tasks
b. The percentage of cost reduction if resources are dynamically provisioned to prioritize Task C

3. Implement a basic machine learning algorithm (e.g., linear regression or decision trees) to predict cloud resource allocation based on workload characteristics such as CPU usage, memory, and network bandwidth. Your project should include:

   a. Data collection and preprocessing
   b. Model training and validation
   c. Analysis of the model's accuracy and how it improves resource allocation

4. Conduct a case study comparing static resource provisioning and dynamic resource provisioning in cloud environments. Your case study should include:

   a. A real-world scenario where user demands fluctuate (e.g., e-commerce websites during sales)
   b. An analysis of resource utilization, cost, and performance under static and dynamic provisioning
   c. A recommendation for the best approach based on your findings

5. Investigate the impact of energy-efficient resource allocation strategies on cloud computing. Write a report that includes:

   a. The importance of energy efficiency in cloud data centers.
   b. An overview of energy-efficient techniques, such as workload consolidation or DVFS (Dynamic Voltage and Frequency Scaling).
   c. Analyze the trade-off between performance and energy efficiency in real-world cloud systems.

6. Develop and implement a heuristic algorithm (e.g., Genetic Algorithm or Particle Swarm Optimization) for optimizing cloud resource allocation. Include:

   a. A description of the algorithm and how it works
   b. A simulation environment where the algorithm allocates resources based on changing workloads
   c. A performance analysis comparing the heuristic algorithm with a traditional allocation method like First Come First Serve (FCFS)

7. Analyze how resource reservation policies can enhance cloud performance in high- demand situations. Specifically, explore how reservation policies affect:

   a. User satisfaction during peak times (e.g., large video streaming events)
   b. Resource utilization and overall system cost
   c. Trade-offs between reserving resources in advance versus on-demand provisioning

8. Design a cloud resource allocation model that ensures Quality of Service (QoS) requirements are met for different types of users (e.g., premium vs. regular users). Your model should include:

a. How resources are prioritized for premium users
b. How to maintain a balance between meeting QoS requirements and optimizing resource use
c. A performance evaluation of your model in terms of response time and service availability

References

1. Pradhan, P., Behera, P.K., Ray, B.N.B.: 6 resource allocation methodologies in cloud computing: a review and analysis. In: Applications of Machine Learning in Big-Data Analytics and Cloud Computing, pp. 115–138. River Publishers (2021)
2. Farooq, J., Zhu, Q.: Revenue maximizing cloud resource allocation. In: Resource Management for On-Demand Mission-Critical Internet of Things Applications, pp. 125–139. IEEE (2021). https://doi.org/10.1002/9781119716112.ch9
3. Liu, F., Huang, J., Wang, X.: Joint task offloading and resource allocation for device-edge-cloud collaboration with subtask dependencies. IEEE Trans. Cloud Comput. **11**(3), 3027–3039 (2023). https://doi.org/10.1109/TCC.2023.3251561
4. Wei, W., Yang, R., Gu, H., Zhao, W., Chen, C., Wan, S.: Multi-objective optimization for resource allocation in vehicular cloud computing networks. IEEE Trans. Intell. Transp. Syst. **23**(12), 25536–25545 (2022). https://doi.org/10.1109/TITS.2021.3091321
5. Saxena, D., Singh, A.K.: An oversubscription and service pricing exploitation-based profit maximization framework for industry cloud resource management. IEEE Trans. Serv. Comput. (2024). https://doi.org/10.1109/TSC.2024.3445379
6. Xu, Y., Gui, G., Gacanin, H., Adachi, F.: A survey on resource allocation for 5g heterogeneous networks: current research, future trends, and challenges. IEEE Commun. Surv. Tutor. **23**(2), 668–695 (2021). https://doi.org/10.1109/COMST.2021.3059896
7. Saidi, K., Bardou, D.: Task scheduling and VM placement to resource allocation in Cloud computing: challenges and opportunities. Cluster Comput. **26**, 3069–3087 (2023)
8. Saxena, D., Singh, A.K.: A comprehensive survey on sustainable resource management in cloud computing environments. Authorea Preprints (2024)
9. Shukur, H., Zeebaree, S., Zebari, R., Zeebaree, D., Ahmed, O., Salih, A.: Cloud computing virtualization of resources allocation for distributed systems. J. Appl. Sci. Technol. Trends **1**(2), 98–105 (2020)
10. Patni, S., Lee, J.: Explainable AI empowered resource management for enhanced communication efficiency in hierarchical federated learning. Comput. Electr. Eng. **117**, 109260 (2024)
11. Chen, J., Xing, H., Xiao, Z., Xu, L., Tao, T.: A DRL agent for jointly optimizing computation offloading and resource allocation in MEC. IEEE Internet Things J. **8**(24), 17508–17524 (2021). https://doi.org/10.1109/JIOT.2021.3081694
12. Chhabra, S., Singh, A.K.: A smart resource management mechanism with trust access control for cloud computing environment. arXiv preprint arXiv:2212.05319 (2022)
13. Swain, S.R., Parashar, A., Singh, A.K., Lee, C.N.: An energy efficient virtual machine placement scheme for intelligent resource management at cloud data center. In: 2023 OITS International Conference on Information Technology (OCIT), pp. 65–70. IEEE, Raipur, India (2023). https://doi.org/10.1109/OCIT59427.2023.10430915
14. Mousavi, S., Mosavi, A., Varkonyi-Koczy, A.R., Fazekas, G.: Dynamic resource allocation in cloud computing. Acta Polytech. Hung. **14**(4), 83–104 (2017)
15. Karimunnisa, S., Pachipala, Y.: An AHP based task scheduling and optimal resource allocation in cloud computing. Int. J. Adv. Comput. Sci. Appl. **14**(3) (2023)

Chapter 4
Dynamic Resource Allocation Models

Abstract Dynamic resource allocation is the real-time adjustment and distribution of computing resources like CPU, memory, storage, and network bandwidth to effectively respond to evolving demands. In this chapter, frameworks are developed to revolve around dynamic resource allocation and load balancing, placing a heightened focus on the optimization of virtual machine placements. These frameworks are designed to address load balancing challenges by mitigating issues such as traffic congestion, reducing system failures, and improving resource utilization. Unlike traditional sequential or random placement methods, the proposed algorithms show superior performance characterized by increased throughput and minimized resource wastage. The chapter covers a detailed performance assessment that demonstrates the impressive results achieved by these innovative algorithms compared to established, widely known approaches.

Keywords Hierarchical load balancer · Application-aware HLB · Resource constraints · Load distribution · Performance optimization · Resource efficiency · Workload management · Adaptive allocation

4.1 Introduction

Effective resource management has become essential in the rapidly changing cloud computing environment to guarantee peak performance, affordability, and user satisfaction. The need for smart and flexible resource allocation solutions has grown as cloud service complexity and scale continue to expand [1]. This chapter explores creative solutions to the problems of resource management in cloud settings by diving into the world of dynamic resource allocation models. The term "dynamic resource allocation" describes how computer resources, including CPU, memory, storage, and network bandwidth, are distributed and adjusted in real time in response to changing needs [2]. Dynamic allocation enables the flexible and effective use of existing resources, responding to the constantly changing demands of users and applications, in contrast to static allocation techniques, which preassign fixed resources. The chapter presents the Hierarchical Load Balancer (HLB) and the

Application-aware Hierarchical Load Balancer (AHLB), two important frameworks intended to optimize resource allocation and load balancing in cloud data centers. These models provide better performance with less resource waste and higher throughput, which is a major improvement over sequential or random placement techniques.

In order to solve load balancing issues [3], the HLB architecture focuses on optimizing VM placements. HLB seeks to maximize system performance while minimizing energy consumption by addressing problems such as traffic congestion, reducing system failures, and increasing resource utilization. This methodology takes into account many resource restrictions, such as CPU, memory, and energy consumption, to determine the ideal physical machine for job distribution. The AHLB scheme, which expands on the HLB model, adds an application-aware element to the resource allocation procedure. This novel method classifies applications as CPU-intensive, memory-intensive, energy-intensive, or bandwidth-intensive based on an analysis of their unique resource needs. AHLB makes resource management more granular and effective, which adjusts the resource allocation method to the particular requirements of each type of application.

Both frameworks are intended to maximize resource utilization and minimize power usage in cloud data centers while satisfying service level agreements (SLAs). These models assist in preventing over-provisioning and unnecessary power usage by dynamically adjusting resource allocation in response to real-time application needs. This helps to save cost and promote environmental sustainability [4]. Through in-depth performance analyses, the chapter offers a thorough examination of these dynamic resource allocation models, showcasing their efficacy. These novel methods yield significant gains in reducer makespan, scalability of traffic, and overall system efficiency compared to conventional methodologies. The creation of complex resource allocation algorithms is essential as cloud computing continues to play a major role in our digital infrastructure. This chapter provides insightful information on the most recent developments in this subject, opening the door to cloud computing systems that are more effective, scalable, and sustainable [5].

4.2 Hierarchical Load Balancer for Cloud Data Centers

A Hierarchical Load Balancer (HLB) is a system that efficiently manages the allocation of tasks across various computing resources, like servers or nodes, in a hierarchical and adaptable manner. This load balancer makes dynamic decisions on where to assign tasks based on factors such as resource availability, capacity, and the current workload. This ensures that computing resources are used efficiently and that performance remains optimal, even in complex and evolving environments [6, 7]. It serves as a unified framework for traffic management by optimizing the placement of VMs in cloud data centers. The primary goal is to minimize energy consumption while improving resource utilization. HLB achieves this by strategically placing VMs to access key performance indicators, including high execution

4.2 Hierarchical Load Balancer for Cloud Data Centers

efficiency, resource utilization, and external service performance. It selects the most suitable host that meets task deployment requirements. The motivation behind the development of HLB is to address the limitations of existing load balancing techniques and provide a more efficient and adaptive solution for cloud data centers. The key objectives of HLB are as follows:

- Minimize energy consumption: By optimizing the placement of VMs on physical servers, HLB aims to reduce the overall energy consumption of the data center. This is achieved by consolidating VMs onto fewer servers and switching off idle servers when possible.
- Improve resource utilization: HLB seeks to maximize the utilization of available resources, such as CPU, memory, and network bandwidth. By intelligently allocating VMs to servers based on their resource requirements and the current system state, HLB ensures that resources are efficiently utilized, reducing waste and improving overall system performance.
- Enhance traffic scalability: As the volume of traffic in cloud data centers continues to grow, it is crucial to have a load balancing mechanism that can scale effectively. HLB is designed to handle high traffic loads by dynamically adjusting the allocation of resources based on the incoming workload.

HLB considers the traffic flow between different hosts in data centers, taking into account resource constraints related to CPU, memory, and energy consumption, prioritizing these factors. It efficiently places VMs by considering the hierarchical network architecture and multidimensional resource constraints, contributing to improved traffic scalability. This approach selects the optimal host that meets multi-dimensional resource constraints related to computing capability and performance. Overall, this method significantly improves traffic scalability compared to sequential and random VM placement strategies [8–10].

4.2.1 System Model

Figure 4.1 illustrates that the system model of HLB consists of the following components:

1. Clients: A set of users or applications that generate requests for cloud services
2. Job requests: The incoming workload from clients, representing the tasks or services to be executed in the cloud environment
3. Servers: Physical machines that host virtual machines and provide computational resources
4. Virtual machines: Software instances running on physical servers, providing the execution environment for client requests
5. Physical hosts: The actual physical machines that host the VMs

HLB as shown operates by mapping job requests from clients to the optimal physical hosts through a mapping function. The mapping function takes into account various

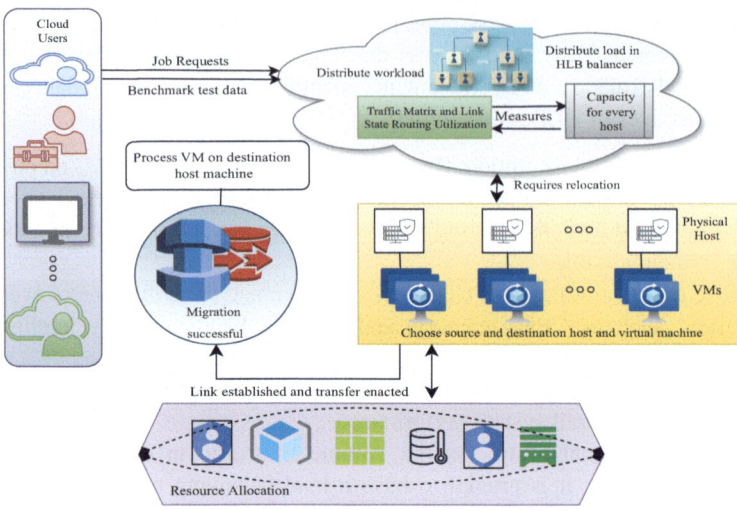

Fig. 4.1 HFL system model

factors, such as the resource requirements of the job requests, the available capacity of the physical hosts, and the current system state.

The system model consists of a set of clients $C = C_1, C_2, \ldots, C_n$, where each client submits a set of job requests $J = J_1, J_2, \ldots, J_j$ to be processed by a set of servers $S = S_1, S_2, \ldots, S_s$. Each server hosts a set of virtual machines $VM = VM_1, VM_2, \ldots, VM_v$, which are responsible for executing the job requests. The physical hosts $PH = PH_1, PH_2, \ldots, PH_m$ reside within the servers and provide the actual computational resources. The allocation of job requests to physical hosts is determined by a mapping function $f : C \times J \to PH$, where $f(C_i, J_j) = PH_m$ indicates that job request J_j from client C_i is allocated to physical host PH_m. The binary variable $x_{j,m}$ represents the allocation decision, with $x_{j,m} = 1$ if job request J_j is allocated to the optimal physical host PH_m, and $x_{j,m} = 0$ otherwise.

4.2.2 Resource Constraints

To ensure a feasible VM placement, the following resource constraints must be satisfied:

$$\sum_{i=1}^{v} y_{i,m} \times \gamma_i \leq \Gamma_m \sum_{i=1}^{v} y_{i,m} \times \mu_i \leq M_m \sum_{i=1}^{v} y_{i,m} \times \epsilon_i \leq E_m \quad \forall m \in PH \tag{4.1}$$

4.2 Hierarchical Load Balancer for Cloud Data Centers

where $y_{i,m}$ is a binary variable indicating whether VM_i is placed on physical host PH_m, γ_i, μ_i, and ϵ_i represent the CPU, memory, and energy consumption of VM_i, respectively, and Γ_m, M_m, and E_m denote the total CPU, memory, and energy resource capacity of physical host PH_m. When allocating tasks [11], the HLB method first checks if the available memory of a physical host is greater than or close to the requested memory of the task. Only then can the task be deployed to that host. This ensures that the total resource consumption of the allocated tasks does not exceed the total capacity of the physical host.

4.2.3 Load Balancing Performance

The HLB method improves load balancing performance by employing a best-fit allocation policy. Instead of randomly selecting a physical host for task deployment, HLB determines the most favorable host based on the resource requirements of the task and the current system state. This optimal allocation is achieved through VM migration, which helps in balancing the load across the system [12]. To prevent overflow conditions on the physical hosts, the following load constraint is introduced:

$$\frac{1}{2}\sum_{i=1}^{v}\sum_{j=1, j\neq i}^{v} \tau_{i,j} \times y_{i,m} \times y_{j,n} \leq \beta_{m,n} \quad \forall m, n \in PH, m \neq n \quad (4.2)$$

where $\tau_{i,j}$ represents the traffic between VM_i and VM_j, $y_{i,m}$ and $y_{j,n}$ are binary variables indicating the placement of VM_i on physical host PH_m and VM_j on physical host PH_n, respectively, and $\beta_{m,n}$ denotes the bandwidth capacity between physical hosts PH_m and PH_n. The coefficient (1/2) in Eq. (4.2) accounts for the fact that the traffic between two VMs is considered twice, once for each direction. Therefore, the load constraint ensures that the total traffic between the VMs placed on different physical hosts does not exceed the available bandwidth capacity. By satisfying these resource and load constraints, the HLB method guarantees that each task is allocated to a single VM on a specific physical host, while optimizing the overall load balancing and resource utilization in the cloud environment.

4.2.4 Resource Allocation

In a hierarchical data center network as shown in Fig. 4.2, the VM capacity is allocated across multiple physical hosts. The proportion of requested resources to the actual capacity is an important metric for evaluating the efficiency of resource utilization. Equation (4.3) calculates this proportion, denoted as Λ, where $\rho_{i,v}^{s}$

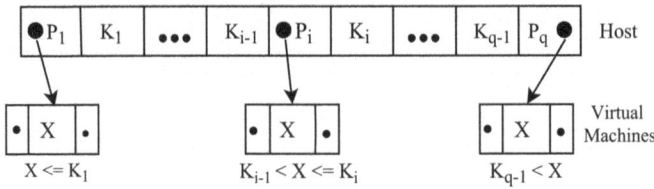

Fig. 4.2 HLB hierarchical structure

represents the served VM capacity and $\rho_{i,v}$ represents the actual capacity. The index i ranges from 1 to q, indicating the number of VMs.

$$\Lambda = \sum_{v \in VM(m)} \frac{\rho^s_{i,v}}{\rho_{i,v}} \quad i \in 1,2,3,\ldots,q \tag{4.3}$$

To assess the traffic load on physical hosts, we define the expected traffic $\tau(s,m)$ for VM_i on physical host $PH_{s,m}$ as the sum of the actual capacities $\rho_{i,v}$ of all VMs assigned to that host, as shown in Eq. (4.4). Similarly, the served traffic $\tau^{(s)}(s,m)$ is calculated by summing the served capacities $\rho^s i, v$ of the VMs on the same host.

$$\tau(s,m) = \sum_{v \in VM(m)} \rho_{i,v} \tag{4.4}$$

$$\tau^{(s)}(s,m) = \sum v \in VM(m) \rho^s_{i,v} \tag{4.5}$$

The available capacity (AC) of resources such as CPU, memory, and energy on each physical host is a crucial factor in determining the feasibility of VM placement. Equation (4.6) calculates the available capacity $\Omega(\Psi)$ by summing the products of the binary variable $\delta^i_{s,m}$ and the corresponding resource capacities γ_i, μ_i, and ϵ_i. The binary variable $\delta^i_{s,m}$ indicates whether VM_i is placed on physical host $PH_{s,m}$.

$$\Omega(\Psi) = \sum_{i=0}^{n} \delta^i_{s,m} \gamma_i \cdot \mu_i \cdot \epsilon_i \tag{4.6}$$

To identify the unoccupied resources, Eq. (4.7) introduces the variable Θ_i, which represents the difference between the total actual capacity and the total served capacity of VMs on a physical host.

$$\Theta_i = \sum_{v \in VM(m)} \rho_{i,v} - \sum_{v \in VM(m)} \rho^s_{i,v} \tag{4.7}$$

The updated available capacity $\Omega_n(\Psi_n)$ is then calculated by adding the unoccupied resources Θ_i to the previous available capacity $\Omega(\Psi)$, as shown in Eq. (4.8).

4.2 Hierarchical Load Balancer for Cloud Data Centers

$$\Omega_n(\Psi_n) = \Omega(\Psi) + \Theta_i \tag{4.8}$$

To optimize the VM placement, a multi-objective approach is employed, considering CPU, memory, and energy consumption. The model allows for a certain level of resource wastage, with tolerance levels set at 20% for CPU, 30% for memory, and 50% for energy. Equation (4.11) calculates the wastage tolerance power ω, where $\rho_{i,v}^s$ represents the served VM capacity.

$$\omega = \rho_{i,v}^s \times (\Gamma \tag{4.9}$$

Finally, Eq. (4.10) determines the allowance parameter α, which is the sum of the served VM capacity $\rho_{i,v}^s$ and the wastage tolerance power ω. This parameter ensures that the resource wastage does not exceed the specified tolerance levels.

$$\alpha = \rho_{i,v}^s + \omega \tag{4.10}$$

4.2.5 Algorithm

The operational summary of the HLB method is presented in Algorithm 1. It aims to provide priority-based resource allocation to tasks, with CPU having higher priority than memory and energy. The algorithm tolerates resource wastage of up to 20%, 30%, and 50% for CPU, memory, and energy, respectively. The study employs a simulated cloud network environment to obtain realistic outcomes, and the experiments are carried out using the JavaEclipse IDE on a computer with an Intel®CoreTM I5 processor running at 2.60GHz and equipped with 8 GB of RAM. To effectively meet the demands of upcoming load simulation scenarios, the evaluation is performed on 200 physical machines with varying configurations.

Algorithm 1 Operational summary of HLB method

1: Initialize J, Γ_m, M_m, and E_m as total CPU, memory, and energy resource amount of PH_m
2: **for all** client's request C_i **do**
3:     Evaluate each job request J_j in J on test data
4:     $\sum_{i=1}^{v} y_{i,m}\gamma_i \leq \Gamma_m \wedge \mu_i \leq M_m \wedge \epsilon_i \leq E_m$
5:     Check $\tau_{i,j} y_{i,m} y_{j,n} \leq \beta_{m,n}$
6: **end for**
7: **if** $y_{i,m}\gamma_i \leq \Gamma_m$ and $y_{i,m}\mu_i \leq M_m$ **then**
8:     Compute served VM capacity/actual VMs
9:     Check current AC of CPU, Memory, and Energy
10:    $\Omega(\Psi) = \sum_{i=0}^{n} \delta_{s,m}^{i} \gamma_i \cdot \mu_i \cdot \epsilon_i$
11: **end if**
12: Evaluate $\Theta_i = \sum_{v \in VM(m)} \rho_{i,v} - \sum_{v \in VM(m)} \rho_{i,v}^s$
13: Update new available capacity Ω_n
14: Update with $\Omega_n(\Psi_n) = \Omega(\Psi) + \Theta_i$
15: **return** optimal PH_m

These machines have different amounts of computing resources available, including CPU, memory, and energy.

4.3 Performance Evaluation

The HLB model's performance is compared against two other VM placement heuristics: sequential placement and random placement. In the sequential placement strategy, VMs are allocated to hosts in a sequential manner, while the random placement strategy selects available physical machines for VM placement requests arbitrarily. Figure 4.3 shows the makespan for requested tasks under three alternative scheduling rules (RND, SEQ, and HLB) for 60 and 100 VMs. The graph indicates that HLB consistently achieves a smaller makespan across all task levels, demonstrating that it is more efficient in task handling than RND and SEQ. Table 4.1 compares the percentage of overflow traffic for RND, SEQ, and HLB over traffic intensity levels ranging from 0 to 200. It displays how each policy handles overflow as traffic volume grows. HLB usually has smaller overflow traffic shares, indicating better performance under larger traffic loads than RND and SEQ. Figure 4.4 depicts the resource utilization percentages for RND, SEQ, and HLB across various numbers of VMs. HLB regularly achieves greater resource utilization rates than RND and SEQ, especially as the number of VMs grows. Notably, HLB has a substantially lower waste rate (21.98%) than RND (38.71%) and SEQ (33.24%), suggesting greater resource efficiency. This graph demonstrates HLB's ability in optimizing resource allocation in cloud environments. The HLB

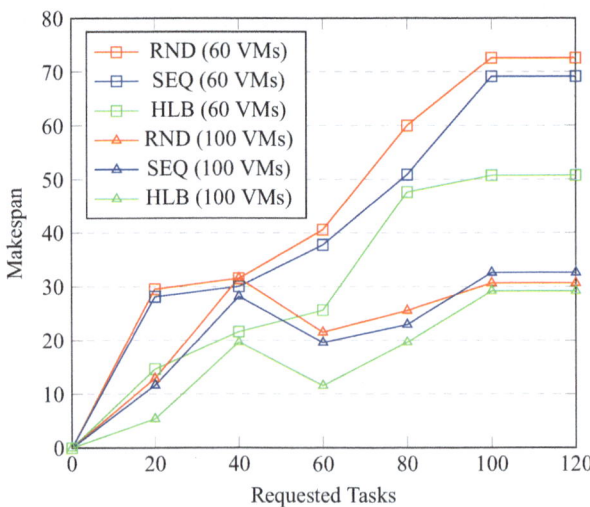

Fig. 4.3 Makespan for requested tasks

4.3 Performance Evaluation

Table 4.1 Comparison of RND, SEQ, and HLB in proportion of overflow traffic

Traffic intensity	0	10	20	30	34	47	54	65	69	70
RND	0.0010	0.0020	0.0024	0.0029	0.0035	0.0043	0.0027	0.0028	0.0031	0.0035
SEQ	0.0005	0.0011	0.0014	0.0017	0.0019	0.0020	0.0029	0.0038	0.0039	0.0039
HLB	0.0002	0.0009	0.0010	0.0012	0.0013	0.0015	0.0019	0.0013	0.0014	0.0016
Traffic intensity	73	76	79	100	120	130	135	140	142	147
RND	0.0037	0.0040	0.0041	0.0045	0.0046	0.0048	0.0049	0.0054	0.0059	0.0060
SEQ	0.0040	0.0040	0.0041	0.0035	0.0036	0.0038	0.0039	0.0034	0.0049	0.0050
HLB	0.0016	0.0018	0.0019	0.0019	0.0020	0.0021	0.0022	0.0023	0.0027	0.0028
Traffic intensity	149	150	164	166	176	177	187	190	200	
RND	0.0062	0.0064	0.0062	0.0069	0.0073	0.0078	0.0080	0.0082	0.0084	
SEQ	0.0052	0.0051	0.0052	0.0049	0.0053	0.0058	0.0060	0.0062	0.0065	
HLB	0.0030	0.0021	0.0022	0.0023	0.0023	0.0028	0.0030	0.0032	0.0035	

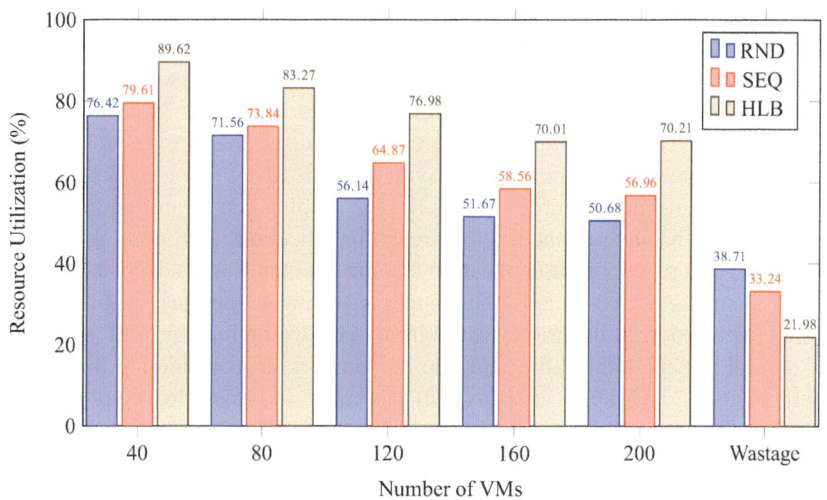

Fig. 4.4 Resource utilization (in %)

consistently outperforms random and sequential allocation algorithms, with shorter makespans and superior overflow traffic control across a wide range of workloads. These findings illustrate HLB's exceptional efficiency in resource utilization and job scheduling, establishing it as a reliable option for optimizing performance in cloud data centers.

4.4 Application-aware Hierarchical Load Balancing

In the rapidly evolving landscape of cloud computing, efficient resource management and load balancing have emerged as critical factors in ensuring optimal performance, cost-effectiveness, and user satisfaction [13, 14]. As cloud service providers strive to maximize their fiscal growth while delivering high-quality services, intelligent resource scaling and allocation strategies have become indispensable. This chapter presents a novel approach to address these challenges through the development of the Application-aware Hierarchical Load Balancer (AHLB) scheme. The AHLB scheme is an innovative solution that aims to optimize resource allocation and load balancing in cloud data centers by analyzing the specific resource requirements of each application and allocating the appropriate number of VMs accordingly. By taking into account the diverse needs of different application types, such as CPU-intensive, memory-intensive, energy-intensive, and bandwidth-intensive applications, AHLB enables a more granular and efficient approach to resource management. The primary objective of the AHLB scheduling model is to enhance the overall performance and user experience while maximizing the profitability of cloud service providers. By intelligently allocating resources based on application requirements, AHLB not only improves resource availability and throughput but also optimizes response times and other key performance metrics. Moreover, by minimizing resource underutilization and over-provisioning, AHLB contributes to significant cost savings for cloud service providers. One of the key distinguishing features of AHLB is its application-aware nature. Unlike traditional load balancing schemes that treat all applications uniformly, AHLB recognizes the heterogeneity of application resource demands and adapts its resource allocation strategies accordingly. This application-aware approach enables AHLB to effectively address the traffic scalability issue by optimizing VM placement and minimizing the total traffic sent into the network. By considering the specific requirements of each application, AHLB can make informed decisions to ensure efficient resource utilization and maintain the desired level of performance [15]. Furthermore, AHLB is designed to meet SLAs and reduce power consumption for each application in cloud data centers. By dynamically adjusting resource allocation based on real-time application demands, AHLB helps in avoiding over-provisioning and unnecessary power consumption. This not only contributes to cost savings but also promotes environmental sustainability in cloud computing environments. The development of AHLB builds upon our previous work, which demonstrated the potential for significant improvements in traffic scalability compared to random and sequential VM placement strategies. In this chapter, we extend our research by introducing the application-aware resource allocation scheme and conducting a comprehensive evaluation of its performance using the widely adopted CloudSim platform. The primary contributions of this chapter are summarized as follows:

1. An application-aware resource allocation strategy is suggested, which analyzes resource needs and assigns a suitable number of VMs to each application in cloud data centers.

4.4 Application-aware Hierarchical Load Balancing

2. AHLB is a method for multi-objective optimization that uses priority-based resource scheduling to find the best physical machine for each task by looking at its CPU, memory, and bandwidth resources.
3. AHLB's performance is measured and assessed using the CloudSim platform, proving that it outperforms conventional load balancing systems.

4.4.1 Design of AHLB

The following scenario might be used to define the suggested issue of optimum task deployment in cloud data centers that use the Infrastructure as a Service (IaaS) architecture. The virtual machines v represent a collection of VMs, where n clients $C = C_1, C_2, \ldots, C_n$ and j job requests $J = J_1, J_2, \ldots, J_j$ are put into virtual machines that are housed on ps physical servers $PS = PS_1, PS_2, \ldots, PS_{ps}$. To achieve multi-objective optimization, several sorts of virtualized resources are taken into consideration, namely CPU, Memory, Energy, and Bandwidth, represented as $R = (r_1, r_2, \ldots, r_q)$, where q is the number of resource categories. To determine if job request J_j is assigned to the cloud service PS_{ps}, let $x_{j,ps}$ be the binary variable. This may be computed as follows:

$$x_{j,ps} = \begin{cases} 1, & \text{if } J_j \text{ is allocated to } PS_{ps}, \\ 0, & \text{otherwise.} \end{cases} \quad (4.11)$$

Nevertheless, the architecture is sufficiently generic to support and take into account a wide range of other resources, like disc and others. This approach places a strong emphasis on selecting the best host to use when deploying the cloudlets in order to use the fewest resources possible. The available quantity and consumption of the resources determine the utilization for each kind of resource. The following illustrates resource utilization for PS_{ps}'s q-th resource type:

$$U_{ps,q} = \frac{1}{A_{ps,q}} \sum_{j=1}^{j} x_{j,ps} r_{j,q} \quad (4.12)$$

The overall utilization of resources that provides cloud services to PS_{ps} can be calculated as

$$U_{ps} = \frac{1}{q} \sum_{q=1}^{q} U_{ps,q} \quad (4.13)$$

where the number of virtualized resource types is denoted by q. In other words, $f(C_i, J_j) = PS_k$ shows that task request J_j from client C_i is allocated to the optimum physical host PS_k. Let f represent the mapping between users and job

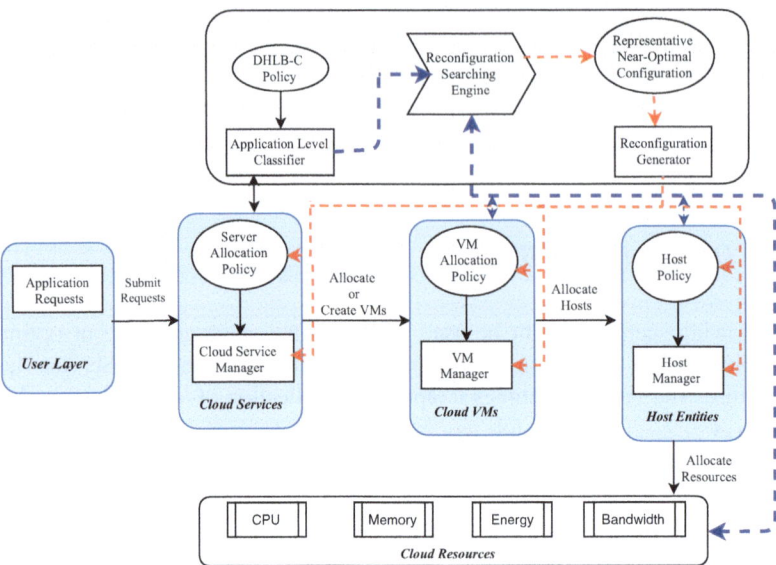

Fig. 4.5 Resource allocation architecture

requests that allocates each physical host, i.e., $f : C \times J \to PS$. The deployment strategy, acquired via vector mapping f, is utilized to determine which job will be deployed onto which physical host PS_k. As seen in Fig. 4.5, it is anticipated that these hosts are diverse and implemented in a dynamic context. In order to assign cloud resources to an application in a reasonable manner, an effort is made to identify the kind of resources and modify them by examining the application's resource requirements. For instance, suppose the application classifier method yields the following weight values for an unknown application: $W_{ci} = 1$, $W_{mi} = 0$, $W_{ei} = 0$, and $W_{bwi} = 0$. This indicates that the application is CPU-intensive. Based on the suggested virtual machine allocation and placement approach, the CPU is the primary resource that the program uses. The virtual machine (VM) should have more CPU resources assigned to it, but other resources like memory, energy, bandwidth, etc., may be used relatively sparingly. This may increase the pace at which physical resources are used and decrease the waste of virtual resources [16, 17]. The following formula serves as the foundation for the resource allocation strategy:

$$f_v = W_{ci}\frac{\rho_{ci}^s - \rho_{ci}}{\rho_{ci}} + W_{mi}\frac{\rho_{mi}^s - \rho_{mi}}{\rho_{mi}} + W_{ei}\frac{\rho_{ei}^s - \rho_{ei}}{\rho_{ei}} + W_{bwi}\frac{\rho_{bwi}^s - \rho_{bwi}}{\rho_{bwi}} \tag{4.14}$$

where ρ_i^s represents the served resources. It should be noted that a feasible VM placement decision should satisfy the following resource constraints and find favorable VMs $y_{i,k}$ as given in Eq. (4.15):

4.4 Application-aware Hierarchical Load Balancing

$$\sum_{i=1}^{v} y_{i,k}(\gamma_i \wedge \mu_i \wedge \epsilon_i \wedge \beta_i) \quad (4.15)$$

where γ_i, μ_i, ϵ_i, and β_i represent the CPU, memory, energy, and bandwidth consumption of VM_i, respectively, and $\gamma_i \leq \Gamma_k$, $\mu_i \leq M_k$, $\epsilon_i \leq E_k$, $\beta_i \leq B_k$. Γ_k, M_k, E_k, and B_k define the total CPU, memory, energy, and bandwidth resource amount of PS_k, respectively. At the time of allocating tasks, it is first checked whether the available memory is greater than or close to the requested amount so that the tasks can be deployed. It ensures that the total required consumption of processors' resource amount should not exceed its total capacity. To avoid overflow conditions on the node servers, the following load constraint is introduced:

$$\frac{1}{2}\sum_{i=1}^{v}\sum_{j=1, j\neq i}^{v} \tau_{i,j} y_{i,k} y_{j,l} \leq \beta_{k,l} \quad \forall k,l \in PS, k \neq l \quad (4.16)$$

where $\beta_{k,l}$ denotes the bandwidth between servers PS_k and PS_l. The coefficient $\frac{1}{2}$ is used for the VM placement pair of respective servers, as it calculates the load twice using Eq. (4.16). It ensures that every application should be deployed on a virtual machine as a respective physical host with specific requests. The AHLB scheme aims to solve the optimal task deployment problem by considering multi-objective optimization of CPU, memory, energy, and bandwidth resources. The application classifier algorithm helps in identifying the resource requirements of applications, allowing for efficient allocation of resources to VMs. By minimizing resource wastage and improving utilization rates, AHLB contributes to the overall performance and cost-effectiveness of cloud data centers.

4.4.2 Optimal Resource Allocation in AHLB

Figure 4.6 shows the AHLB architecture for best host selection and deployment. It displays the communication, which is crucial to the architecture, between AHLB and other entities. To classify the resource needs (CPU, memory, energy, and bandwidth utilization) for each application in accordance with the Service Level Agreement (SLA), an application-level classifier is used. Load balancing kicks in when customers request a fresh batch of tasks to arrive at the cloud system. Following their initialization and monitoring of the test data, load managers gather data on the quantity of requested (ρ_i) and available (A_i) resources of m physical hosts in the cloud data centers. Equation (4.17) displays the ratio of the served virtual machine capacity to the actual capacity of the resources, with $\rho_{i,v}^s$ representing the served VM capacity and $\rho_{i,v}$ representing the real capacity. The served traffic to physical host PH_p is defined as $\tau^{(s)}p = \sum v \in VM(m)\rho_{i,v}^s$, where

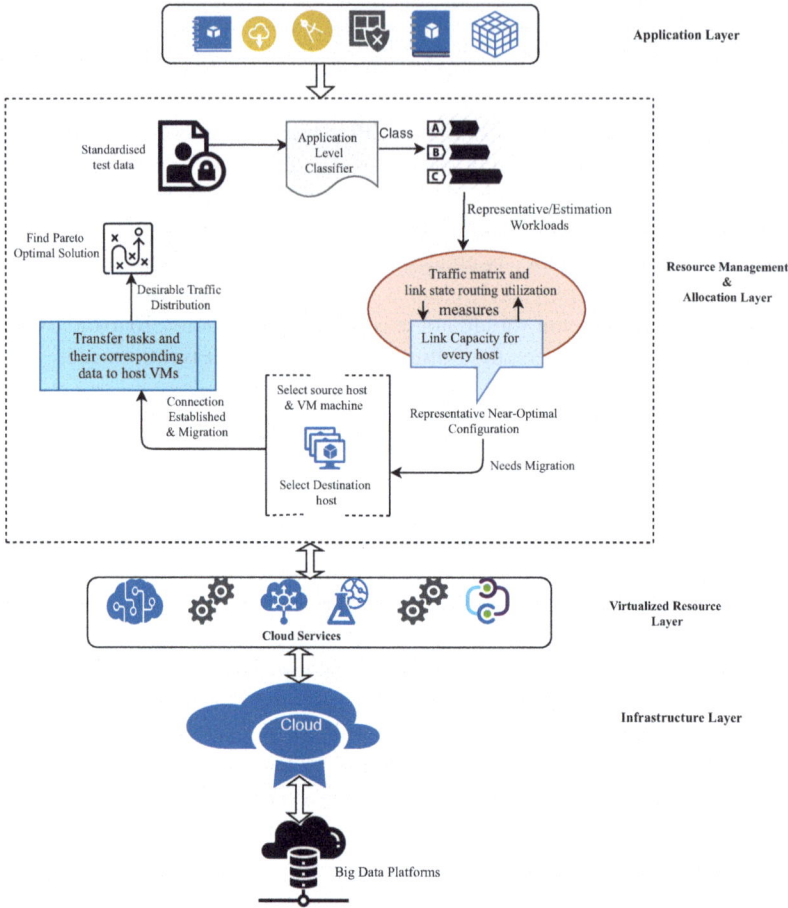

Fig. 4.6 AHLB architecture

$\rho_{i,v}^s$ is the actual traffic rate from VM_i to VM_v. The expected traffic for VM_i to physical host $PH_{s,m}$ is defined as $\tau(s,m) = \sum_{v \in VM(m)} \rho_{i,v}$.

$$\Lambda = \sum_{v \in VM(m)} \frac{\rho_{i,v}^s}{\rho_{i,v}} \quad i \in 1,2,3,\ldots,q \quad (4.17)$$

The Available Capacity (AC) of respective resources (CPU, Memory, Energy, and Bandwidth) is given in Eq. (4.18). Using Eq. (4.19), the unoccupied resources that are remaining can be determined.

4.5 Results and Analysis

$$\Omega(\Psi) = \sum_{i=0}^{n} \delta_p^i \gamma_i \cdot \mu_i \cdot \epsilon_i \cdot \beta_i \qquad (4.18)$$

$$\Theta_i = \sum_{v \in VM(m)} \rho_{i,v} - \sum_{v \in VM(m)} \rho_{i,v}^s \qquad (4.19)$$

$$\Omega_n(\Psi_n) = \Omega(\Psi) + \Theta_i \qquad (4.20)$$

AHLB uses a priority-based technique to take into account multi-objective optimization using resources like CPU, Memory, Energy, and Bandwidth per VM. Since the right virtual machines (VMs) are assigned depending on the kind of resource-intensive application, this paradigm allows for the waste of CPU, Memory, Energy, and Bandwidth. Equation (4.21) provides the best VMs for task deployment based on priority-based resource scheduling and computes the waste tolerance power ω. This upper limit on the amount of waste allowed by the allowance parameter α is shown in Eq. (4.22).

$$\omega = \rho_{i,v}^s \times (\Gamma \qquad (4.21)$$

$$\alpha = \rho_{i,v}^s + \omega \qquad (4.22)$$

The AHLB architecture efficiently handles the optimal host selection and deployment process by leveraging the application-level classifier and considering multi-objective optimization of resources. It actively monitors the requested and available resources, calculates the proportion of served VM capacity to actual capacity, and determines the available capacity of each resource type. By utilizing priority-based resource scheduling and allowing for a certain level of resource wastage based on the application type, AHLB ensures the allocation of appropriate VMs to maximize resource utilization and minimize wastage. The architecture's ability to adapt to the specific requirements of different resource-intensive applications contributes to its effectiveness in optimizing task deployment and improving overall system performance in cloud data centers.

4.5 Results and Analysis

The scatter plot in Fig. 4.7 illustrates the makespan for requested tasks using four different scheduling policies (RND, SEQ, HLB, and AHLB) for varying numbers of tasks (20, 40, 60, 80, and 100). Each policy is represented by a distinct marker, providing a clear visual comparison of their performance. The plot reveals that C-HLB consistently achieves the lowest makespan across all task levels, indicating its superior efficiency in handling tasks compared to the other policies [18]. Table 4.2 shows a detailed comparison of the amount of overflow traffic for four different

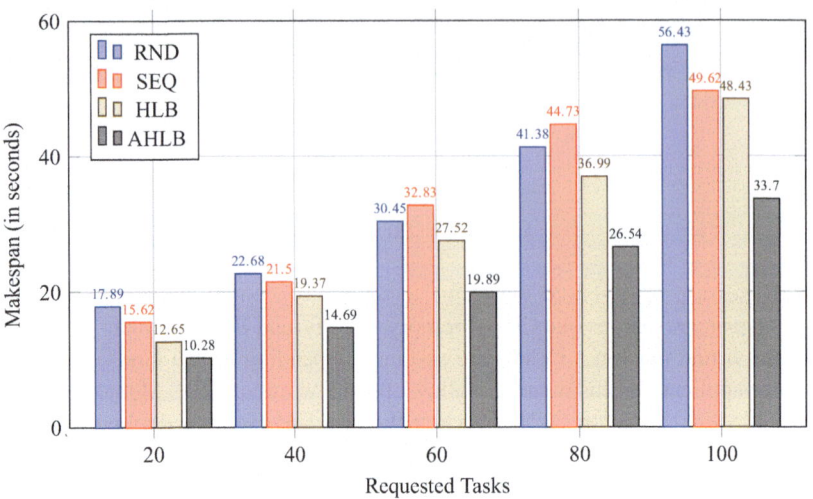

Fig. 4.7 Makespan for requested tasks (60 VMs)

Table 4.2 Comparison of proportion of overflow traffic for different allocation policies

Traffic intensity	Policy	Mean	Std Dev	Min	Max
20	RND	0.0024	0.0002	0.0020	0.0028
	SEQ	0.0014	0.0001	0.0012	0.0016
	HLB	0.0010	0.0001	0.0008	0.0012
	AHLB	0.0005	0.0001	0.0004	0.0006
40	RND	0.0035	0.0003	0.0030	0.0040
	SEQ	0.0029	0.0002	0.0026	0.0032
	HLB	0.0019	0.0002	0.0016	0.0022
	AHLB	0.0010	0.0002	0.0008	0.0012
60	RND	0.0043	0.0004	0.0038	0.0048
	SEQ	0.0038	0.0003	0.0034	0.0042
	HLB	0.0028	0.0003	0.0024	0.0032
	AHLB	0.0019	0.0002	0.0016	0.0022
80	RND	0.0048	0.0005	0.0043	0.0053
	SEQ	0.0042	0.0004	0.0038	0.0046
	HLB	0.0032	0.0003	0.0028	0.0036
	AHLB	0.0022	0.0003	0.0019	0.0025
100	RND	0.0054	0.0006	0.0048	0.0060
	SEQ	0.0052	0.0005	0.0047	0.0057
	HLB	0.0034	0.0004	0.0030	0.0038
	AHLB	0.0034	0.0004	0.0030	0.0038

(continued)

4.6 Summary

Table 4.2 (continued)

Traffic intensity	Policy	Mean	Std Dev	Min	Max
120	RND	0.0058	0.0006	0.0052	0.0064
	SEQ	0.0048	0.0005	0.0043	0.0053
	HLB	0.0024	0.0003	0.0020	0.0028
	AHLB	0.0016	0.0002	0.0013	0.0019
140	RND	0.0068	0.0007	0.0061	0.0075
	SEQ	0.0058	0.0006	0.0052	0.0064
	HLB	0.0028	0.0003	0.0025	0.0031
	AHLB	0.0022	0.0003	0.0019	0.0025
160	RND	0.0078	0.0008	0.0070	0.0086
	SEQ	0.0058	0.0006	0.0052	0.0064
	HLB	0.0023	0.0003	0.0020	0.0026
	AHLB	0.0019	0.0002	0.0016	0.0022
180	RND	0.0086	0.0009	0.0077	0.0095
	SEQ	0.0062	0.0006	0.0056	0.0068
	HLB	0.0025	0.0003	0.0022	0.0028
	AHLB	0.0023	0.0003	0.0020	0.0026
200	RND	0.0096	0.0010	0.0086	0.0106
	SEQ	0.0065	0.0007	0.0058	0.0072
	HLB	0.0028	0.0003	0.0025	0.0031
	AHLB	0.0029	0.0003	0.0026	0.0032

allocation policies (RND, SEQ, HLB, and AHLB) at different traffic levels (from 0 to 200, with 20-minute breaks between each level). It showcases how each policy manages overflow as the traffic intensity increases, providing insights into their relative efficiency. HLB and AHLB generally show lower proportions of overflow traffic, indicating better performance under higher traffic loads compared to RND and SEQ.

Figure 4.8 depicts a scatter plot comparing the proportion of overflow traffic for four different allocation policies (RND, SEQ, HLB, and C-HLB) across various traffic intensities ranging from 0 to 200. Each policy is represented by a distinct marker style, allowing for easy visual differentiation. The plot shows how each policy performs in terms of handling overflow traffic as the traffic intensity increases.

4.6 Summary

Innovative methods for dynamic resource allocation in cloud computing have been discussed in this chapter, with particular attention to the HLB and AHLB models. These frameworks surpass conventional techniques in optimizing virtual machine placements and system efficiency, making important advancements in resource management and load balancing in cloud settings. The HLB model efficiently

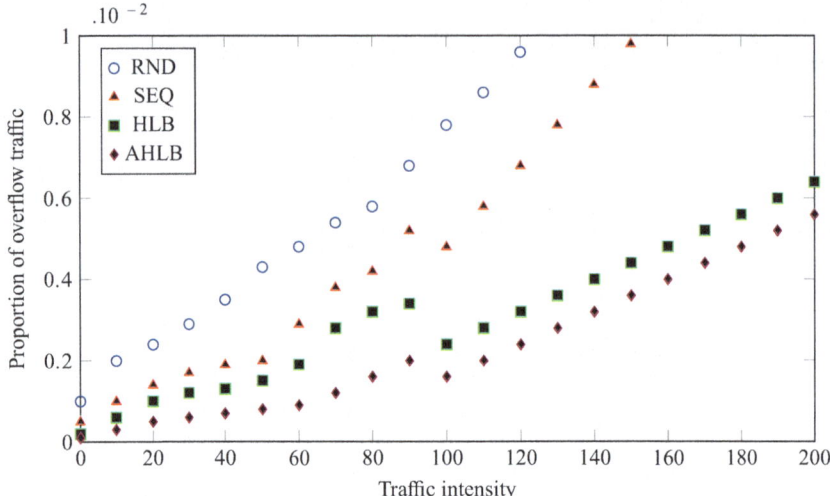

Fig. 4.8 Comparison of proportion of overflow traffic for different allocation policies

reduces energy usage and enhances resource utilization by taking into account multidimensional resource restrictions. This is expanded upon by the AHLB, which offers application-specific allocation, allowing for more precise management suited to a range of application requirements. Performance assessments show constant advantages over traditional approaches in terms of scalability under different traffic intensities, makespan reduction, and overflow traffic minimization. Both methods support sustainable cloud operations by lowering energy usage and increasing resource utilization rates. As network intensity rises, they become more useful in controlling traffic, reducing bottlenecks and improving overall efficiency. These models will be essential in developing more effective, scalable, and long-lasting infrastructures as cloud computing develops. Subsequent investigations might concentrate on optimizing algorithms for classifying applications and investigating the suitability of these models in developing computer paradigms.

4.7 Exercises

1. Compare the performance of the HLB (Heuristic Load Balancing) and AHLB (Adaptive Heuristic Load Balancing) models with traditional VM placement methods like random placement or sequential placement. Your analysis should focus on:
    - Throughput
    - Energy efficiency
    - Resource wastage

4.7 Exercises

Present your findings using graphs and charts.
2. Consider a cloud environment with three servers handling traffic loads. Servers 1, 2, and 3 have the following maximum capacities:

   - Server 1: 500 requests/sec
   - Server 2: 600 requests/sec
   - Server 3: 400 requests/sec

   The incoming traffic load is 1200 requests/sec. Using the AHLB model, calculate how traffic should be distributed across the servers to minimize overflow traffic and system bottlenecks. Compare this with a simple round robin allocation method.
3. Assume that the energy consumption rate of servers in a cloud environment increases quadratically with CPU utilization. For three servers, the utilization levels with the HLB model are 70%, 80%, and 60%. The energy consumption function is

$$E(x) = 0.05 \times (x^2)$$

   where x is the CPU utilization in percentage:

   a. Calculate the total energy consumption for these three servers.
   b. Compare this to the energy consumption with random allocation where utilizations are 90%, 70%, and 80%.
4. Design a project to simulate the AHLB model for application-specific dynamic resource allocation. Your project should include:

   a. Application classification based on resource needs (e.g., CPU-intensive vs. memory-intensive)
   b. An algorithm that allocates resources dynamically based on application-specific requirements
   c. A performance comparison of this method with traditional resource allocation models in terms of scalability, makespan, and resource utilization

5. Load balancing and traffic overflow minimization: Write a research-based assignment on how the HLB and AHLB models minimize traffic overflow and system failures in high-intensity network environments. Your report should include:

   a. A detailed explanation of how these models distribute loads across cloud resources
   b. A comparison with existing load balancing methods, like Round Robin or Least Connections
   c. An evaluation of their performance under varying traffic conditions (low, medium, high)

6. Case study on scalability of AHLB model: Conduct a case study to evaluate the scalability of the AHLB model under different traffic intensities. Your study should include:

a. An analysis of how the model performs when the traffic intensity increases from low (500 requests/sec) to high (1500 requests/sec)

b. A discussion of the impact on makespan, throughput, and energy consumption

7. Future directions for dynamic resource allocation: Discuss potential future research directions for optimizing dynamic resource allocation models, such as HLB and AHLB, in evolving computing paradigms like edge computing and IoT. Address the following points:

    a. How these models can be adapted to meet the needs of decentralized environments

    b. The role of machine learning in further enhancing resource allocation efficiency

    c. Possible challenges in implementing these models in real-world IoT scenarios

8. Algorithm improvement for resource utilization: Develop and propose an improvement to the AHLB model that incorporates machine learning techniques (e.g., reinforcement learning) for better resource utilization. Your project should include:

    a. An explanation of how machine learning can enhance dynamic resource allocation

    b. A detailed description of the learning algorithm used and how it adapts over time

    c. A performance comparison with the existing AHLB model in terms of energy efficiency and traffic management

References

1. Haji, L.M., Zeebaree, S., Ahmed, O.M., Sallow, A.B., Jacksi, K., Zeabri, R.R.: Dynamic resource allocation for distributed systems and cloud computing. TEST Eng. Manag. **83**, 22417–22426 (2020)
2. Praveenchandar, J., Tamilarasi, A.: Retracted article: dynamic resource allocation with optimized task scheduling and improved power management in cloud computing. J. Ambient Intell. Humaniz. Comput. **12**(3), 4147–4159 (2021)
3. Du, J., Jiang, C., Benslimane, A., Guo, S., Ren, Y.: SDN-based resource allocation in edge and cloud computing systems: an evolutionary stackelberg differential game approach. IEEE/ACM Trans. Netw. **30**(4), 1613–1628 (2022). https://doi.org/10.1109/TNET.2022.3152150
4. Naha, R.K., Garg, S., Chan, A., Battula, S.K.: Deadline-based dynamic resource allocation and provisioning algorithms in fog-cloud environment. Future Gener. Comput. Syst. **104**, 131–141 (2020)
5. Shang, Q.: A dynamic resource allocation algorithm in cloud computing based on workflow and resource clustering. J. Internet Technol. **22**(2), 403–411 (2021)
6. Gupta, I., Saxena, D., Singh, A.K., Lee, C.-N.: A multiple controlled Toffoli driven adaptive quantum neural network model for dynamic workload prediction in cloud environments. IEEE Trans. Pattern Anal. Mach. Intell. (2024). https://doi.org/10.1109/TPAMI.2024.3402061

7. Liang, H., et al.: Reinforcement learning enabled dynamic resource allocation in the Internet of vehicles. IEEE Trans. Ind. Inform. **17**(7), 4957–4967 (2021). https://doi.org/10.1109/TII.2020.3019386
8. Chhabra, S., Singh, A.K.: Dynamic resource allocation method for load balance scheduling over cloud data center networks. J. Web Eng. **20**(8), 2269–2284 (2021)
9. Li, Q., Jia, X., Huang, C., Bao, H.: A dynamic combinatorial double auction model for cloud resource allocation. IEEE Trans. Cloud Comput. **11**(3), 2873–2884 (2023). https://doi.org/10.1109/TCC.2022.3231249
10. Mireslami, S., Rakai, L., Wang, M., Far, B.H.: Dynamic cloud resource allocation considering demand uncertainty. IEEE Trans. Cloud Comput. **9**(3), 981–994 (2021). https://doi.org/10.1109/TCC.2019.2897304
11. Habiba, U., Maghsudi, S., Hossain, E.: A repeated auction model for load-aware dynamic resource allocation in multi-access edge computing. IEEE Trans. Mobile Comput. **23**(7), 7801–7817 (2024). https://doi.org/10.1109/TMC.2023.3338602
12. Chhabra, S., Singh, A.K.: Dynamic hierarchical load balancing model for cloud data centre networks. Electron. Lett. **55**, 94–96 (2019). https://doi.org/10.1049/el.2018.5427
13. Geeta, K., Kamakshi Prasad, V.: Multi-objective cloud load-balancing with hybrid optimization. Int. J. Comput. Appl. **45**(10), 611–625 (2023). https://doi.org/10.1080/1206212X.2023.2260616
14. Adewojo, A.A., Bass, J.M.: A novel weight-assignment load balancing algorithm for cloud applications. SN Comput. Sci. **4**, 270 (2023). https://doi.org/10.1007/s42979-023-01702-7
15. Hu, J., Luo, W., He, Y., Wang, J., Zhang, D.: Deep reinforcement learning based load balancing for heterogeneous traffic in datacenter networks (2024)
16. Rozehkhani, S.M., Mahan, F., Pedrycz, W.: Efficient cloud data center: an adaptive framework for dynamic virtual machine consolidation. J. Netw. Comput. Appl. **226**, 103885 (2024)
17. Saxena, D., Singh, A.K., Lindenstruth, V.: A latency aware and dynamic caching model for heterogeneous datalake environments. In: 2024 IEEE 48th Annual Computers, Software, and Applications Conference (COMPSAC), pp. 2302–2307. IEEE, Osaka, Japan (2024). https://doi.org/10.1109/COMPSAC61105.2024.00370
18. Zhang, J., Yu, H., Fan, G., Li, Z., Xu, J., Li, J.: Handling hierarchy in cloud data centers: a hyper-heuristic approach for resource contention and energy-aware Virtual Machine management. Expert Syst. Appl. **249**, 123528 (2024)

Chapter 5
Secure Cloud Resource Management

Abstract This chapter covers the essential concerns of security in multi-tenant cloud settings and proposes the Robust Tenant Identification Framework (RTIF) as an innovative solution. We first review core cloud security ideas, concentrating on the special threats given by multi-tenancy, including side-channel attacks and VM escape vulnerabilities. RTIF is then offered as a complete security framework that incorporates sophisticated user identification mechanisms with intelligent load balancing algorithms. By evaluating user behavior, access patterns, and historical data, RTIF generates secure user profiles for intelligent resource allocation and access control choices. The framework's mathematical underpinnings are explained, proving its potential to maximize security and resource consumption concurrently. Performance assessments illustrate RTIF's efficacy in minimizing security concerns while maintaining efficient resource utilization in shared cloud settings. This study helps greatly to strengthen the security and efficiency of multi-tenant cloud computing systems.

Keywords Multi-tenancy security · Colocation risks · Tenant identification Access control · Security monitoring · Resource isolation · Threat prevention · Security framework

5.1 Introduction

Cloud computing offers previously unheard-of levels of scalability, flexibility, and cost-effectiveness, and it has completely changed how businesses install and manage their IT resources. To preserve the availability, confidentiality, and integrity of data and apps, cloud environments' shared nature presents serious security issues that need to be resolved [1]. A vast array of procedures, tools, and regulations are included in cloud security, all with the goal of safeguarding the cloud computing environment. A number of basic ideas, including data security, network security, application security, operational security, and disaster recovery, lie at the heart of cloud security [2]. Together, these components provide a strong security posture that is resistant to the many threats that contemporary cloud infrastructures face.

One of the distinguishing features of cloud computing is multi-tenancy, which creates special security issues since several users share the same physical resources. Vulnerabilities like resource freeing, VM escape, and side-channel attacks that result from this shared environment may jeopardize the security of tenants who share a space [3, 4].

Researchers have created a variety of security models and frameworks to solve these issues. The RTIF for Shared Cloud Environments is one such cutting-edge method. RTIF is a noteworthy development in cloud security, providing a multi-objective method that combines sophisticated user identification techniques with clever load balancing algorithms. RTIF creates trustworthy and secure user profiles via the analysis of user behavior, access patterns, and historical data. These user profiles provide the basis for well-informed decisions about resource allocation and access control. The innovative load balancing method from RTIF takes efficiency and security criteria into account. It determines client dependability by looking at historical performance and evaluates virtual machine safety when allocating resources. This makes it possible to quickly identify secure physical computers for load balancing and threat avoidance, greatly improving multi-tenant cloud system's security posture while preserving ideal resource use. Frameworks like RTIF will be essential in helping to handle the complicated security environment as cloud computing develops, opening the door for safer and more effective cloud services that can satisfy the expanding needs of businesses all over the globe.

5.2 Cloud Security Fundamentals

A crucial component of contemporary computer infrastructures is cloud security. It includes a variety of procedures, tools, and measures used to safeguard information, programs, and cloud computing infrastructure [5].

5.2.1 Cloud Security Types

Here is a summary of the basic ideas and the main categories of cloud security are as follows:

5.2.1.1 Data Security

Ensuring data integrity and safeguarding cloud-stored data from unauthorized access are all part of data security. This comprises:

5.2 Cloud Security Fundamentals

- Data encryption both in transport and at rest
- Authentication and access restrictions
- Consistent data recovery and backup protocols

5.2.1.2 Network Security

In cloud contexts, network security is primarily concerned with safeguarding the network infrastructure itself. Important elements consist of:

- Intrusion detection/prevention systems and firewalls
- VPNs or virtual private networks
- Micro- and network-level segmentation

5.2.1.3 Applications Security

Protecting cloud-based apps against attacks is known as application security. This comprises:

- Secure application development methods
- Regular security testing and vulnerability assessments
- Web application firewalls

5.2.1.4 Operation Security

The procedures and choices made for managing and safeguarding digital assets are part of operational security [6]. This comprises:

- Security guidelines and protocols
- Training and awareness initiatives for employees
- Responding to and managing incidents

5.2.1.5 Business Continuity and Disaster Recovery

In the event of a catastrophe, this feature of cloud security guarantees the recovery of data and applications. It consists of:

- Frequent backups of data
- Redundancy and failover systems
- Planning and testing for disaster recovery

5.2.2 Fundamental Equations and Concepts of Cloud Security

5.2.2.1 Tenant Sharing

One of the core ideas of cloud computing is multi-tenancy [7], which is described as

$$\text{Multi-Tenancy} = \text{Virtualization} + \text{Resource Sharing} \quad (5.1)$$

There are particular security issues with this paradigm that must be addressed.

5.2.2.2 Evaluation of Risk

In cloud settings, risk is often defined as

$$\text{Risk} = \text{Threat} \times \text{Vulnerability} \times \text{Impact} \quad (5.2)$$

where Threat is the possibility of harm, Vulnerability is a weakness that might be exploited, and Impact is the possible harm in the event that a threat exploits vulnerability.

5.2.2.3 Security

One essential component of data security is encryption. An elementary illustration of encryption may be

$$C = E(P, K) \quad (5.3)$$

where C is the ciphertext (encrypted data), E is the encryption algorithm, P is the plaintext (original data), and K is the encryption key.

5.2.2.4 Control of Access

The least privilege concept is often the foundation of access control. An easy-to-understand paradigm for access choices looks like this:

$$\text{Access Granted} = \text{User Authentication} \times \text{User Authorization} \quad (5.4)$$

where access can only be allowed if both authorization and authentication are valid.

5.2.2.5 Accessibility

The idea of "nines" is often used to quantify availability in cloud systems. For instance, the availability of "five nines" is determined by

$$\text{Availability } (\%) = \frac{\text{Total Time} - \text{Downtime}}{\text{Total Time}} \times 100 \quad (5.5)$$

A "five nines" availability rate of 99.999% means that there are only around 5.26 minutes of downtime annually.

5.2.3 Cloud Security Difficulties

- Data breaches
- Insecure APIs
- Vulnerabilities in systems and applications
- Theft of accounts
- Insider fraud
- APTs, or Advanced Persistent Threats
- Loss of data
- Inadequate diligence
- Cloud Service Abuse and Malicious Use
- Denial of Service

Businesses may strengthen the security of their cloud-based assets and data by comprehending these core elements of cloud security. It is noteworthy that cloud security is a joint obligation of the cloud service provider and the client, and the particular security precautions required may differ according to the cloud service type (IaaS, PaaS, or SaaS) that is being used [8, 9].

5.3 Cloud Security Essentials: Multi-tenancy Attacks and Safe Load Balancing

5.3.1 Multi-tenancy Attacks

Multi-tenancy, a crucial aspect of cloud computing, enables multiple users to share a single physical infrastructure [10]. This approach, while efficient, introduces several security challenges.

5.3.1.1 Concept and Definition

In cloud computing, multi-tenancy combines virtualization and resource sharing. This can be expressed as

$$\text{Multi-Tenancy} = \text{Virtualization} + \text{Resource Sharing} \tag{5.6}$$

This model potentially creates vulnerabilities when multiple tenants share the same physical resources.

5.3.1.2 Types of Attacks Against Multiple Tenancy

1. Side-Channel Attacks

These attacks exploit shared resources to obtain data about other tenants. Examples include cache-based, power analysis, and timing attacks. The risk of a successful side-channel attack (R_{SC}) can be modeled as

$$R_{SC} = f(V_{shared}, I_{leak}, D_{tenant}) \tag{5.7}$$

where V_{shared} is the vulnerability of shared resources, I_{leak} is the amount of information leakage, and D_{tenant} is the proximity between tenants [11].

2. VM Escape Attacks

In these attacks, a malicious tenant attempts to break out of their VM to access the underlying system or other tenants' VMs. The probability of a successful VM escape (P_{VME}) can be represented as

$$P_{VME} = g(V_{hypervisor}, S_{isolation}, C_{attack}) \tag{5.8}$$

where $V_{hypervisor}$ represents hypervisor vulnerabilities, $S_{isolation}$ is the strength of VM isolation, and C_{attack} is the complexity of the attack.

3. Resource Freeing Attacks

These occur when a malicious tenant manipulates shared resources to improve their own performance at the expense of others. The impact of such an attack (I_{RFA}) can be modeled as

$$I_{RFA} = h(R_{consumed}, E_{other}, T_{duration}) \tag{5.9}$$

5.3 Cloud Security Essentials: Multi-tenancy Attacks and Safe Load Balancing

where $R_{consumed}$ is the amount of resources consumed by the attacker, E_{other} is the efficiency loss for other tenants, and $T_{duration}$ is the duration of the attack.

5.3.1.3 Strategies for Mitigation

To counter multi-tenancy threats, cloud providers can [17]:

- Improve isolation techniques
- Conduct regular security audits
- Implement advanced intrusion detection systems
- Monitor resource usage and detect anomalies

The effectiveness of these mitigation strategies (E_{mit}) can be expressed as

$$E_{mit} = k(S_{implemented}, D_{detection}, R_{response}) \tag{5.10}$$

where $S_{implemented}$ represents the security measures implemented, $D_{detection}$ is the detection capability, and $R_{response}$ is the response time to potential threats.

5.3.2 Secure Load Balancing

Secure load balancing is crucial in cloud environments to ensure optimal resource utilization while maintaining security. It involves distributing workloads across multiple computing resources to maximize performance and minimize security risks [12].

5.3.2.1 The Secure Load Balancing Goals

The primary objectives of secure load balancing can be summarized as

$$O_{SLB} = \max(P_{performance}, S_{security}, R_{reliability}) \tag{5.11}$$

where $P_{performance}$ is system performance, $S_{security}$ is the security level, and $R_{reliability}$ is system reliability.

5.3.2.2 Safe Load Distribution Techniques

1. Round Robin with Security Checks

This technique assigns requests sequentially to each server in the pool but includes security checks [13]. The selection of the next server (S_{next}) can be represented as

$$S_{next} = (S_{current} + 1) \mod N \quad \text{if} \quad SC(S_{next}) = true \tag{5.12}$$

where N is the total number of servers and $SC(S_{next})$ is a security check function for the next server.

2. Least Connections with Risk Assessment

This algorithm selects the server with the least number of active connections, factoring in a risk assessment. The server selection ($S_{selected}$) can be modeled as

$$S_{selected} = \arg\min_i (C_i + \alpha R_i) \tag{5.13}$$

where C_i is the number of connections to server i, R_i is the risk factor for server i, and α is a weighting factor.

3. Weighted Secure Distribution

Servers are assigned weights based on their capacity and security level. The probability of selecting server i (P_i) is given by

$$P_i = \frac{W_i \cdot S_i}{\sum_{j=1}^{N} W_j \cdot S_j} \tag{5.14}$$

where W_i is the weight of server i and S_i is its security score.

5.3.2.3 Security Factors to Be Aware of When Load Balancing

Key security considerations include:

- Encrypting data sent between load balancers and servers
- Implementing strong authentication and access control
- Regularly updating and patching the load balancing system
- Monitoring and logging activities to identify threats

5.3.2.4 Secure Load Balancing Performance Measurements

The effectiveness of secure load balancing (E_{SLB}) can be evaluated using various metrics:

$$E_{SLB} = f(T_{response}, L_{distribution}, S_{incidents}, R_{availability}) \tag{5.15}$$

where $T_{response}$ is the average response time, $L_{distribution}$ is the load distribution fairness, $S_{incidents}$ is the number of security incidents, and $R_{availability}$ is the overall system availability. By implementing secure load balancing, cloud providers can ensure efficient resource utilization while maintaining high security, thus addressing both performance and protection challenges in multi-tenant cloud environments.

5.4 Robust Tenant Identification Framework for Shared Cloud Environments

The RTIF for Shared Cloud Environments is an innovative multi-objective technique designed to address the critical challenges of security and load balancing in multi-tenant cloud computing systems. As cloud computing continues to evolve, the shared nature of multi-tenant environments presents significant security risks and resource allocation complexities. RTIF aims to mitigate these concerns by integrating advanced user identification mechanisms with intelligent load balancing algorithms. At its core, RTIF leverages sophisticated user identification techniques that analyze user behavior, access patterns, and historical data to establish reliable and secure user profiles. These profiles serve as the foundation for making informed decisions regarding resource allocation and access control, minimizing the risk of unauthorized access and potential security breaches [14]. The framework incorporates a novel approach to load balancing by considering both security and efficiency metrics. It assesses whether virtual machines (VMs) are in safe or dangerous situations during resource allocation and calculates client dependability based on past performance. This enables RTIF to swiftly identify safe physical machines for load balancing and threat avoidance when cloud data centers receive task deployment requests. RTIF's load balancing algorithms dynamically distribute workloads across available resources, taking into account factors such as resource utilization, performance metrics, and security constraints. This ensures optimal resource allocation while minimizing the impact of potential threats. The framework's ability to adapt to dynamic workloads and evolving security threats makes it particularly valuable in the context of multi-tenancy, where resource sharing and virtualization are essential components. Mathematically, multi-tenancy in cloud computing can be expressed as:

$$Virtualization + ResourceSharing = Multi - Tenancy \qquad (5.16)$$

RTIF addresses the inherent risks of this model by implementing resource provisioning VM allocation algorithms based on time-shared or space-shared indicators. This approach significantly reduces the number of virtual machines cotenanted on the same physical host while adhering to both security and workload balancing requirements. Through extensive experimentation in real-world multi-tenant cloud environments, RTIF has demonstrated its effectiveness in enhancing

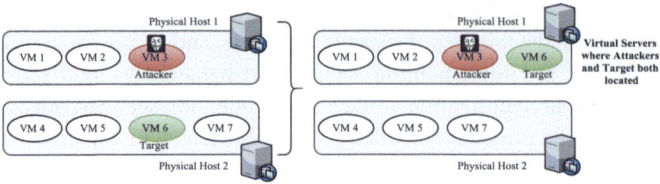

Fig. 5.1 Malicious coresidency exploitation in load distribution processes

security, improving load balancing, and optimizing resource utilization. Its modular architecture allows for seamless integration with existing cloud infrastructures, making it an accessible and powerful tool for cloud service providers and users alike. By offering a comprehensive solution that balances security concerns with efficient resource allocation, RTIF represents a significant advancement in cloud computing technology, addressing the complex challenges of multi-tenant environments and paving the way for safer, more efficient cloud services.

5.4.1 Security Assumptions for Cloud Load Balancing

This scheme considers several assumptions based on anticipated outcomes. The cloud service provider and clients are aware of potential attack vectors but cannot pinpoint the attacker's location [15].

Assumption 5.1 Cloud Service Providers ($CSPs_k$) handle every VM request with equal consideration, having no previous knowledge of the attacker's capabilities as shown in Fig. 5.1. Target VMs may be indirectly compromised by an attacker, but CSP_k cannot foresee this. This vulnerability affects not only renters but also business users who depend more and more on cloud-based services. Cloud tenants are assumed to have sensitive data, including cryptographic keys, business data, database records, and personal information. Attackers use load balancing to find the VMs of their target cotenant. They take full use of the VMs they have been allotted, including the construction and termination of VMs.

Assumption 5.2 The Intrusion Detection System (IDS) automatically detects attacks and determines if the current virtual machine state is safe or compromised. This is why VM live migration is taken into consideration. The resource manager confirms the security status in the load balancing background model before attempting to migrate virtual machines based on workload data. The state is regarded as safe if two VMs of interest colocate for more than τ_{thresh} for a time frame Δt; if not, it is regarded as compromised.

Assumption 5.3 Only servers with enough available resources (qualified hosts) are taken into consideration when clients submit new task requests to the resource manager for deployment. Qualified hosts are defined as follows:

5.4 Robust Tenant Identification Framework for Shared Cloud Environments

$$\sum_{i=1}^{N} \alpha_{i,r,m} C_i \leq X_{r,m} \quad \text{and} \quad M_i \leq Y_{r,m} \quad \text{represents VM}_i$$

This just takes into account the status of the system at the moment and the outstanding work requests for each incoming client request. The physical hosts $PH_{r,m}$ are used to assess CPU and memory resources, respectively. Only eligible physical hosts with sufficient remaining resources are taken into account while processing a new request. The main goal is to create an algorithm that would choose the best host while maintaining safe load balancing.

- k: index for cloud service providers
- r: index for physical hosts
- m: index for resource types (e.g., CPU, memory)
- N: total number of VMs
- $\alpha_{i,r,m}$: binary variable indicating if VM_i is allocated to physical host r for resource type m
- C_i: CPU requirement of VM_i
- M_i: memory requirement of VM_i
- $X_{r,m}$: available CPU capacity of physical host r
- $Y_{r,m}$: available memory capacity of physical host r
- τ_{thresh}: threshold time for colocation
- Δt: time window for security state evaluation

5.4.2 RTIF

Figure 5.2 illustrates the RTIF framework that integrates user identification, job request processing, and resource management in cloud environments. It employs a multistage approach involving job requests, resource allocation, and VM selection and placement while incorporating safety assessments and state calculations to enhance security and efficiency in multi-tenant cloud systems. With an emphasis on preventing coresident assaults during load balancing operations, we provide a thorough model for safe VM allocation in a multi-tenant cloud environment in this section. Consider a cloud architecture where many physical servers support several VMs. Here is how the system is defined: Let $\mathcal{U} = \{u_1, u_2, \ldots, u_N\}$ denote the set of N clients, $\mathcal{J} = \{j_1, j_2, \ldots, j_Q\}$ represents the set of Q job requests, $\mathcal{H} = \{h_1, h_2, \ldots, h_M\}$ is the set of M physical hosts, $\mathcal{S} = \{s_1, s_2, \ldots, s_K\}$ denotes the set of K servers, and $\mathcal{V} = \{v_1, v_2, \ldots, v_L\}$ represents the set of L virtual machines. Our allocation mapping $\Phi : \mathcal{U} \times \mathcal{J} \to \mathcal{H}$ designates a physical host for every task request received from a client. There is a binary variable that represents this mapping:

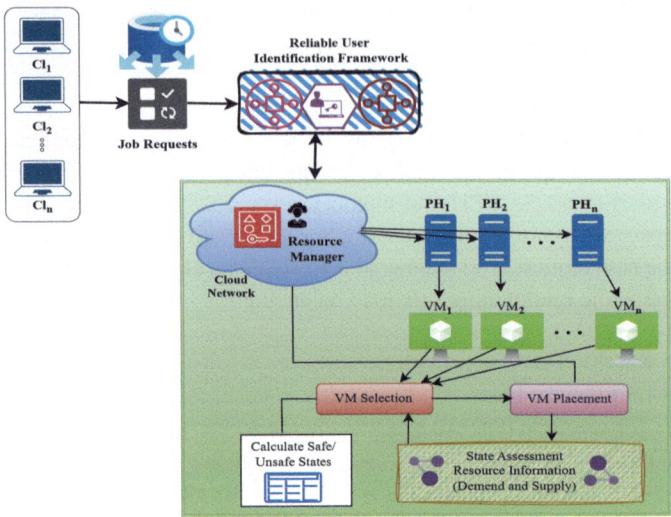

Fig. 5.2 RTIF framework

$$\Phi_{u,j,h} = \begin{cases} 1 & \text{if job request } j \text{ of client } u \text{ is allocated to safe host } h \\ 0 & \text{otherwise} \end{cases}$$

In order to preserve a safe state, the resultant allocation method Φ chooses which tasks to distribute to which physical hosts. We need to take into account resource limits because of the dynamic environment and the varied character of the hosts. Assume that a binary variable $\alpha_{v,h}$ indicates whether or not VM v is installed on host h. The following is the formulation of the resource constraints:

$$\sum_{v=1}^{L} \alpha_{v,h} C_v \leq X_h \quad \forall h \in \mathcal{H} \tag{5.17}$$

$$\sum_{v=1}^{L} \alpha_{v,h} M_v \leq Y_h \quad \forall h \in \mathcal{H} \tag{5.18}$$

where C_v and M_v represent the CPU and memory consumption of VM v, respectively. X_h and Y_h define the total CPU and memory resource capacity of host h, respectively. These limitations make sure that the overall amount of CPU and memory resources needed does not surpass the entire amount of space available on each physical host. We show a load allocation matrix Λ to illustrate how virtual machines are distributed across physical hosts. Let $\lambda_{i,j}$ be a matrix Λ element. The load allocation between v_i and v_j is defined by $\lambda_{i,j}$.

5.4.2.1 Security Considerations

Protecting physical hosts against coresident attacks—coarse-grained or fine-grained side-channel attacks—is the main objective of this paradigm. Our system, implemented inside a stochastic framework, determines the safest physical machine for deployment using its algorithmic method when the cloud data center gets a request for task deployment. We include real-time monitoring and modification capabilities in our approach to accommodate the dynamic nature of cloud settings. This makes possible:

- Constant assessment of every physical host's security condition
- Real-time VM placement adjustments in reaction to threats identified or variations in resource use
- Proactive VM migration to preserve the ideal mix between security and performance

Our safe virtual machine allocation policy's ultimate goal is to maximize resource efficiency while reducing the likelihood of successful coresident assaults. This may be expressed as an optimization problem with many objectives:

$$\min_{\Phi} \{\text{Risk}(\Phi), -\text{Utilization}(\Phi)\} \tag{5.19}$$

subject to the resource restrictions (1) and (2), where Utilization(Φ) gauges the effectiveness of resource consumption and Risk(Φ) quantifies the security risk connected to a certain allocation approach. This all-inclusive model addresses the crucial problem of striking a balance between performance and security in contemporary cloud computing infrastructures by providing a basis for the development of sophisticated algorithms that guarantee safe and effective VM allocation in multi-tenant cloud environments. Consider VM i located by tenant u as $v_i(u)$, and VM j found by tenant w, where w may be malevolent, as $v_j(w)$. We clarify:

- CoTenant$_{u,i,w,j}(\Delta t)$: a Boolean value indicating whether $v_i(u)$ and $v_j(w)$ are cotenants at time Δt
- CoHost$_{v_i(u),h}(\Delta t)$: a Boolean value indicating whether $v_i(u)$ is deployed on host h at time Δt

By minimizing hazardous states throughout the allocation process, our secure virtual machine allocation approach seeks to reduce the potential of multi-tenancy attacks. The VM placement and VM selection procedures are affected by the policy. When resource managers receive work requests from customers $u_i \in \mathcal{U}$, the RTIF classifies states as dependable or unreliable. The set of all feasible VMs $v_i \in \mathcal{V}$ that RTIF keeps track of is as follows:

$$\bigcup_{i=1,u=1}^{L,N} v_i(u) = (v_1(u_1), v_2(u_2), \ldots, v_i(u_i), \ldots, v_L(u_N)) \tag{5.20}$$

To determine the secure deployment of requests, we present the notions of safe and unsafe states. We use the cotenancy history of tenants to determine their dependability for safe states:

$$[\text{CoTenant}_{i(u)} \times \text{Favorable}_{i(u)}](\Delta t) > \gamma \tau_{thresh} \quad (5.21)$$

where τ_{thresh} is the time threshold to identify malicious VMs among cotenant VMs, and γ is a safety factor. For trustworthy hosts,

$$[\text{CoTenant}_{i(u)} \times \text{Favorable}_{i(u)} \times \text{KnownHost}_{i(u)}](\Delta t) > \gamma \tau_{host} \quad (5.22)$$

where τ_{host} is the time it takes for the intrusion detection system to determine whether a host can securely deploy virtual machine tasks. Unsafe states are calculated to identify potential leakage points:

$$\text{Unsafe}_{v_i(u) \to v_j(w)}(\Delta t, T_m) = \sum (\text{CoTenant}_{v_i(u), v_j(w)}(\Delta t)$$
$$\times \text{Favorable}_{v_i(u), v_j(w)}(\Delta t)) \quad (5.23)$$

where T_m is the monitoring time window. The total unsafe states for the cloud environment are calculated as

$$\text{Unsafe}_{\text{total}}(\Delta t, T_m) = \sum_{u \in \mathcal{U}} \text{Unsafe}_u(\Delta t, T_m) \quad (5.24)$$

where

$$\text{Unsafe}_u(\Delta t, T_m) = \sum_{w \in \mathcal{U}, w \neq u} \text{Unsafe}_{u \to w}(\Delta t, T_m) + \sum_{h \in \mathcal{H}} \text{Unsafe}_{u \to h}(\Delta t, T_m)$$
$$(5.25)$$

The load balancing problem is formulated as an optimization of task deployment over time Δt from a long-term perspective. The objective is to minimize the total unsafe states while maximizing resource utilization:

$$\min_{\Phi} \{\text{Unsafe}_{\text{total}}(\Delta t, T_m), -\text{Utilization}(\Phi)\} \quad (5.26)$$

subject to the resource constraints defined in Eqs. (5.1) and (5.2) of the previous section. The RTIF enhances security in multi-tenant cloud environments by identifying potentially malicious tenants and optimizing VM placement to minimize security risks. Through constant observation of tenant interactions and behavior [16], the RTIF algorithm improves security in multi-tenant cloud systems. Based on cotenancy trends, it evaluates tenant risk, assigns new task requests to hosts that decrease security concerns, and optimizes VM placement on a regular basis to lower system vulnerability. In order to maintain a safe cloud environment, our method adapts to changing tenant behaviors and system states while balancing effective resource utilization with strong security measures. This algorithm

Algorithm 2 Reliable Tenant Identification Framework (RTIF)

Require: $\mathcal{U}, \mathcal{V}, \mathcal{H}, \mathcal{J}, \tau_{thresh}, \tau_{host}, T_m, \gamma$
Ensure: Secure VM allocation Φ
1: **function** RTIF($\mathcal{U}, \mathcal{V}, \mathcal{H}, \mathcal{J}$)
2:     TenantScores $\leftarrow$ InitializeTenantScores($\mathcal{U}$)
3:     **for** each time interval Δt **do**
4:         UpdateTenantBehavior($\mathcal{U}, \Delta t$)
5:         CoTenancyMatrix $\leftarrow$ UpdateCoTenancy($\mathcal{V}, \Delta t$)
6:         **for** each $u \in \mathcal{U}$ **do**
7:             TenantScores[u] $\leftarrow$ AssessTenantRisk(u, CoTenancyMatrix, τ_{thresh})
8:         **end for**
9:         **for** each $j \in \mathcal{J}$ **do**
10:            $h^* \leftarrow$ FindOptimalHost(j, GetRequestingTenant(j), $\mathcal{H}$, TenantScores, τ_{host})
11:            **if** $h^* \neq$ null **then**
12:                 $\Phi \leftarrow \Phi \cup \{(j, h^*)\}$
13:                 UpdateResourceUtilization(h^*)
14:            **end if**
15:         **end for**
16:         **if** CalculateTotalUnsafeStates(Φ, T_m) $>$ threshold **then**
17:            $\Phi \leftarrow$ OptimizeAllocation(Φ, TenantScores, $\mathcal{H}$)
18:         **end if**
19:     **end for**
20:     **return** Φ
21: **end function**
22: **function** ASSESSTENANTRISK(u, CoTenancyMatrix, τ_{thresh})
23:     risk $\leftarrow \sum_{v_i \in \text{TenantsVMs}(u)} \sum_{v_j \notin \text{TenantsVMs}(u)} [\text{CoTenancyMatrix}[v_i][v_j] > \gamma \tau_{thresh}]$
24:     **return** NormalizeRisk(risk)
25: **end function**
26: **function** FINDOPTIMALHOST($j, u, \mathcal{H}$, TenantScores, τ_{host})
27:     **return** $_{h \in \mathcal{H}}\{\text{TenantScores}[u] + \sum_{v \in \text{VMsOnHost}(h)}[\text{CoHost}_{v,h}(\Delta t)] < \gamma \tau_{host}] \cdot$ TenantScores[TenantOfVM(v)]$\}$
28: **end function**
29: **function** OPTIMIZEALLOCATION(Φ, TenantScores, $\mathcal{H}$)
30:     **for** each $(j, h) \in \Phi$ where TenantScores[GetRequestingTenant(j)] $>$ highRiskThreshold **do**
31:         $h_{new} \leftarrow$ FindSaferHost(j, GetRequestingTenant(j), $\mathcal{H}$, TenantScores)
32:         **if** $h_{new} \neq$ null **then**
33:             $\Phi \leftarrow (\Phi \setminus \{(j, h)\}) \cup \{(j, h_{new})\}$
34:         **end if**
35:     **end for**
36:     **return** Φ
37: **end function**

efficiently balances resource utilization and security risk minimization in multi-tenant cloud environments. The RTIF algorithm shown in Algorithm 2 dynamically assesses tenant risk and optimizes VM allocation in shared cloud environments. It continuously updates tenant behavior scores, evaluates cotenancy risks, and adjusts resource allocation to maintain security while optimizing performance, employing functions like AssessTenantRisk, FindOptimalHost, and OptimizeAllocation to achieve these objectives.

Table 5.1 Parameters used in simulation

Parameters	Value
Host memory (MB)	204800
Host storage (GB)	10000
Host bandwidth (Mbps)	100000
System architecture	x86
Operating system	Linux
MIPS	250–350
VM image size (MB)	1000–5000
VM memory (RAM) (MB)	2048
VM bandwidth (Mbps)	1000–2000
VMM name	Xen
Number of hosts	100
Number of VMs	1000
Simulation duration (hours)	24

5.4.3 Performance Evaluation and Analysis

One hundred real computers with various configurations that can effectively meet the demands of impending load simulation circumstances are used to examine and assess the simulated cloud network. Each physical machine has a unique VMId that changes in value based on the dynamic deployment of cloudlets. The machines are divided into a number of clusters in space-shared mode, and each cluster is assigned a single task and shares memory. When using time sharing, many users split up the processing power, and each work runs for a certain amount of time. Cloudlet completion times under time-shared and space-shared allocation policies are compared. The CPU and memory amounts that are accessible on each of these 100 physical machines vary. These physical computers are home to 50 cloudlets that are always in operation. Table 5.1 provides a summary of the data that is recorded about these devices and tasks on the RTIF global blackboard. As shown in Fig. 5.3, when the number of cloudlets in the safe state varies, the processing time of the time-shared policy executes faster for fewer tasks than the space-shared policy.

The CloudSim 3.0.3 simulator is used in this study to calculate the number of failed tasks during task scheduling and deployment. It is only feasible to locate these failure nodes in the dynamic environment when the selected physical machine is unable to meet certain requirements of the assigned jobs. The likelihood of failures rises steadily as the amount of required tasks grows since handling duties will get harder over time. The primary purpose of this evaluation's load balancing metrics is to assess how well the system performs in terms of service. These efficient metrics often include job management skills, task request calculation response times, service completion rates per unit of time, etc. The cloud system computes the throughput rate based on these factors, which aids in assessing the performance of the external service over time. As seen in Fig. 5.4, the throughput is calculated among different numbers of requested jobs by taking cloudlets as 1000, 2000, 3000, and 4000. The impact of certain requested tasks on the corresponding cloudlet completion time in a time-shared scheduler policy is shown in Fig. 5.5. The host, virtual machine, and

5.4 Robust Tenant Identification Framework for Shared Cloud Environments 105

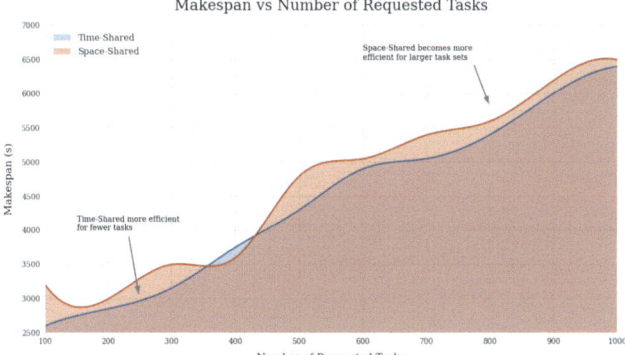

Fig. 5.3 Comparison of the Makespan of time-shared and space-shared resource allocation

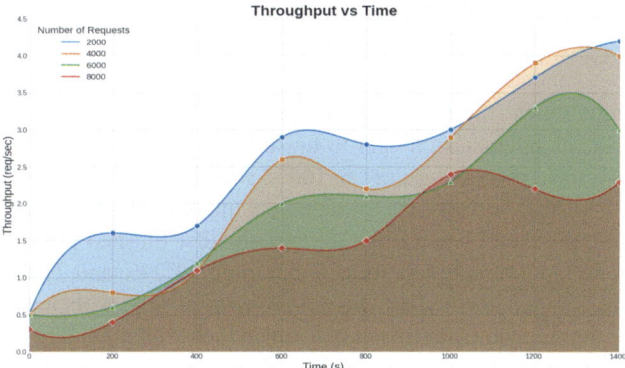

Fig. 5.4 Comparison of throughput in different number of requested tasks

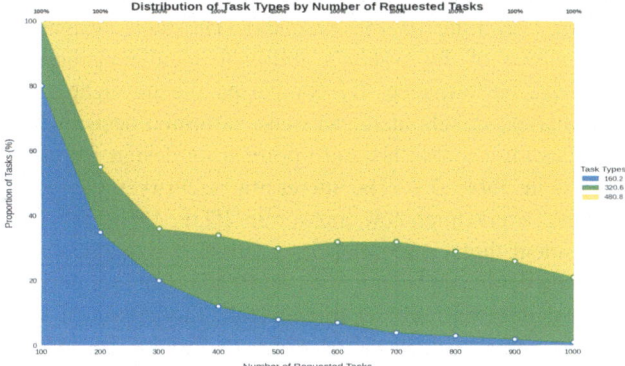

Fig. 5.5 Amount of work requested in the normal state

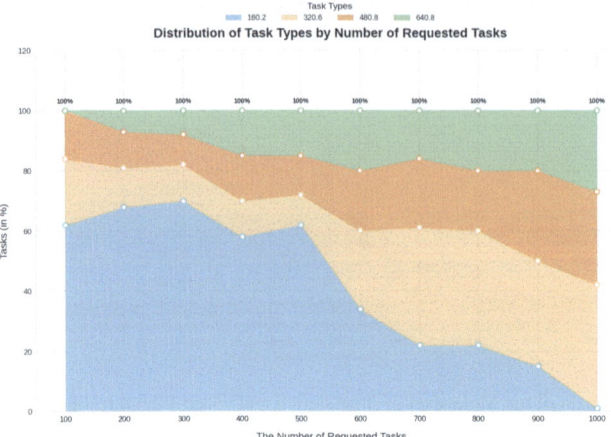

Fig. 5.6 Amount of work requested in the safe state

cloudlet configurations stay the same; however as the number of tasks rises from 100 to 1000, the cloudlets take longer to finish the tasks. At $n = 800$, only 6% of cloudlets finish their processing in $t = 160$ s, while the remaining 94% finish in 320.6 or 480.8 s. At $n = 100$, 80% of cloudlets finish their processing in time $= 160.2$ s. In a similar vein, when $n = 100$, no cloudlet finished processing in 160 seconds, although in a typical condition, a maximum of 29% and 71% of cloudlets finished processing in 320.6 and 480.8 seconds, respectively. Although some of the cloudlets take longer than 640.8 seconds to finish their execution, Fig. 5.6 is a safer graph than the one before it. It indicates if it requires additional time or guarantees that the consumers may exchange resources without feeling unsafe.

In this evaluation, the load balancing performance of the cloud system is assessed using a table that presents the throughput values for different numbers of requested tasks (1000–8000) over time (0–140 seconds). The table format allows for a comprehensive analysis of the system's ability to handle increasing workloads and maintain service performance. By comparing the throughput values across different load scenarios, stakeholders can make informed decisions regarding the system's load balancing capabilities and optimize its design for efficient service delivery as shown in Table 5.2. The increasing security issues in multi-tenant cloud settings have a potential new answer in RTIF. RTIF provides a holistic approach to coresident threat mitigation by combining dynamic risk assessment, adaptive resource allocation, and continuous tenant behavior monitoring. In addition to improving cloud infrastructure security overall, this approach keeps resource efficiency and performance in check. In order to foster trust and dependability in shared computing environments and pave the way for more efficient and secure cloud services, techniques such as RTIF will be more important as cloud computing develops. RTIF is a big step forward in tackling the complicated security environment of contemporary cloud computing, even if further study and practical applications are required to completely confirm its efficacy.

5.4 Robust Tenant Identification Framework for Shared Cloud Environments

Table 5.2 Throughput in a different number of requested tasks

Time (s)	1000 tasks	2000 tasks	3000 tasks	4000 tasks	5000 tasks	6000 tasks	7000 tasks	8000 tasks
0	0.52	0.31	0.29	0.23	0.20	0.18	0.16	0.14
10	0.85	0.62	0.53	0.45	0.39	0.35	0.31	0.28
20	1.12	0.89	0.75	0.64	0.56	0.50	0.45	0.41
30	1.37	1.13	0.96	0.83	0.73	0.65	0.59	0.54
40	1.65	1.38	1.18	1.02	0.90	0.81	0.73	0.67
50	1.91	1.62	1.39	1.21	1.07	0.96	0.87	0.80
60	2.14	1.82	1.57	1.38	1.22	1.10	1.00	0.92
70	2.37	2.03	1.76	1.55	1.38	1.24	1.13	1.04
80	2.59	2.23	1.94	1.71	1.53	1.38	1.26	1.16
90	2.80	2.43	2.12	1.87	1.67	1.52	1.39	1.28
100	3.01	2.61	2.29	2.03	1.82	1.65	1.51	1.39
110	3.21	2.80	2.46	2.19	1.96	1.78	1.63	1.51
120	3.41	2.97	2.62	2.33	2.10	1.91	1.75	1.62
130	3.60	3.15	2.78	2.48	2.23	2.04	1.87	1.73
140	3.79	3.32	2.93	2.62	2.37	2.16	1.99	1.84

5.5 Summary

This chapter has examined the crucial field of cloud security, emphasizing the particular difficulties presented by multi-tenant setups and offering the RTIF as a creative solution. Starting with the fundamentals of cloud security, we looked at operational safety, network security, and data protection, emphasizing the hazards that come with shared cloud infrastructures. In tackling these security issues, the implementation of RTIF is a major change. RTIF provides a dynamic and adaptable method of safeguarding multi-tenant cloud systems by combining clever load balancing algorithms with advanced user identification mechanisms. Robust user profiles may be created using the framework's analysis of user behavior, access patterns, and historical data. These user profiles serve as the foundation for choices about access control and safe resource allocation. Performance reviews have shown how well RTIF works to reduce security threats while retaining high levels of resource use. The framework has the potential to completely transform cloud security procedures because of its multi-objective optimization methodology, which strikes a balance between efficiency and security concerns.

5.6 Exercises

1. Security Threats in Multi-tenant Cloud Environments: Identify and analyze the primary security threats in multi-tenant cloud environments, such as side-channel attacks and VM escape vulnerabilities. Write a detailed report discussing how RTIF addresses these specific threats compared to conventional cloud security models.
2. Mathematical Modeling of RTIF for Security Optimization: RTIF's framework optimizes both security and resource consumption using multi-objective optimization. Assume RTIF uses the following utility functions for security (S) and resource consumption (R):
    - S = 100 (Risk Factor × Vulnerability Exposure)
    - R = Resource Utilization <Dmathdollar>—Overhead Penalty

    Given a cloud scenario with a risk factor of 0.7, vulnerability exposure of 50, resource utilization of 80%, and an overhead penalty of 10, calculate the security and resource consumption values. Discuss how the results balance security with resource usage.
3. Project-Based Exploration of RTIF's Load Balancing Algorithms: Develop a project that simulates the intelligent load balancing algorithms used in RTIF. Your project should:

    a. Define different cloud tenants with varying resource needs and behaviors
    b. Implement RTIF's load balancing algorithm to allocate resources based on user profiles

c. Compare the resource utilization and security performance of RTIF's approach against a traditional round robin load balancing method
4. Security vs. Efficiency Trade-Off in RTIF: Write a research-based report discussing the trade-off between security and efficiency in multi-tenant cloud systems. Use RTIF as a case study, focusing on how it balances these conflicting objectives and how its multi-objective optimization method ensures both high security and efficient resource usage.
5. Case Study on RTIF's Performance in Reducing Side-Channel Attacks: Conduct a case study that evaluates RTIF's effectiveness in reducing side-channel attacks in a multi-tenant cloud system. Your study should:

   a. Explain the side-channel attack method
   b. Simulate a cloud environment where a side-channel attack is attempted both with and without RTIF in place
   c. Measure the effectiveness of RTIF in detecting and preventing the attack
6. Comparative Study of RTIF and Conventional Cloud Security Models: Conduct a comparative study that highlights the differences between RTIF and conventional cloud security models (e.g., Role-Based Access Control, VM isolation). Your study should focus on:

   a. User identification mechanisms
   b. Resource allocation strategies
   c. Effectiveness in preventing common cloud-based attacks
7. Future Research Directions for RTIF: Discuss potential future research directions for RTIF, focusing on its integration with emerging technologies such as Blockchain, Federated Learning, or AI-based threat detection. Your report should cover:

   a. How these technologies can enhance RTIF's security framework
   b. Possible challenges in integrating these technologies into RTIF
   c. The impact of these enhancements on multi-tenant cloud security

References

1. Parast, F.K., Sindhav, C., Nikam, S., Yekta, H.I., Kent, K.B., Hakak, S.: Cloud computing security: A survey of service-based models. Comput. Secur. **114**, 102580 (2022)
2. Abdulsalam, Y.S., Hedabou, M.: Security and privacy in cloud computing: technical review. Future Internet **14**(1), 11 (2021)
3. Thabit, F., Alhomdy, S., Al-Ahdal, A.H., Jagtap, S.: A new lightweight cryptographic algorithm for enhancing data security in cloud computing. Glob. Transit. Proc. **2**(1), 91–99 (2021)
4. Edwards, J., Weaver, G.: Cloud Security. In: The Cybersecurity Guide to Governance, Risk, and Compliance, pp. 481–496. Wiley (2024). https://doi.org/10.1002/9781394250226.ch27

5. Pallavi, G.B., Jayarekha, P.: Secure and efficient multi-tenant database management system for cloud computing environment. Int. J. Inf. Technol. **14**, 703–711 (2022). https://doi.org/10.1007/s41870-019-00416-5
6. Kumar, P., Kumar Bhatt, A.: Enhancing multi-tenancy security in the cloud computing using hybrid ECC-based data encryption approach. IET Commun. **14**(18), 3212–3222 (2020)
7. Jia, R., Yang, Y., Grundy, J., Keung, J., Hao, L.: A systematic review of scheduling approaches on multi-tenancy cloud platforms. Inf. Softw. Technol. **132**, 106478 (2021)
8. Ramegowda, A., Agarkhed, J., Patil, S.R.: Adaptive task scheduling method in multi-tenant cloud computing. Int. J. Inf. Technol. **12**(4), 1093–1102 (2020)
9. Singh, A.K., Chhabra, S., Gupta, R., et al.: A Reliable Client Detection System during Load Balancing for Multi-tenant Cloud Environment. SN Comput. Sci. **4**, 86 (2023). https://doi.org/10.1007/s42979-022-01504-3
10. Saxena, D., Gupta, I., Kumar, J., Singh, A.K., Wen, X.: A Secure and Multiobjective Virtual Machine Placement Framework for Cloud Data Center. IEEE Syst. J. **16**(2), 3163–3174 (2022). https://doi.org/10.1109/JSYST.2021.3092521
11. Zhu, X., Shen, P., Dai, Y., Xu, L., Hu, J.: Privacy-Preserving and Trusted Keyword Search for Multi-Tenancy Cloud. IEEE Trans. Inf. Forensics Secur. **19**, 4316–4330 (2024). https://doi.org/10.1109/TIFS.2024.3377549
12. Geeta, K., Kamakshi Prasad, V.: Multi-objective cloud load-balancing with hybrid optimization. Int. J. Comput. Appl. **45**(10), 611–625 (2023). https://doi.org/10.1080/1206212X.2023.2260616
13. Adewojo, A.A., Bass, J.M.: A Novel Weight-Assignment Load Balancing Algorithm for Cloud Applications. SN Comput. Sci. **4**, 270 (2023). https://doi.org/10.1007/s42979-023-01702-7
14. Singh, A.K., Kumar, J.: Secure and energy-conscious load balancing framework for cloud data center networks. Electron. Lett. **55**(9), 540–541 (2019)
15. Han, J., Yun, I., Kim, S., Kim, T., Son, S., Han, D.: Scalable and Secure Virtualization of HSM With ScaleTrust. IEEE/ACM Trans. Netw. **31**(4), 1595–1610 (2023). https://doi.org/10.1109/TNET.2022.3220427
16. Yassin, M., Ould-Slimane, H., Talhi, C., Boucheneb, H.: Multi-Tenant Intrusion Detection Framework as a Service for SaaS. IEEE Trans. Serv. Comput. **15**(5), 2925–2938 (2022). https://doi.org/10.1109/TSC.2021.3077852
17. Majumdar, S., et al.: ProSAS: Proactive Security Auditing System for Clouds. IEEE Trans. Dependable Secure Comput. **19**(4), 2517–2534 (2022). https://doi.org/10.1109/TDSC.2021.3062204

Chapter 6
Heuristic Models for Optimal Host Selection

Abstract Advanced heuristic methods for the best host selection and resource distribution in cloud computing environments are presented in this chapter. The probabilistic framework for IaaS design, Adaptive Resource Allocation with Predictive Modeling (ARAPM), and multi-objective virtual machine optimizer (MOVMO) are the three main methodologies that are the focus of this study. These models tackle important issues in cloud infrastructure management, such as load balancing, resource optimization, and job scheduling. A lot of simulations and comparisons show that the suggested methods, especially MOVMO, are much better than current methods when it comes to reducing makespan, optimizing load distribution, saving energy, and improving overall system performance. Reduced VM downtime, higher failure rates, adaptable resource allocation to changing workloads, avoidance of over- or underutilization of hosts, and increased traffic scalability are some of the major accomplishments. These models provide strong solutions that can handle the growing complexity of contemporary cloud settings by combining probabilistic approaches, predictive modeling, and multi-objective optimization. This opens the door for more effective, resilient, and responsive cloud infrastructures.

Keywords Host selection · Resource optimization · Predictive modeling · Virtual machine placement · Performance metrics · Resource utilization · Energy efficiency · Workload distribution

6.1 Introduction

In the rapidly evolving landscape of cloud computing, efficient task scheduling and optimal host selection have become critical factors in maximizing resource utilization and minimizing makespan time [1]. This chapter delves into the realm of heuristic models designed to address these challenges, focusing on techniques that not only optimize task deployment but also enhance the overall performance of cloud data centers. The increasing complexity of cloud environments, characterized by heterogeneous virtual machines and dynamic workloads, necessitates sophisticated approaches to load balancing and resource allocation [2]. Traditional methods often fall short in adapting to the fluid nature of cloud infrastructures, leading to suboptimal resource utilization and compromised service quality. In response to these challenges, researchers have developed a suite of heuristic models that leverage probabilistic frameworks, machine learning techniques, and speculative approaches to achieve more efficient and responsive cloud operations [3, 4]. This chapter presents an in-depth exploration of two key heuristic models: the Probabilistic Framework for IaaS architecture the Adaptive Resource Allocation with Predictive Modeling (ARAPM), and the Multi-objective Virtual Machine Optimizer (MOVMO). Each of these models addresses specific aspects of the host selection problem, offering innovative solutions to enhance execution efficiency, resource utilization, and external service performance of cloud data centers.

The Probabilistic Framework for IaaS architecture introduces a novel approach to modeling client request services in environments with heterogeneous virtual machines. This model recognizes the inherent variability in cloud workloads and resource availability, employing probabilistic techniques to make informed decisions about task allocation. By considering the stochastic nature of cloud environments, this framework aims to achieve a more balanced distribution of workloads across available resources, ultimately leading to improved overall system performance [5, 6]. Building on this foundation, the ARAPM takes a step further by incorporating machine learning techniques to achieve immediate load balancing effects in dynamic environments. This approach leverages historical data and real-time metrics to predict resource requirements and optimize task placement. The ARAPM model's ability to adapt quickly to changing conditions makes it particularly well-suited for cloud environments with fluctuating workloads and resource availability [7]. The second model, MOVMO, addresses the specific needs of parallel and distributed applications. By formulating the problem within a speculative framework that considers CPU usage, memory consumption, and energy efficiency, MOVMO aims to optimize throughput while minimizing failure rates. This model's comprehensive approach to resource estimation allows for more accurate predictions of application performance, leading to more efficient VM placement decisions.

Figure 6.1 depicts the process of optimal host selection in a cloud environment using three heuristic models: Probabilistic Framework, ARAPM, and MOVMO. It illustrates how these models analyze incoming tasks and intelligently allocate them to appropriate hosts, demonstrating the concept of efficient task scheduling and resource optimization in cloud computing [8].

These heuristic models represent a significant advancement in the field of cloud resource management. By moving beyond traditional, static approaches to host selection and load balancing, these models offer more nuanced and adaptive solutions to the challenges posed by modern cloud environments [9]. Their ability to consider multiple factors simultaneously—including execution efficiency, resource utilization, and external service performance—enables cloud providers to make more informed decisions about task scheduling and resource allocation. The realization that optimal host selection involves more than just distributing tasks evenly among available resources is what inspired the creation of these

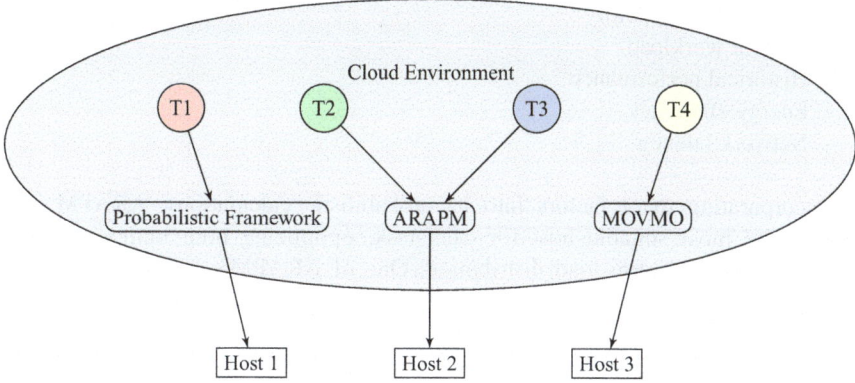

Fig. 6.1 Heuristic models for optimal host selection in cloud environment

models. Instead, it requires a deep understanding of the complex interplay between various system components, workload characteristics, and performance metrics. By incorporating probabilistic reasoning, machine learning techniques, and speculative analysis, these heuristic models provide a more holistic approach to cloud resource management. As cloud computing continues to evolve and expand, the importance of efficient task scheduling and optimal host selection will only grow. The heuristic models presented in this chapter offer a glimpse into the future of cloud resource management, where adaptive, intelligent systems work in real time to optimize performance and resource utilization. By embracing these advanced techniques, cloud providers can enhance the reliability, efficiency, and scalability of their services, ultimately delivering greater value to their clients and end users [10].

6.2 Adaptive Resource Allocation with Predictive Modeling

It is an advanced approach designed to optimize task allocation in Infrastructure as a Service (IaaS) architectures with heterogeneous virtual machines. This model builds upon the foundations of probabilistic frameworks to enhance load balancing and resource utilization in cloud data centers. ARAPM employs a two-stage process for optimal host selection:

- **Qualification Stage**: Initially, ARAPM filters the available hosts to create a set of qualified candidates that meet the minimum requirements for task deployment. This preselection process ensures that only capable hosts are considered for further analysis, reducing computational overhead.
- **Probabilistic Optimization**: In the second stage, ARAPM applies a sophisticated probabilistic model to the qualified host set. This model evaluates each host based on multiple factors, including:

- Computing capability
- Current workload
- Historical performance
- Energy efficiency
- Network latency

By incorporating these factors into its probabilistic calculations, ARAPM can identify the most suitable host for each task, optimizing both immediate performance and long-term load distribution. One of ARAPM's key innovations is its predictive modeling component. This feature allows the system to anticipate upcoming workloads and resource demands based on historical data and current trends. By leveraging machine learning techniques, ARAPM can:

- Forecast peak usage periods.
- Predict potential resource bottlenecks.
- Estimate task completion times on different hosts.

This predictive capability enables ARAPM to make proactive allocation decisions, preventing imbalances before they occur and maintaining optimal performance across the cloud infrastructure. Moreover, ARAPM's adaptive nature allows it to continuously refine its decision-making process. As it gathers more data on task performance and host behavior, the model updates its probabilistic estimations, leading to increasingly accurate and efficient allocations over time. The ARAPM approach offers several benefits:

- Improved long-term load balancing by uniformly distributing tasks across servers.
- Enhanced overall system performance through optimal host selection.
- Reduced communication overhead due to accurate workload estimations.
- Increased energy efficiency by considering power consumption in allocation decisions.
- Better scalability and adaptability to changing cloud environments.

6.2.1 Problem Formulation

The ARAPM model employs probabilistic methods to optimize various parameters, including makespan time, throughput, and other service performance criteria. Traditionally, when clients submit requests to cloud data centers, these requests are often deployed to physical hosts randomly. However, ARAPM's approach of selecting the optimal host significantly enhances load balancing and resource utilization [11]. In this model, a probabilistic framework is developed to identify the optimal host with the highest probability of efficiently deploying tasks. The load balancer manager (LBM) ensures that the requested resources do not exceed available resources. While multiple physical hosts may meet the basic resource requirements, ARAPM

6.2 Adaptive Resource Allocation with Predictive Modeling

identifies the optimal one based on factors such as high probability, maximum resource utilization, reduced makespan time, and high throughput. The cloud archetype in ARAPM consists of N clients: $C = \{C_1, C_2, \ldots, C_n\}$, M job requests: $J = \{J_1, J_2, \ldots, J_m\}$, and P physical hosts: $H = \{H_1, H_2, \ldots, H_p\}$. The model aims to find a mapping function $f : C \times J \rightarrow H$ that assigns requests to optimal physical hosts. This can be represented as:

$$f\{C \times J \times H\} = \{f_{i,j,k} | f_{i,j,k} = 1 \text{ iff job request } J_j \text{ from } C_i \text{ is allocated to optimal } H_k\} \quad (6.1)$$

This formulation determines which task should be deployed to which physical host optimally in the heterogeneous cloud environment. To streamline the process and reduce communication overhead, ARAPM utilizes a Dynamic Resource State (DRS) table. This table maintains records of:

- Free and under-processed hosts
- Virtual machines per host
- Allocated hosts
- Non-assigned hosts

When new tasks arrive for deployment, the LBM can quickly identify the optimal host using the DUI table, significantly reducing communication overheads. The ARAPM model's probabilistic approach considers various factors in its decision-making process:

- Current host utilization: U_k
- Historical performance: P_k
- Energy efficiency: E_k
- Network latency: L_k

The probability of selecting a host H_k for a job J_j can be represented as:

$$P(H_k|J_j) = \frac{w_1 U_k + w_2 P_k + w_3 E_k + w_4 L_k}{\sum_{i=1}^{p}(w_1 U_i + w_2 P_i + w_3 E_i + w_4 L_i)} \quad (6.2)$$

where w_1, w_2, w_3, and w_4 are weighting factors that can be adjusted based on specific cloud environment priorities. By incorporating these probabilistic calculations and maintaining the DUI table, ARAPM achieves:

- Improved load distribution across physical hosts.
- Enhanced resource utilization.
- Reduced makespan time for task completion.
- Increased overall system throughput.

This approach represents a significant advancement in cloud resource management, offering a more intelligent and efficient method for task allocation in heterogeneous cloud environments.

6.2.2 Architecture of ARAPM

The Adaptive Resource Allocation with Predictive Modeling (ARAPM) is defined by an octatuple $\omega = \{J, H, C, CPU_{avl}, MEM_{avl}, CPU_{req}, MEM_{req}, E\}$, where $J = \{J_1, J_2, \ldots, J_m\}$ defines the set of job requests for task deployment, $H(p, t_0) = \{H_1, H_2, \ldots, H_p\}$ represents the set of available physical hosts, where t_0 is the starting time for task deployment, and $C(n, \Delta t, t) = \{C_1, C_2, \ldots, C_n\}$ describes the client requests within a particular time interval Δt. $CPU_{avl} = \{CPU_{avl}^1, CPU_{avl}^2, \ldots, CPU_{avl}^p\}$ and $MEM_{avl} = \{MEM_{avl}^1, MEM_{avl}^2, \ldots, MEM_{avl}^p\}$ represent the current available CPU and memory resources of the p physical hosts, $CPU_{req}(n, t) = \{CPU_{req}^1, CPU_{req}^2, \ldots, CPU_{req}^n\}$ is the requested CPU resource amount for deploying n tasks in J, and E represents energy consumption. ARAPM employs a predictive modeling approach to optimize resource allocation and load balancing in dynamic cloud environments. It uses historical data and current system state to forecast resource requirements and make proactive allocation decisions.

An illustration of the ARAPM system design for cloud settings may be seen in Fig. 6.2. This demonstrates the flow of information from client requests to the ARAPM Controller, which includes both resource allocation management and predictive modeling. For the purpose of selecting the most suitable hosts for task

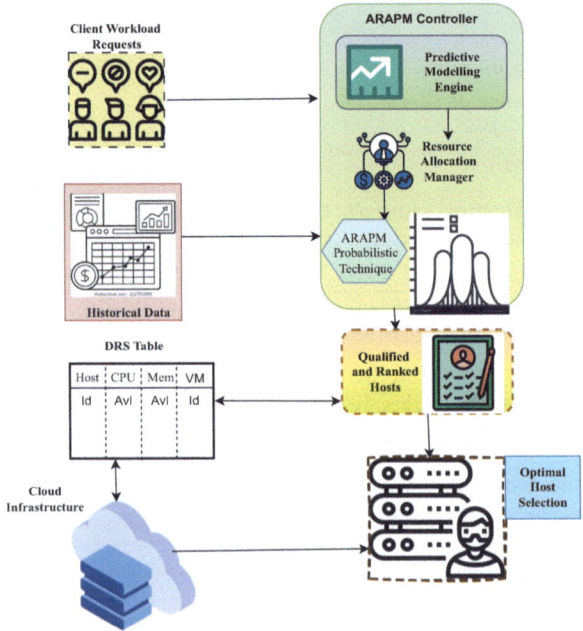

Fig. 6.2 ARAPM architecture

6.2 Adaptive Resource Allocation with Predictive Modeling

deployment, the system engages in interaction with a Dynamic Resource State Table as well as the cloud architecture that lies behind it. In order to ensure effective management of cloud resources, this design places a strong emphasis on the integration of historical data analysis, real-time resource monitoring, and adaptive decision-making. The objective function of ARAPM can be represented as

$$\omega_r = \sum_{i=1}^{n}\sum_{j=1}^{m} P(H_j|J_i), \quad i \in \{1,2,\ldots,n\}, j \in \{1,2,\ldots,m\}, r \in \{1,2,\ldots,N\} \tag{6.3}$$

where $P(H_j|J_i)$ denotes the probability of selecting host H_j for job J_i, calculated using our predictive model:

$$P(H_j|J_i) = \frac{w_1 U_j + w_2 P_j + w_3 E_j + w_4 L_j}{\sum_{k=1}^{p}(w_1 U_k + w_2 P_k + w_3 E_k + w_4 L_k)} \tag{6.4}$$

Here, U_j, P_j, E_j, and L_j represent the utilization, performance history, energy efficiency, and network latency of host H_j, respectively, with w_1, w_2, w_3, and w_4 as corresponding weight factors. The qualification function for host selection in ARAPM is defined as

$$Qual(H_j, J_i) = \begin{cases} 1 & \text{if } (CPU_{req}^i \leq CPU_{avl}^j) \wedge (MEM_{req}^i \leq MEM_{avl}^j) \\ 0 & \text{otherwise} \end{cases} \tag{6.5}$$

ARAPM aims to optimize multiple objectives simultaneously:

$$\min(T_{exec}, E_{cons}, L_{bal}) \tag{6.6}$$

where T_{exec} is the execution time, E_{cons} is energy consumption, and L_{bal} represents the load balance across hosts. The predictive component of ARAPM uses machine learning techniques to forecast future resource demands:

$$R_{pred}(t + \Delta t) = f(R_{hist}, S_{current}, W_{pattern}) \tag{6.7}$$

where $R_{pred}(t + \Delta t)$ is the predicted resource demand at time $t + \Delta t$, R_{hist} is the historical resource usage data, $S_{current}$ is the current system state, and $W_{pattern}$ represents identified workload patterns. By incorporating these predictive elements, ARAPM achieves more efficient resource allocation, reduced response times, and improved overall system performance in dynamic cloud environments. In the ARAPM model, we define the availability index of a host H_i as:

$$A_i = \phi CPU_{avl}^i + \psi MEM_{avl}^i + \eta E_{eff}^i \tag{6.8}$$

where CPU_{avl}^i and MEM_{avl}^i define the available computing power of CPU and memory, respectively, and E_{eff}^i represents the energy efficiency of the host. The coefficients ϕ, ψ, and η are weighting factors. The ARAPM probabilistic model relies on a particular set of data and performance constraints. The qualified set of hosts is defined as

$$Qual\{H_1, H_2, \ldots, H_n | \Xi\} = \prod_{i=1}^{n} Qual(H_i | \Xi) \tag{6.9}$$

where Ξ represents the set of parameters (CPU, memory, and energy efficiency). For each host, we define a likelihood function:

$$\lambda(\Xi; H_1, H_2, \ldots, H_n) = \prod_{i=1}^{n} Qual(H_i | \Xi) \tag{6.10}$$

Here, the semicolon separates parameters Ξ from observations $H_1, H_2, \ldots, H_n$. The ARAPM model calculates the probability of each qualified host handling tasks effectively. We define a suitability ratio Υ for each host:

$$\Upsilon_i = \frac{CPU_{req}^i}{CPU_{avl}^i} \times \frac{MEM_{req}^i}{MEM_{avl}^i} \times \frac{E_{req}^i}{E_{eff}^i}; \quad i \in \{1, 2, 3, \ldots, q\} \tag{6.11}$$

where q is the number of qualified hosts, and CPU_{req}^i, MEM_{req}^i, and E_{req}^i represent the required CPU, memory, and energy for the task. The ARAPM model then selects the optimal host with the maximum probability:

$$H_{OPT} = {}_{i=1}^{q}\{\Upsilon_i \cdot P(H_i | J)\} \tag{6.12}$$

where $P(H_i | J)$ is the probability of selecting host H_i for job J, as defined in our earlier equation. To enhance the predictive capabilities of ARAPM, we incorporate a time series forecasting component:

$$R_{pred}^i(t + \Delta t) = f(R_{hist}^i, S_{current}^i, W_{pattern}) + \epsilon_t \tag{6.13}$$

where $R_{pred}^i(t + \Delta t)$ is the predicted resource demand for host H_i at time $t + \Delta t$, R_{hist}^i is the historical resource usage data, $S_{current}^i$ is the current system state, $W_{pattern}$ represents identified workload patterns, and ϵ_t is the error term. The final optimization problem in ARAPM can be formulated as

$$\min_{H_i}\{w_1 T_{exec} + w_2 E_{cons} + w_3 L_{imb}\} \tag{6.14}$$

$$\text{subject to: } \Upsilon_i \leq 1, \quad \forall i \in \{1, 2, \ldots, q\} \tag{6.15}$$

6.2 Adaptive Resource Allocation with Predictive Modeling

where T_{exec} is the execution time, E_{cons} is energy consumption, L_{imb} is load imbalance, and w_1, w_2, w_3 are weighting factors. This ARAPM architecture combines probabilistic host selection with predictive modeling to achieve optimal task deployment in cloud data centers, minimizing execution time and enhancing resource utilization while considering future resource demands. Algorithm 3 shows the ARAPM algorithm that is designed to show the fundamental capabilities of the Adaptive Resource Allocation with Predictive Modeling system, which is designed for use in cloud settings. It handles incoming task requests by anticipating resource needs, identifying qualified hosts, and picking the ideal host based on a mix of suitability ratios and probabilistic selection. In addition, it identifies qualified hosts. It is the algorithm's responsibility to distribute resources, continually update a Dynamic Resource State Table, and make periodic adjustments to its parameters and prediction model in order to ensure that it continues to function effectively. For the purpose of optimizing task deployment across heterogeneous cloud infrastructures, this technique combines real-time resource management with predictive analytics.

6.2.3 Performance Evaluation

Within the context of the cloudsim simulation environment, the experiments are carried out by providing assistance for the dynamic creation. Assessing the effects of these long-term studies on actual infrastructures is a task that is fraught with intense difficulty. For the purpose of getting improved performance while simultaneously gaining appropriate testing findings, the simulated cloud network is being explored. The ARAPM system is being evaluated experimentally using a simulated cloud environment that has certain hardware and software characteristics. The host computers have 204,800 MB of RAM, 10,000,000 MB of storage, and a 100,000 Mbps bandwidth. These are very powerful machines. These hosts provide a realistic cloud infrastructure configuration, running an ×86 Linux operating system. The hosts can process data at speeds ranging from 250 to 350 MIPS (Million Instructions Per Second), which permits the performance fluctuations common in cloud systems with different topologies. The VMs that are deployed on these hosts have RAM allotment of 2048 MB, and their image sizes vary from 1000 to 5000 MB. The virtual machine's bandwidth is adjusted between 1000 and 2000 Mbps to replicate various network scenarios. Every physical system has a single CPU core installed, and all VMs are overseen by the Xen hypervisor (VMM). This configuration offers a realistic and varied environment to evaluate the efficiency of the ARAPM system in scheduling tasks and allocating resources in various cloud computing situations. MakeSpan is the overall amount of time required to process the jobs from start to finish. It is mostly used in scheduling contexts where work requests are assigned to physical hosts. As the number of requested jobs increases, the makespan will also grow. The Random Deployment (RD) technique uses randomized jobs to handle data in cloud data centers. Compared to these, this ARAPM completes the necessary

---
Algorithm 3 ARAPM (adaptive resource allocation with predictive modeling)

Require:
1: $J = \{J_1, J_2, \ldots, J_m\}$ ▷ Set of incoming job requests
2: $H = \{H_1, H_2, \ldots, H_p\}$ ▷ Set of available hosts
3: R_{hist} ▷ Historical resource usage data
4: Δt ▷ Time interval for prediction

Ensure: Optimal host allocation for each job
5: Initialize Dynamic Resource State Table (DRST)
6: **for** each time interval t **do**
7:     Update DRST with current resource states of all hosts in H
8: **end for**
9: **for** each job request J_i in J **do**
10:     Extract job requirements: CPU_{req}^i, MEM_{req}^i, E_{req}^i
11:     $R_{pred} \leftarrow$ PredictResourceDemand(R_{hist}, DRST, Δt)
12:     $Q \leftarrow \{\}$ ▷ Set of qualified hosts
13:     **for** each host H_j in H **do**
14:       **if** $(CPU_{avl}^j \geq CPU_{req}^i) \wedge (MEM_{avl}^j \geq MEM_{req}^i) \wedge (E_{eff}^j \geq E_{req}^i)$ **then**
15:         $Q \leftarrow Q \cup \{H_j\}$
16:       **end if**
17:     **end for**
18:     **if** Q is empty **then**
19:       Wait or reject job J_i
20:       **continue** to next job
21:     **end if**
22:     **for** each qualified host H_j in Q **do**
23:       Calculate Suitability Ratio:
24:       $\Upsilon_j \leftarrow \frac{CPU_{req}^i}{CPU_{avl}^j} \times \frac{MEM_{req}^i}{MEM_{avl}^j} \times \frac{E_{req}^i}{E_{eff}^j}$
25:       Calculate Selection Probability:
26:       $P(H_j|J_i) \leftarrow \frac{w_1 U_j + w_2 P_j + w_3 E_j + w_4 L_j}{\sum_{k \in Q}(w_1 U_k + w_2 P_k + w_3 E_k + w_4 L_k)}$
27:     **end for**
28:     Select Optimal Host:
29:     $H_{OPT} \leftarrow {}_{j \in Q}\{\Upsilon_j \cdot P(H_j|J_i)\}$
30:     Allocate job J_i to host H_{OPT}
31:     Update DRST:
32:     $CPU_{avl}^{OPT} \leftarrow CPU_{avl}^{OPT} - CPU_{req}^i$
33:     $MEM_{avl}^{OPT} \leftarrow MEM_{avl}^{OPT} - MEM_{req}^i$
34:     Update other relevant metrics
35: **end for**
36: Periodically:
37:     Evaluate overall system performance
38:     Adjust weighting factors w_1, w_2, w_3, w_4 if necessary
39:     Retrain predictive model with new historical data
40: Repeat steps 2–4 until no more jobs or system shutdown
---

tasks in less time. Table 6.1 displays the comparative experimental outcomes of these four methods.

The number of failure nodes that occur throughout the deployment procedure in this dynamic environment is used to assess the trials. When the selected host is unable to meet the computational needs of the assigned tasks, it might

6.2 Adaptive Resource Allocation with Predictive Modeling

Table 6.1 Makespan comparison (mean and standard deviation) for various task loads and allocation methods

Tasks	RD (s)	DLB (s)	ARAPM (s)
10	1285.67 ± 42.31	1102.45 ± 35.78	987.23 ± 29.56
20	2876.34 ± 65.87	2435.78 ± 54.32	2187.56 ± 47.89
30	4567.89 ± 89.43	3876.23 ± 76.54	3432.12 ± 68.76
40	6789.34 ± 123.87	5643.78 ± 98.76	4987.56 ± 87.45
50	9234.56 ± 167.54	7654.32 ± 134.65	6765.43 ± 118.90
60	11987.45 ± 198.76	9876.54 ± 165.43	8654.32 ± 145.67
70	14567.89 ± 234.56	11987.45 ± 198.76	10543.21 ± 176.54
80	17654.32 ± 276.54	14567.89 ± 232.12	12765.43 ± 204.32
90	21098.76 ± 312.87	17432.10 ± 265.43	15234.56 ± 234.56
100	25432.12 ± 356.78	20987.65 ± 298.76	18765.43 ± 267.89

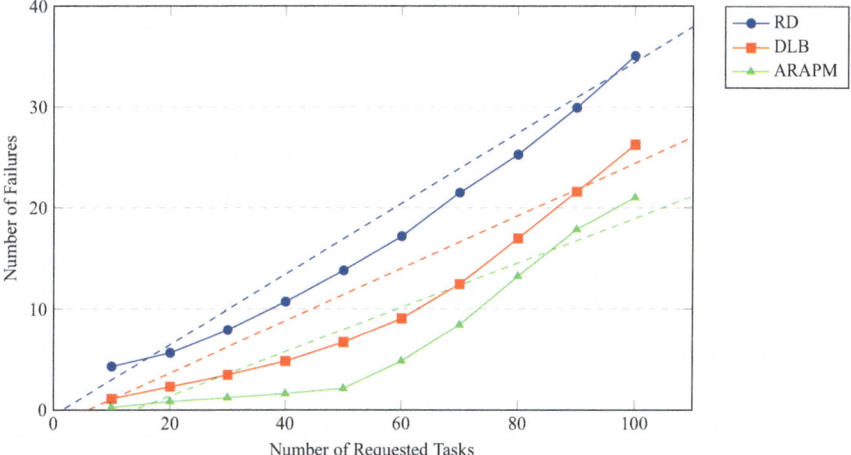

Fig. 6.3 Number of failures vs. requested tasks with predictive trends

happen. The likelihood of failure nodes will steadily grow as the number of jobs requested increases. A comparison of failure nodes with RD and DLB is shown in Fig. 6.3. According to the findings, ARAPM is more reliable and efficient for cloud data centers. Table 6.2 shows the assessment of throughput, which is based on completed services per unit time and reaction time per host, indicating the higher performance of ARAPM over RD and DLB approaches. Throughput is consistently higher with ARAPM, and performance steadily improves over time. The reason for this advantage is the predictive modeling capabilities of ARAPM, which enables proactive and effective resource allocation. Because ARAPM is adaptive, it can continually optimize job allocation based on past data and real-time system performance. Through the consideration of several aspects such as CPU utilization, memory utilization, and network latency, ARAPM is able to minimize resource

Table 6.2 Throughput comparison of resource allocation methods over time

Time (s)	RD	DLB	OPH-LB	ARAPM
0	1.32	0.78	0.65	1.45
100	1.45	0.95	0.89	1.68
200	1.58	1.12	1.35	1.92
300	2.73	1.65	1.82	2.85
400	1.62	2.18	1.95	2.98
500	2.85	2.75	2.65	3.15
600	1.58	2.95	2.85	3.28
700	1.65	2.15	2.35	3.42
800	1.75	2.25	2.18	3.55
900	2.15	2.32	1.85	3.68
1000	3.75	2.35	2.65	3.82
1100	2.45	2.38	2.55	3.95
1200	2.35	2.45	1.95	4.08
1300	2.28	2.55	2.15	4.22
1400	2.35	2.65	1.92	4.35

contention and achieve more efficient load balancing. Moreover, ARAPM's capacity to learn from past data results in predictions and allocation choices that are optimally made over time, which helps to maintain a greater throughput than other techniques.

6.3 Multi-Objective Virtual Machine Optimizer

The MOVMO approach focuses on finding the optimal host and meeting performance criteria to achieve long-term load balancing for cloud data centers [12, 13]. The authors have developed a multi-objective model that optimally manages key parameters: CPU utilization, memory usage, and energy consumption. This multimodal problem addresses multiple specifications to find the node that minimizes these three critical factors. The objective function can be expressed as

$$\omega_r = \sum_{i=1}^{n} \sum_{j=1}^{m} H_i^j, \quad i \in \{1, 2, \ldots, n\}, j \in \{1, 2, \ldots, m\}, r \in \{1, 2, \ldots, N\}$$
(6.16)

where H_i^j denotes the optimal host selection for the i-th VM on the j-th host, defined as

6.3 Multi-Objective Virtual Machine Optimizer

$$H_i^j = \begin{cases} 1 & \text{if optimal VM}_i \text{ is found and } MEM_{req} \leq MEM_{avl}, i \in \{1, 2, \ldots, n\} \\ 0 & \text{if optimal VM}_i \text{ is not found or } MEM_{req} > MEM_{avl}, i \in \{1, 2, \ldots, n\} \\ \text{Invalid} & \text{if VM}_i \text{ has not been allocated to Host}_j \end{cases} \quad (6.17)$$

To obtain better results, MOVMO emphasizes finding the best host that utilizes the least amount of resources for efficient cloudlet deployment. We define the available resource amount of a physical host as

$$A_i = \phi CPU_{avl}^i + \psi MEM_{avl}^i + E_i \quad (6.18)$$

where $\phi + \psi = 1$. CPU_{avl}^i and MEM_{avl}^i represent the available computing power of CPU and memory, respectively. E_i estimates the energy consumed during deployment. ϕ and ψ are weighting factors. When tasks are queued for deployment, multiple hosts may meet the configuration requirements. However, MOVMO employs a maximum likelihood approach to identify the optimal host, ensuring accurate decisions with reduced communication overhead. This maximum likelihood algorithm is a statistical method that maximizes parameter likelihood estimations based on a particular dataset. It considers various physical hosts H_i with different configurations, having a joint density function:

$$f(H_1, H_2, \ldots, H_n | \Xi) = f(H_1 | \Xi) \times f(H_2 | \Xi) \times \ldots \times f(H_n | \Xi) \quad (6.19)$$

where Ξ represents the parameters (CPU, memory, and energy consumption). The likelihood function for each host is defined as

$$\lambda(\Xi; H_1, H_2, \ldots, H_n) = f(H_1, H_2, \ldots, H_n | \Xi) = \prod_{i=1}^{n} f(H_i | \Xi) \quad (6.20)$$

Here, the semicolon separates two types of inputs: parameters Ξ and observations $H_1, H_2, \ldots, H_n$. The MOVMO approach optimizes virtual machine placement by considering multiple objectives simultaneously, leading to improved load balancing, resource utilization, and energy efficiency in cloud environments.

6.3.1 Advanced Maximum Likelihood Estimation in MOVMO

MOVMO applies a natural logarithm to the likelihood function, resulting in a log-likelihood function defined as

$$\ln \lambda(\Xi; H_1, H_2, \ldots, H_n) = \sum_{i=1}^{n} \ln f(H_i|\Xi) \qquad (6.21)$$

An average calculation of this log likelihood is expressed as

$$\ell = \frac{1}{n} \ln \lambda \qquad (6.22)$$

The objective of this maximum likelihood method is to achieve efficient workload balancing by estimating Ξ_{MLE} and finding a value of Ξ that maximizes $\ell(\Xi; H)$. The maximum performance value is defined as the node that fulfills the maximum requested resource amount in the set of task requests RQ_i:

$$\{\Xi_{MLE}\} = \{\max_{i=1}^{n} RQ_i \ell(\Xi; H_1, H_2, \ldots, H_n)\} \qquad (6.23)$$

Here, RQ_i represents the requested resource amount of the i-th task:

$$RQ_i = \phi RQC_i + \psi RQM_i \qquad (6.24)$$

To measure the load balancing degree of a cloud data center, MOVMO utilizes a probability density function, observing the mean and standard deviation of all hosts:

$$\mu = \frac{\sum_{i=1}^{n} H_i}{N} \qquad (6.25)$$

$$\sigma = \sqrt{\frac{\sum_{i=1}^{n}(H_i - \mu)^2}{N}} \qquad (6.26)$$

The remaining load scale of a host is calculated as

$$RM_i = \frac{Load_i}{Total_i}, \quad i \in \{1, 2, 3, \ldots, n\} \qquad (6.27)$$

where $Total_i$ denotes the computing power of physical hosts:

$$Total_i = \phi TC_i + \psi TM_i; \quad i \in \{1, 2, 3, \ldots, n\} \qquad (6.28)$$

TC_i and TM_i define the total computing power of CPU and memory of host i. The probability of processing a particular task request set to achieve the optimal physical host is calculated using a normal distribution $q(\mu, \sigma^2)$:

$$P(H|\mu, \sigma^2) = \frac{1}{\sqrt{2\pi\sigma^2}} \exp\left(-\frac{(H-\mu)^2}{2\sigma^2}\right) \qquad (6.29)$$

6.3 Multi-Objective Virtual Machine Optimizer

For n independent identically distributed physical hosts, the corresponding density function is

$$f(H_1, H_2, \ldots, H_n | \sigma^2) = (\frac{1}{2\pi\sigma^2})^{n/2} \exp\left(-\frac{\sum_{i=1}^{n}(H_i - \mu)^2}{2\sigma^2}\right) \quad (6.30)$$

or alternatively:

$$f(H_1, H_2, \ldots, H_n | \sigma^2) = \left(\frac{1}{2\pi\sigma^2}\right)^{n/2} \exp\left(-\frac{\prod_{i=1}^{n}(H_i - x_0)^2 + n(x_0 - \mu)^2}{2\sigma^2}\right) \quad (6.31)$$

MOVMO determines the most advantageous physical host for task deployment by choosing the model parameter set that maximizes the probability function using the observed data [14]. By using this approach, the probability of the observed data under the final distribution is maximized. In order to choose the best host for deployment, the Dynamic Load Balancing module must communicate with other entities. The load balancing mechanism kicks in when fresh work requests come in. In the process of gathering data on the requested (RQ_i) and available (A_i) resources of m physical hosts in cloud data centers, load managers keep an eye on and initiate these tasks. Based on this data, the model creates a deployment plan that is sent to the deployment controller. MOVMO chooses suitable hosts with low resource use and a high deployment probability from among all physical hosts. The load management distributes the burden across the system by selecting which hosts to utilize for deployment as fresh batches of jobs come in. This dynamic technique has drawbacks since every new task might lead to imbalances, necessitating a lot of communication between processors and perhaps producing oscillation problems. For the best host selection and deployment, job requests (jr_i) that have collected over a time period Δt are taken into account. The MOVMO approach is shown in Fig. 6.4 for effective resource allocation in cloud systems. It starts with client workload task requests sent into the cloud system, which the MOVMO manager oversees. Two concurrent processes—resource information collecting and the MOVMO Core—are fed from these initial requests, which are also analyzed Found central in the system, and the MOVMO Core manages multi-objective optimization and deployment strategy development. It finds suitable physical hosts depending on the investigated needs and resources. The procedure then uses maximum likelihood estimate to choose the best host and entails inter-host communication overhead analysis. This all-encompassing strategy takes host capabilities, system-wide efficiency, and resource needs all at once. Emphasizing MOVMO's complex decision-making process—which balances many goals to attain optimum VM placement and load distribution throughout the cloud infrastructure—this helps to maximize resource use and system performance.

Advanced methods of resource management in cloud computing are embodied by the MOVMO and related Job Reallocation algorithm in Algorithms 4 and 5. Using maximum likelihood estimate and probability-based selection, MOVMO

Fig. 6.4 MOVMO architecture

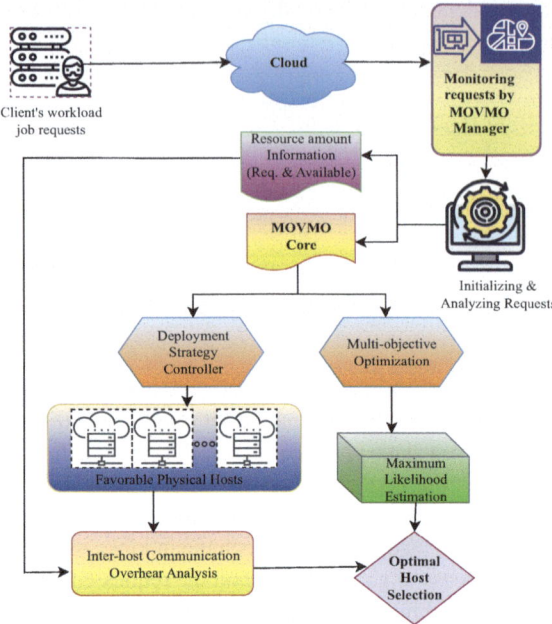

Algorithm 4 MOVMO (Multi-objective virtual machine optimizer)

Require:
1: $J = \{J_1, J_2, \ldots, J_m\}$ ▷ Set of job requests
2: $H = \{H_1, H_2, \ldots, H_n\}$ ▷ Set of available hosts
3: $RQ = \{RQ_1, RQ_2, \ldots, RQ_m\}$ ▷ Resource requirements for jobs
4: $A = \{A_1, A_2, \ldots, A_n\}$ ▷ Available resources on hosts

Ensure: Optimal host allocation for each job
5: **for** each job request J_i in J **do**
6:     Calculate $RQ_i = \phi RQC_i + \psi RQM_i$
7:     $F \leftarrow \{\}$ ▷ Set of favorable hosts
8:     **for** each host H_j in H **do**
9:         **if** $A_j \geq RQ_i$ **then**
10:             $F \leftarrow F \cup \{H_j\}$
11:         **end if**
12:     **end for**
13:     Calculate μ and σ for F using Eqs. (5.18) and (5.19)
14:     $\Xi_{MLE} \leftarrow_{H_j \in F} RQ_i \cdot \ell(\Xi; H_j)$
15:     $P(H_j|\mu, \sigma^2) \leftarrow \frac{1}{\sqrt{2\pi\sigma^2}} \exp(-\frac{(H_j - \mu)^2}{2\sigma^2})$
16:     $H_{opt} \leftarrow_{H_j \in F} P(H_j|\mu, \sigma^2)$
17:     Allocate J_i to H_{opt}
18:     Update A_{opt}
19: **end for**

maximizes VM allocation across many hosts by concurrently evaluating several goals. It computes resource needs, finds suitable hosts, and uses statistical analysis to decide where best to deploy objects. Using same ideas but with an eye

6.3 Multi-Objective Virtual Machine Optimizer

Algorithm 5 Job reallocation based on MOVMO

Require:
1: $J_{overload}$ ▷ Job to be reallocated
2: $H_{current}$ ▷ Current overloaded host
3: $H = \{H_1, H_2, \ldots, H_n\}$ ▷ Set of available hosts
4: $A = \{A_1, A_2, \ldots, A_n\}$ ▷ Available resources on hosts
5: $RQ_{overload}$ ▷ Resource requirement of overloaded job

Ensure: New host for job reallocation
6:   $F \leftarrow \{\}$ ▷ Set of favorable hosts
7:   **for** each host H_j in $H \setminus \{H_{current}\}$ **do**
8:     **if** $A_j \geq RQ_{overload}$ **then**
9:       $F \leftarrow F \cup \{H_j\}$
10:    **end if**
11: **end for**
12: **if** F is empty **then**
13:    **return** No suitable host found
14: **end if**
15: Calculate μ and σ for F using Eqs. (5.18) and (5.19)
16: **for** each host H_j in F **do**
17:    Calculate RM_j using Eq. (5.20)
18:    $P(H_j|\mu, \sigma^2) \leftarrow \frac{1}{\sqrt{2\pi\sigma^2}} \exp(-\frac{(H_j-\mu)^2}{2\sigma^2})$
19: **end for**
20: $H_{new} \leftarrow {}_{H_j \in F} P(H_j|\mu, \sigma^2) \cdot (1 - RM_j)$
21: Reallocate $J_{overload}$ to H_{new}
22: Update A_{new} and $A_{current}$
23: **return** H_{new}

---

toward system balance, the Job Reallocation algorithm enhances MOVMO by effectively moving work from overburdened hosts. Both systems use advanced statistical techniques and multi-objective optimization to guide choices, thereby optimizing resource use and increasing capacity to manage changing workloads. Taken together, they provide a strong, flexible solution for resource management in cloud contexts, hence much improving conventional load balancing methods.

6.3.2 Results and Analysis for MOVMO

The CPU and memory amounts that are accessible on each of these 100 physical machines vary. These physical computers are home to 50 cloudlets that are operating continuously. The simulation setup needed for the suggested approach's performance study is provided in the section above. This study computes the MakeSpan and is analyzed and contrasted with the random deployment (RD), the best possible deployment approach (BPD), and load balancing with Bayes and Clustering (LB-BC) techniques. The RD technique uses randomized jobs to handle data in cloud data centers. It seems sense that the system's ability to handle so many jobs would eventually wear out if the amount of requests for work increases and the selection

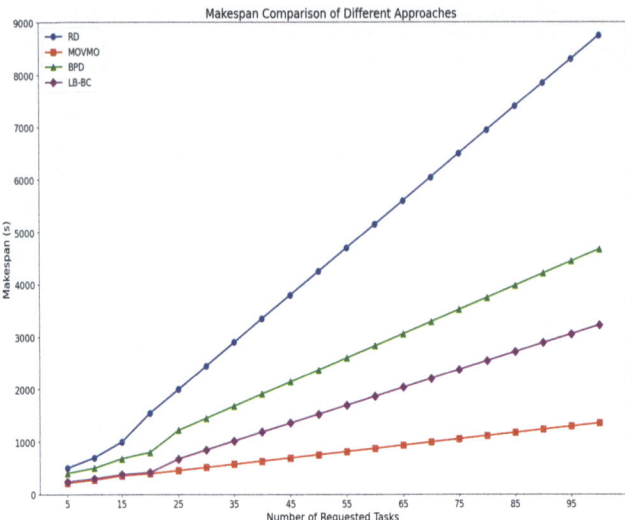

Fig. 6.5 Comparison of RD, BPD, LB-BC, and MOVMO in terms of Makespan

process is random. The prediction model serves as the foundation for this BPD strategy, which is also based on some repository knowledge and past experience. A further method known as LB-BC, which is based on Bayes and Clustering, also handles the tasks for each iteration and determines how long each job request takes to process.

Figure 6.5 illustrates that these solutions usually need more processing time overall than the MOVMO approach. The reason for this is because, given identical circumstances, the MOVMO technique may rapidly identify the best host based on the amount of resources needed, resulting in a shorter makespan than the others. Even yet, this MOVMO completes the same number of jobs in less time than these. Additionally, it reduces the cost of resource utilization and, in turn, lowers the power consumption of cloud data centers.

The cloudsim simulator was used in this study to determine the amount of failed tasks that occurred during task scheduling and deployment. Only when part of the demands of the required tasks cannot be met by the selected physical machine will it be able to locate these failure nodes in the dynamic environment. Because task management capacity deteriorates progressively, the likelihood of more failures rises as the number of requested tasks grows [15]. The model is contrasted with various methods currently in use based on the amount of jobs that fail during deployment in the cloud network data center simulation, as seen in Table 6.3. Because the RD technique deploys at random, it has a large number of failure sets in this figure. In contrast, the BPD approach has less failures than the RD approach because to its knowledge repository experimental values. However, these failures are not able to be handled in real time. Another method, known as LB-BC, yielded excellent results and could dynamically and adaptively identify the ideal

6.3 Multi-Objective Virtual Machine Optimizer

Table 6.3 Number of failures in task deployment events for various allocation methods

Number of requested tasks	RD	LB-BC	BPD	MOVMO
10	4.32	0.27	0.65	0.89
20	5.68	0.42	0.98	2.15
30	9.21	0.61	0.32	4.23
40	11.34	0.79	0.75	5.12
50	14.27	1.05	1.23	9.34
60	17.12	1.43	2.87	12.15
70	21.36	1.82	3.45	15.78
80	25.12	2.34	4.12	21.23
90	29.87	2.98	7.23	24.12
100	34.95	3.45	10.12	26.34

Table 6.4 Standard deviation for load balancing over time

Time (s)	RD	LB-BC	BPD	MOVMO
100	0.3012	0.2523	0.2487	0.0723
200	0.3021	0.2876	0.2589	0.0701
300	0.3154	0.2432	0.2412	0.0689
400	0.3598	0.1876	0.1901	0.0512
500	0.2812	0.1687	0.1898	0.0456
600	0.2123	0.1798	0.1823	0.0434
700	0.1532	0.0687	0.0978	0.0401
800	0.1423	0.0654	0.0912	0.0387
900	0.1165	0.0701	0.0876	0.0365
1000	0.1187	0.0623	0.0798	0.0342
1100	0.1201	0.0512	0.0687	0.0321
1200	0.1098	0.0498	0.0601	0.0309
1300	0.0798	0.0432	0.0523	0.0287

physical host for the deployment. It considerably lowers the failure rate. However, in the MOVMO experiment, it was discovered that no failure node occurred for up to 35 requested jobs. Just <5 or a small number of tasks fail when there are 100 tasks. In summary, the findings indicate that for large-scale cloud data centers, the MOVMO offers superior efficacy and stability. Table 6.4 displays the standard deviation value for estimating the degree of load balancing. In terms of time, the balancing impact is contrasted with RD, BPO, LB-BC, and MOVMO. It is clear that in cloud data centers, a smaller standard deviation number indicates better load balancing. The RD method is always bigger than three specific techniques, as Table 6.4 illustrates, and the standard deviation of ODS and LB-BC correspondingly lowers. BPO's standard deviation is initially lower than LB-BC's. Yet, LB-BC is improving when time = 600 and the two SD values are equal. However, MOVMO is always superior than other methods since it rapidly determines the best host based on the amount of processing power left. The results demonstrate that MOVMO has a greater load balancing impact and may thus enhance the cloud data center's resource

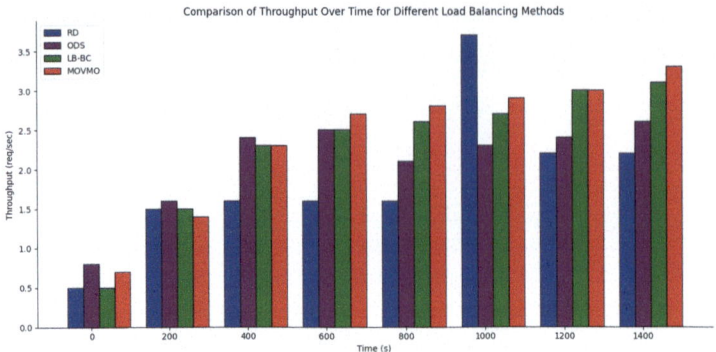

Fig. 6.6 Comparison of RD, BPD, LB-BC, and MOVMO in terms of throughput

utilization efficiently. This assessment measure analyzes and assesses the approach's suitability in terms of service performance using the effective load balancing metric. The capacity to handle tasks, the time it takes to compute a task request, the quantity of services done in a certain amount of time, etc., are some of these useful metrics. These factors are used in the cloud system to determine throughput rate and assess the performance of external services as time increases. To enhance and optimize the algorithm, the suggested MOVMO method is validated and contrasted with other methods. As illustrated in Fig. 6.6, the findings were compared with the proposed methodology. Overall, the MOVMO approach demonstrates superior performance. Initially, both RD and BDO outperform MOVMO, as shown in the graph. However, after 200 seconds, their performance steadily stabilizes with increasing time, surpassing BPO and RD with longer durations. Based on past projections and repository knowledge, the BDO method determines the best host. It provides an estimate of each physical host's load state. As a result, MOVMO has greatly increased the need for task deployment. In summary, it can be said that the MOVMO technique offers superior efficiency and stability. Based on this analysis, an auxiliary experiment is proposed and carried out in a dynamic cloud environment to determine the best host and the amount of energy used during the load balancing procedure. It takes into account that 10–100 required jobs are executing over the whole cloud data center rather than on a physical host. In this dynamic setup, the cloudsim simulator uses the getpower() method to calculate the energy. It can quickly determine how many kilowatts of electricity were used overall. The suggested method locates the best node for efficiently deploying desired jobs. That the ideal node uses less electricity is thus easily understood. These findings provide a comparative study of the overall power consumption with and without the use of DLB-ML, as shown in Fig. 6.7. It will take longer if we cannot automatically identify the best node for deployment, and power will also be destroyed if more time is spent. It comes to the conclusion that load balancing via server switching maximizes the resource's energy usage. Thus, identify the best node first, and then deploy into them. After that, the price will automatically drop. All things

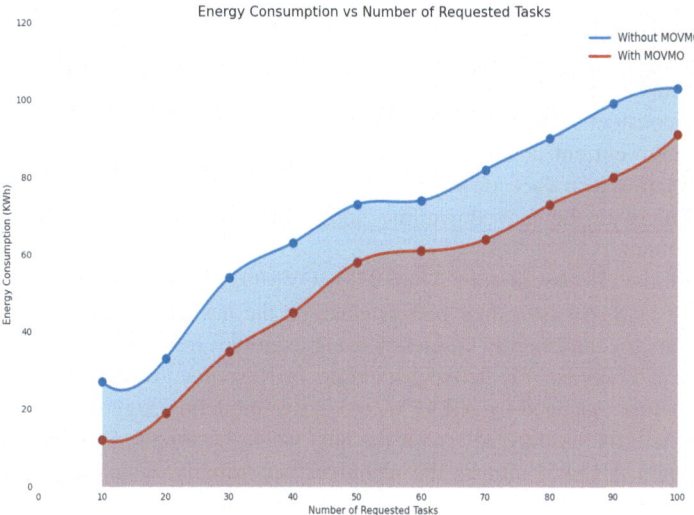

Fig. 6.7 Comparison of RD, BPD, LB-BC, and MOVMO in terms of energy consumption

considered, it aids in lowering carbon dioxide emissions as well as operational and infrastructural costs.

6.4 Summary

This chapter focused on the Probabilistic Framework for IaaS architecture ARAPM, and MOVMO, and provided a thorough examination of sophisticated heuristic models for the best host selection and resource allocation in cloud computing settings. These models tackle important issues in cloud infrastructure management, such as load balancing, resource optimization, and job scheduling. The suggested techniques, especially MOVMO, showed significant gains over the state of the art in terms of makespan reduction, load distribution optimization, energy efficiency, and overall system performance via thorough simulations and comparative analysis. Reduced VM downtime, higher failure rates, adaptable resource allocation to changing workloads, avoidance of over- or underutilization of hosts, and increased traffic scalability are some of the major accomplishments. Through the use of multi-objective optimization, predictive modeling, and probabilistic methodologies, these models provide reliable answers that can manage the growing complexity of contemporary cloud systems. The developments discussed in this chapter have a major impact on cloud computing and open the door to cloud infrastructures that are more responsive, sustainable, and efficient. In order to further improve the capabilities of cloud resource management systems, future research areas may examine the integration of machine learning methods and the deployment of these models in edge and fog computing situations.

6.5 Exercises

1. Numerical Exercise: VM Downtime and Energy Efficiency: Using the MOVMO model, consider a cloud system where reducing VM downtime is critical. Assume the current downtime is 8% with a failure rate of 5%. The MOVMO model claims to reduce downtime by 30% and improve energy efficiency by 15%. Calculate the new downtime and assess the overall energy efficiency improvement.
2. Compare the effectiveness of ARAPM, MOVMO, and the Probabilistic Framework for IaaS. Analyze their performance on the basis of makespan reduction, load balancing, and energy efficiency using examples from relevant case studies.
3. Numerical Exercise: Predictive Modeling in Resource Allocation: In a cloud infrastructure managed by ARAPM, predictive modeling suggests that resource demand will increase by 25% over the next week. If current resource utilization is 70% and ARAPM adjusts the resources accordingly, what will be the new resource utilization? Discuss how this predictive approach helps avoid under- or overutilization.
4. Simulation of Load Balancing Using MOVMO: Implement a basic simulation to demonstrate how MOVMO optimizes load balancing in a cloud environment. Measure the system's performance before and after applying MOVMO by evaluating metrics such as makespan, load distribution, and energy consumption.
5. Future Integration of ML in Cloud Resource Allocation: Explore the potential integration of machine learning (ML) techniques into the MOVMO and ARAPM models. Discuss how ML could improve predictive modeling and multi-objective optimization for resource allocation in cloud environments.
6. Case Study: Traffic Scalability in Cloud Systems: Using the case of increased traffic scalability, explain how the Probabilistic Framework for IaaS handles traffic overflow and prevents bottlenecks. Provide a specific scenario where this framework enhances system responsiveness during peak traffic times.
7. Numerical Exercise: Over/Underutilization in Resource Allocation: In a cloud environment managed by ARAPM, assume current resource utilization is at 90% during peak times and 40% during off-peak hours. ARAPM aims to reduce overutilization by 20% during peak hours and improve resource utilization by 30% during off-peak hours. Calculate the new utilization levels and assess the benefits.
8. Energy Efficiency with MOVMO: Simulate a cloud environment where MOVMO is applied to reduce energy consumption. Calculate the energy savings in kilowatt hours (kWh) assuming a baseline consumption of 500 kWh per day. MOVMO claims to reduce consumption by 15%. What are the new energy savings?

References

1. Zhao, J., Hu, L., Ding, Y., Xu, G., Hu, M.: A heuristic placement selection of live virtual machine migration for energy-saving in cloud computing environment. PLoS ONE **9**(9), e108275 (2014). https://doi.org/10.1371/journal.pone.0108275
2. Zhao, J., Yang, K., Wei, X., Ding, Y., Hu, L., Xu, G.: A heuristic clustering-based task deployment approach for load balancing using Bayes theorem in cloud environment. IEEE Trans. Parallel Distrib. Syst. **27**(2), 305–316 (2016). https://doi.org/10.1109/TPDS.2015.2402655
3. Annie Poornima Princess, G., Radhamani, A.S.: A hybrid meta-heuristic for optimal load balancing in cloud computing. J. Grid Comput. **19**, 21 (2021). https://doi.org/10.1007/s10723-021-09560-4
4. Tuli, K., Malhotra, M.: Optimal meta-heuristic elastic scheduling (OMES) for VM selection and migration in cloud computing. Multimed. Tools Appl. **83**, 34601–34627 (2024). https://doi.org/10.1007/s11042-023-16820-w
5. Hussain, A.J., Chunlin, L., Hammad-Ur-Rehman, Q.: Adaptive threshold detection based on current demand for efficient utilization of cloud resources. In: 2019 IEEE 4th International Conference on Computer and Communication Systems (ICCCS), pp. 341–346. IEEE, Singapore (2019). https://doi.org/10.1109/CCOMS.2019.8821759
6. Liu, J., Wang, S., Zhou, A., Kumar, S.A.P., Yang, F., Buyya, R.: Using proactive fault-tolerance approach to enhance cloud service reliability. IEEE Trans. Cloud Comput. **6**(4), 1191–1202 (2018). https://doi.org/10.1109/TCC.2016.2567392
7. Chhabra, S., Singh, A.K.: OPH-LB: Optimal physical host for load balancing in cloud environment. Pertanika J. Sci. Technol. **26**(3) (2018)
8. Yadav, R., Zhang, W., Li, K., et al.: An adaptive heuristic for managing energy consumption and overloaded hosts in a cloud data center. Wirel. Netw. **26**, 1905–1919 (2020). https://doi.org/10.1007/s11276-018-1874-1
9. Kaur, A., Kaur, B.: Load balancing optimization based on hybrid heuristic-metaheuristic techniques in cloud environment. J. King Saud Univ. Comput. Inf. Sci. **34**(3), 813–824 (2022)
10. Lipsa, S., Dash, R.K., Ivković, N., Cengiz, K.: Task scheduling in cloud computing: a priority-based heuristic approach. IEEE Access **11**, 27111–27126 (2023). https://doi.org/10.1109/ACCESS.2023.3255781
11. Patni, S., Singh, A.K.: An optimal host allocation and load distribution framework using maximum likelihood in cloud environment. SN Comput. Sci. **4**, 572 (2023). https://doi.org/10.1007/s42979-023-01939-2
12. Aburukba, R.O., Landolsi, T., Omer, D.: A heuristic scheduling approach for fog-cloud computing environment with stationary IoT devices. J. Netw. Comput. Appl. **180**, 102994 (2021)
13. Chhabra, S., Singh, A.K.: A probabilistic model for finding an optimal host framework and load distribution in cloud environment. Procedia Comput. Sci. **125**, 683–690 (2018)
14. Kumar, J., Singh, A.K., Mohan, A.: Resource-efficient load-balancing framework for cloud data center networks. ETRI J. **43**(1), 53–63 (2021)
15. Patil, A., Patil, R.: An optimal heuristic model for greedy and efficient consolidation process in cloud datacenters. In: 2020 3rd International Conference on Intelligent Sustainable Systems (ICISS), pp. 1308–1313. IEEE, Thoothukudi, India (2020). https://doi.org/10.1109/ICISS49785.2020.9316026

Chapter 7
Secure and Energy-Efficient Cloud Traffic Management Schemes

Abstract This chapter introduces two novel frameworks, the Secure Resource Distribution Framework (SRDF) and Adaptive Multi-tier Traffic Distributor (AMultiTD) that solve important issues in multi-tenant cloud settings. By reducing colocation threats, SRDF dramatically improves security—a 40.63% decrease is achieved while retaining optimum resource utilization. AMultiTD reduces energy consumption by 25.89% without sacrificing security measures in order to strike a balance between security and energy savings. By means of in-depth simulations, both frameworks are thoroughly assessed while taking into account different operational characteristics. Comprehensive studies of theoretical underpinnings, performance indicators, and implementation methodologies are provided by the study. The results regularly show significant gains in energy saving, resource efficiency, and security enhancement over conventional methods. These frameworks provide cloud service providers useful tools to increase the security, effectiveness, and sustainability of their infrastructure. The approaches and results discussed here have a major impact on the development of cloud computing, opening the door for more reliable, effective, and ecologically friendly cloud services in an increasingly digitized society.

Keywords Traffic management · Energy optimization · Security controls · Resource distribution · Network efficiency · Multi-tier architecture · Load balancing · Power management

7.1 Introduction

The rise of cloud computing has instigated a seismic shift in how computing resources are procured and used by companies and private users alike. With a compound annual growth rate (CAGR) of 17.9% from 2023 to 2030, the worldwide cloud computing industry is expected to reach $ 832.1 billion by 2024 [1]. The need for effective and secure cloud management solutions is highlighted by this fast rise. However, new difficulties in striking a balance between resource utilization, energy efficiency, and security arise as cloud infrastructures becoming more complicated and multi-tenant scenarios become more common [2]. The convergence of resource usage, energy efficiency, and security in relation to VM deployment and load balancing is a critical but sometimes disregarded component of cloud computing that is covered in this chapter. Although a lot of study has been done on energy conservation and resource optimization [3], it has been said about how these practices may affect security, especially in situations where there are several tenants. The current issue is complex. To cut down on operating expenses and environmental effect, cloud service providers aim to optimize resource utilization and minimize energy use [4]. Conversely, they have to guarantee the safety and segregation of their customers' assets in communal settings. The introduction of sophisticated assaults that take use of cloud systems' inherent multi-tenancy further complicates this balancing effort. According to recent surveys, at least one security issue has occurred in almost 80.6% of organizations that use public cloud services [5]. Vulnerabilities resulting from inefficient resource allocation and load balancing techniques account for a considerable fraction of these instances. This concerning figure emphasizes how urgently more sophisticated and safe cloud traffic control solutions are needed [6]. To get around these problems, this chapter presents a new way to solve the resource consumption traffic imbalance issue by rewriting it as a combinatorial security strategy for VM deployment with multiple resource limitations [7]. In contrast to the majority of current methods, which concentrate mostly on energy and resource use, our study adopts a security-first approach, addressing the security threats that cloud customers encounter in the context of virtual machine load balancing that are often disregarded [8]. Our key innovation is how we enhance the VM allocation rules to make it more harder for attackers to continue sharing a virtual machine with their targets. By doing this, we hope to stop assaults known as multi-tenancy attacks, in which malevolent parties try to set up shop on the same physical server as their intended targets [9]. In order to do this, we provide and examine secure resource allocation strategies that surpass conventional load balancing goals. During VM allocations, our multi-objective techniques continually assess the safety states, implementing a secure load balancing approach. By being proactive, we want to lessen the likelihood of assaults from many users that use the same cloud infrastructure. We will examine two different models in this chapter that deal with different facets of this intricate issue: (1) Secure resource distribution framework for mitigating colocation risks (SRDF) and (2)Adaptive Multi-tier Traffic Distributor for Security and Energy Optimization (AMultiTD). Our overall objective is to create cloud environments that are more dependable, efficient, and secure, and each of these models helps to achieve that aim.

7.2 Secure Resource Distribution for Mitigating Colocation Risks

The difficulties of VM coresidency in multi-tenant cloud environments are addressed with an advanced technique called the Secure Resource Distribution

7.2 Secure Resource Distribution for Mitigating Colocation Risks

Framework for Mitigating Colocation Risks (SRDF). Building on the fundamental ideas of the previously described RTIF, this framework focuses on resource distribution and allocation tactics that reduce colocation concerns. Although it is financially advantageous for cloud service providers, virtual machine coresidency raises serious security issues. It happens when a physical computer is shared by many customers, including possible attackers. By streamlining the first VM allocation procedure within a data center, SRDF seeks to reduce these risks.

7.2.1 Probabilistic Model

The framework employs a probabilistic model to evaluate and mitigate coresidency risks:

$$P(\text{co-resident}) = P(A) \times P(L) \tag{7.1}$$

where:

$$P(A) = \frac{A \in \sum_{i=1}^{N} S_i}{|U|}$$

$$P(L) = \frac{L \in \sum_{i=1}^{N} S_i}{|U|}$$

where S_i represents the servers, $|U|$ is the total number of users, and A and L denote attacker and legitimate users, respectively. The SRDF employs several key metrics to quantify and mitigate coresidency risks in multi-tenant cloud environments. These metrics provide a mathematical foundation for assessing and improving security in VM allocation strategies [10]. The first metric calculates the probability of attacker VMs coresiding with at least one target VM:

$$G(S, A) = \frac{|\text{pm}_i(\text{Succ}_N(A : \text{Tar}))|}{N(A : \text{Tar})} \tag{7.2}$$

where pm_i represents physical machines, $\text{Succ}_N(A : \text{Tar})$ denotes successful coresidency events between attacker and target VMs, and $N(A : \text{Tar})$ is the total number of attacker VMs. Similarly, the probability of legitimate user VMs coresiding with targets is measured by

$$G(S, L) = \frac{|\text{pm}_i(\text{Succ}_N(L : \text{Tar}))|}{\text{Tar}} \tag{7.3}$$

Tar being the total number of target VMs. These equations help in understanding the likelihood of potential attacks and normal coresidency patterns. The framework also considers the coresidency probability excluding attackers, given by

$$P(\text{co-resident}(L, \text{Tar})) = \frac{|\text{pm}_i(\text{Succ}_N(L : \text{Tar}))|}{N(L : \text{Tar})} \qquad (7.4)$$

which establishes a baseline for detecting anomalies that might indicate an attack. Crucially, SRDF evaluates the attack success rate using:

$$\text{SuccRate}(A : \text{Tar}) = \frac{|\text{VMs}((\text{Succ}_{\text{Target}} N(A : \text{Tar})))|}{\text{Tar}} \qquad (7.5)$$

where pm_i represents physical machines, Tar denotes targets $N(A : \text{Tar})$, and $N(L : \text{Tar})$ represent the number of attacker and legitimate VMs, respectively. It is measuring the proportion of target VMs successfully colocated with attacker VMs. This metric is vital for assessing the potential impact and effectiveness of attacks. By continuously monitoring and analyzing these metrics, SRDF can dynamically adjust its VM allocation strategy to minimize security risks while maintaining efficient resource utilization. This adaptive approach enables SRDF to balance performance requirements with robust security measures, making it an effective solution for protecting multi-tenant cloud environments against sophisticated colocation-based attacks. The framework's ability to quantify these risks and make data-driven decisions sets it apart as a comprehensive security solution for modern cloud infrastructures. These criteria are used by SRDF as part of an all-encompassing resource allocation plan. Upon receiving requests for task deployment from the cloud data center, the framework:

1. Identifies all possible VMs (v_i) for selection and placement.
2. Calculates safe and unsafe states for all feasible migration paths.
3. Evaluates the security advantage of each potential allocation based on the number of unsafe states.
4. Identifies favorable hosts based on required and available resources for safe states.

Figure 7.1 shows the proposed framework of SRDF that aims to mitigate colocation risks in cloud environments. It processes client workload submissions through a resource coordinator, which considers resource availability and needs. The framework incorporates past usage records, VM utilization data, and user type identification to check coresidency and determine the most suitable host for workload placement, categorizing hosts as more or less secure based on this analysis [11]. To further enhance security, SRDF incorporates dynamic resource constraints:

$$\sum_{i=1}^{V} \alpha_{i,s,m} C_i \leqslant X_{s,m} \quad \forall s_t \in s \quad \forall m \in M \qquad (7.6)$$

$$\sum_{i=1}^{V} \alpha_{i,s,m} M_i \leqslant Y_{s,m} \quad \forall s_t \in s \quad \forall m \in M \qquad (7.7)$$

7.2 Secure Resource Distribution for Mitigating Colocation Risks

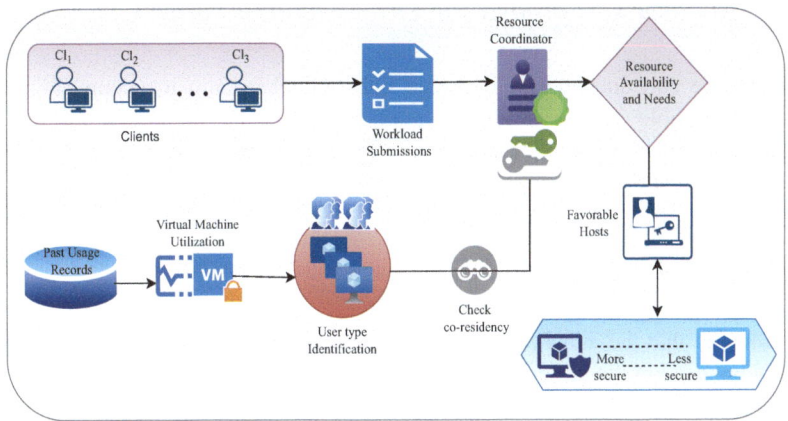

Fig. 7.1 SRDF

$$\sum_{i=1}^{V} \alpha_{i,s,m} E_i \leqslant Z_{s,m} \quad \forall s_t \in s \quad \forall m \in M \tag{7.8}$$

where $\alpha_{i,s,m}$ is a binary variable indicating VM placement, C_i, M_i, and E_i represent CPU, Memory, and Energy consumption of VM_i, and $X_{s,m}$, $Y_{s,m}$, and $Z_{s,m}$ define the total CPU, memory, and energy resources of $pm_{s,m}$. SRDF employs a maximum likelihood estimation method to achieve efficient workload balancing:

$$\{\Xi_M\} = \{\max_{i=1}^{n} RQ_i \ell(\Xi; \phi_1, \phi_2, ..., \phi_n)\} \tag{7.9}$$

where RQ_i represents the requested resource amount of the i-th task, Ξ are the parameters (CPU, memory, energy consumption), and ϕ_i are the observations (physical machines). By implementing these strategies, SRDF aims to:

1. Reduce the probability of successful coresident attacks.
2. Minimize information leakage during load balancing.
3. Enhance overall cloud security without significantly impacting performance.
4. Provide a robust framework for secure VM allocation in multi-tenant environments.

The framework's effectiveness is evaluated through extensive simulations in comparison to current allocation strategies. Results reveal that SRDF effectively minimizes the danger of coresident assaults while maintaining efficient resource usage and load balancing. SRDF represents a significant advancement in securing multi-tenant cloud environments. It offers a proactive approach to cloud security by tackling the crucial problem of virtual machine coresidency at the allocation stage, in line with the expanding demand for reliable, secure cloud computing solutions in an increasingly interconnected digital landscape.

7.2.2 Attacker's Approach for VM Allocation Policies

To maximize coresidency and coverage rates, attackers aim to occupy as many servers as possible with the minimum number of VMs [12]. This section examines various VM allocation policies and the strategies attackers might employ to exploit them. The attacker's primary objectives are:

- Maximize coresidency rate.
- Maximize coverage rate.
- Minimize the number of VMs used.

It is assumed that the attacker can deduce the VM allocation policy (or at least its type) being used in the system and optimize their strategy accordingly.

7.2.2.1 Least VM Allocation Policy (LVMP)

Under LVMP, the attacker should start as many VMs as possible simultaneously, as a server will not be selected twice within a short period.

$$Pr_i = \frac{Tar}{N - (i - 1)} \quad (7.10)$$

where Pr_i is the probability of coresidency for the i-th VM, Tar is the number of target VMs, and N is the total number of servers.

7.2.2.2 Most VM Allocation Policy (MVMP)

For MVMP, the attacker should start VMs in batches of size M, where $M < |VM(A, Tar)|$, repeating $|VM(A, Tar)|/M$ times.

$$Pr_i = \frac{Tar}{N - (i - 1) \bmod D} \quad (7.11)$$

where D is a small constant representing the batch size and $N'_i = N - (i-1) \bmod D$ represents the number of available servers for the i-th VM.

7.2.2.3 Round Robin VM Allocation Policy (RRVMP)

RRVMP is based on the distribution of CPU time among scheduled tasks. It uses a queue system where each task gets a small unit of CPU time (quantum, typically 10–100 milliseconds).

7.2 Secure Resource Distribution for Mitigating Colocation Risks

$$Pr_i = \frac{N \times (N-1)}{2} \quad (7.12)$$

The efficiency of RRVMP depends on the selection of quantum time. In an enhanced version, the quantum time changes in each round:

$$Quantum = \frac{Mean(processes) + Median(processes)}{2} \quad (7.13)$$

The framework selects the most favorable physical host for task deployment by maximizing the likelihood function with the observed data. This process involves:

1. Estimating model parameters based on observed data
2. Calculating the likelihood of observed data under different parameter values
3. Selecting the parameter set that maximizes this likelihood
4. Identifying the safest and most optimal host for deployment

This approach not only ensures efficient resource allocation but also enhances security by considering the potential for attacker exploitation of VM allocation policies. Understanding these allocation policies and potential attacker strategies allows cloud service providers to implement more robust security measures. By anticipating attacker behavior, providers can design allocation strategies that balance performance needs with security considerations, thereby reducing the risk of successful coresidency attacks. The whole process of SRDF is illustrated in Algorithm 6.

7.2.3 Results and Analysis

The parameters that specify the features of the datacentre environment and the activities to be completed form the basis of the simulation results. Three different VM allocation policies—Least VM Allocation Policy (LVMP), Round Robin VM Allocation Policy (RRVMP), and Most VM Allocation Policy (MVMP)—can be compared using these parameters, which are listed in Table 6.6. The data center configuration comprises VMs with different computational capacities, with CPU computing capacities ranging from 1860 MIPs to 2660 MIPs. Each VM has 10 GB of storage, 4096 MB of RAM, a 100 M/s bandwidth, and 8 GB of disc I/O capability. A realistic simulation of a diverse cloud environment is possible with this arrangement. The data center receives tasks that have different CPU needs (250–1000 MIPs), file sizes (100–2000 MB), and output sizes (memory requirements) (20–40 MB). This broad task profile allows a thorough assessment of the performance of each allocation strategy under different workload scenarios. Three VM allocation strategies are compared in the study:

- Least VM Allocation Policy (LVMP): This scheduler uses the least-utilized VM at the moment of job arrival to determine which VMs are most suited to receive

Algorithm 6 Secure resource distribution framework (SRDF)

Require: Set of hosts H, Set of VMs V, Set of tasks T, Security threshold θ
Ensure: Secure VM allocation A
1: **function** SRDF(H, V, T, θ)
2:     Initialize allocation $A \leftarrow \emptyset$
3:     Calculate initial co-residency probabilities P_{co} for all $(h, v) \in H \times V$
4:     **for** each task $t \in T$ **do**
5:         $candidates \leftarrow \emptyset$
6:         **for** each host $h \in H$ **do**
7:             **if** h has sufficient resources for t **then**
8:                 $v \leftarrow$ CreateVM(t)
9:                 $risk \leftarrow$ CalculateRisk(h, v, P_{co})
10:                **if** $risk < \theta$ **then**
11:                    $candidates \leftarrow candidates \cup \{(h, v, risk)\}$
12:                **end if**
13:             **end if**
14:         **end for**
15:         **if** $candidates \neq \emptyset$ **then**
16:             $(h^*, v^*, risk^*) \leftarrow \arg\min_{(h,v,risk) \in candidates} risk$
17:             $A \leftarrow A \cup \{(h^*, v^*)\}$
18:             UpdateCoResidencyProbabilities(P_{co}, h^*, v^*)
19:         **else**
20:             RejectTask(t)
21:         **end if**
22:     **end for**
23:     **return** A
24: **end function**
25: **function** CALCULATERISK(h, v, P_{co})
26:     $G(S, A) \leftarrow \frac{|\text{Succ}_N(A:\text{Tar})|}{N(A:\text{Tar})}$ for h
27:     $P(\text{co-resident}) \leftarrow \frac{|\text{Succ}_N(L:\text{Tar})|}{N(L:\text{Tar})}$ for h
28:     SuccRate $\leftarrow \frac{|\text{VMs}(\text{Succ}_{\text{Target}} N(A:\text{Tar}))|}{|\text{Tar}|}$ for h
29:     **return** $w_1 \cdot G(S, A) + w_2 \cdot P(\text{co-resident}) + w_3 \cdot$ SuccRate
30: **end function**
31: **function** UPDATECORESIDENCYPROBABILITIES(P_{co}, h, v)
32:     **for** each VM v' on host h **do**
33:         Update $P_{co}(v, v')$ based on new co-location
34:     **end for**
35: **end function**

incoming workloads. It gives less-used resources priority in an effort to balance the load.

- The Round Robin VM Allocation Policy (RRVMP) method dispatches tasks to the subsequent VM in the queue, irrespective of the virtual machine's present load. It guarantees that jobs are evenly distributed across all VMs that are available.
- Most VM Allocation Policy (MVMP): This policy uses the Intrusion Detection System (IDS) to identify which secure VM is most used for arriving tasks. It seeks to balance resource conservation with security.

7.2 Secure Resource Distribution for Mitigating Colocation Risks

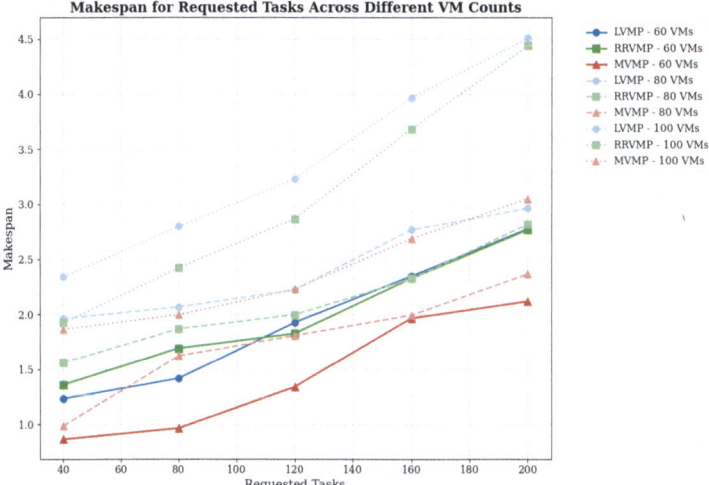

Fig. 7.2 Makespan performance comparison of VM allocation policies

The research aims to assess the efficiency, security, and overall system utilization of these rules by simulating them using the given parameters. This comparison will shed light on the advantages and disadvantages of each strategy in a cloud computing setting, especially in situations where security and performance are crucial factors. Three VM allocation strategies are shown in Fig. 7.2, along with their makespan performance, for varying amounts of requested tasks and VM counts: LVMP, RRVMP, and Most MVMP. The y-axis displays the makespan in any time unit, while the x-axis indicates the number of jobs requested, which ranges from 40 to 200. Using varying line styles, 60, 80, and 100 VMs are used to evaluate each policy. A comparative study of the effectiveness and scalability of each allocation approach in a cloud computing context is made possible by the graph, which shows how makespan changes with increasing task load and VM availability. With different numbers of VMs in a cloud computing environment, the resource utilization efficiency of three VM allocation policies—RRVMP, LVMP, and MVMP—is shown in Fig. 7.3. The number of VMs ranges from 40 to 200 on the x-axis, while the resource utilization % is shown on the y-axis. To provide obvious distinction, each policy is represented by a distinctive color and marker type. The graph shows how, for each allocation approach, resource utilization varies as VM numbers rise. Furthermore, each policy's average waste is shown, giving users an understanding of how effective they are overall. With an average waste of 21.11%, MVMP exhibits the lowest wastage, followed by LVMP (31.24%) and RRVMP (34.71%). The performances of the rules in terms of resource use and efficiency at various VM deployment sizes are compared. In Table 7.1, two host configurations—one with 16 CPU cores and 24 GB RAM, and the other with 12 CPU cores and 48 GB RAM—are compared for Coresidency Efficiency of LVMP, MVMP, and

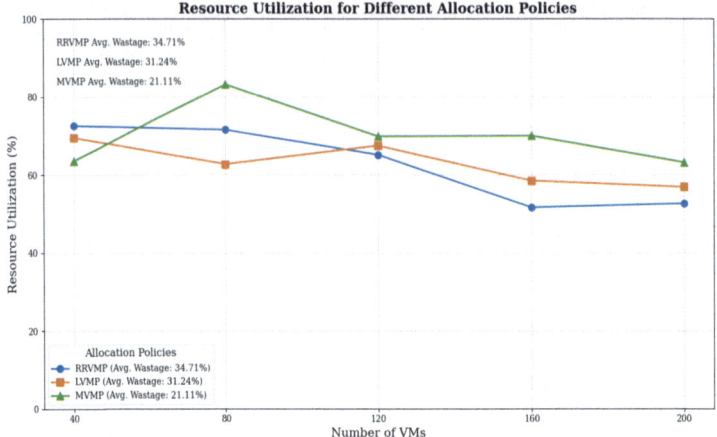

Fig. 7.3 Resource utilization comparison of VM allocation policies

RRVMP. For every setup, the data displays differences in efficiency measures under various VM(A,t) values.

Table 7.1 Coresidency efficiency comparison, configuration 1: 16 CPU cores, 24 GB RAM, Configuration 2: 12 CPU cores, 48 GB RAM

VM (A,t)	MVMP Conf 1	LVMP Conf 1	RRVMP Conf 1	MVMP Conf 2	LVMP Conf 2	RRVMP Conf 2
10	1.5	5.0	9.5	0.5	3.0	6.0
20	3.0	6.5	9.8	1.0	3.5	6.5
40	3.0	7.0	9.2	1.2	4.0	7.0
60	3.0	8.0	8.5	1.5	3.5	8.0
80	3.0	8.5	8.8	1.2	3.8	8.5
100	3.0	9.0	9.0	1.0	4.5	9.0

Coresidency Success Rates for MVMP, LVMP, and RRVMP are compared between two distinct host configurations—Configuration 1 with 16 CPU cores and 24 GB RAM, and Configuration 2 with 12 CPU cores and 48 GB RAM—in this table. Table 7.2 shows that RRVMP exhibits greater efficiency in coresidency as it continuously obtains the greatest success rates across all VM(A,t) levels in both setups. Because there is more RAM available in Configuration 2, LVMP operates somewhat better. On the other hand, MVMP has very low success rates in every scenario, which suggests that it is ineffective in obtaining coresidency success in the evaluated circumstances. In general, Configuration 2 improves coresidency success rates for all approaches, especially LVMP and RRVMP, indicating that memory expansion is a major factor in better coresidency outcomes.

Table 7.2 Coresidency success rate comparison: Configuration 1: 16 CPU cores, 24 GB RAM, Configuration 2: 12 CPU cores, 48 GB RAM

VM (A,t)	MVMP Conf 1	LVMP Conf 1	RRVMP Conf 1	MVMP Conf 2	LVMP Conf 2	RRVMP Conf 2
10	1	0	10	0	5	15
20	2	5	15	0	5	20
40	0	10	20	0	10	25
60	1	10	30	0	10	35
80	1	15	35	0	15	45
100	0	20	45	0	20	55

7.3 Adaptive Multi-tier Traffic Distributor for Security and Energy Optimization

Cloud computing has emerged as a transformative force in the IT sector, academia, financial services, and storage industries, offering minimal capital investment and maximum scalability. However, there are now serious issues with resource management, energy efficiency, and security as a result of the rising use of cloud services [13]. Our proposal, known as the Adaptive Multi-tier Traffic Distributor for Security and Energy Optimization (AMultiTD) architecture, aims to tackle these issues. Data centers must include scalable traffic engineering to maximize storage, energy efficiency, bandwidth, and processing power due to the growing workload in cloud settings. In addition to addressing the pressing problems of energy inefficiency and security flaws that afflict existing cloud infrastructures, AMultiTD seeks to manage this expanding demand. Conventional methods of placing VMs often result in either an excessive or insufficient use of resources, which causes them to be wasted and use too much power. Furthermore, dangers like VM assaults, data breaches, and coresident attacks that might jeopardize sensitive data are introduced by the sharing and multiplexing of resources in cloud settings. By using a multi-tiered traffic distribution strategy and dynamically modifying resource allocation in response to energy consumption trends and real-time security concerns, AMultiTD addresses these issues. Real cloud service providers often do not tell specific customers about the VM placement procedure and do not consider the possibility of security breaches when allocating virtual machines at cloud data centers [14], as seen in Fig. 7.4. Another difficult operation in the cloud context is mapping virtual machines (VMs) to the real host. The available resources on the host computers are taken into consideration while doing this mapping.

The AMultiTD framework expands on earlier theories, such as load balancing strategies and safe VM placement algorithms, to provide a holistic solution that maximizes energy efficiency and security precautions at many levels of the cloud architecture. AMultiTD seeks to provide a strong defense against side-channel assaults while guaranteeing effective use of computer resources by fusing energy-

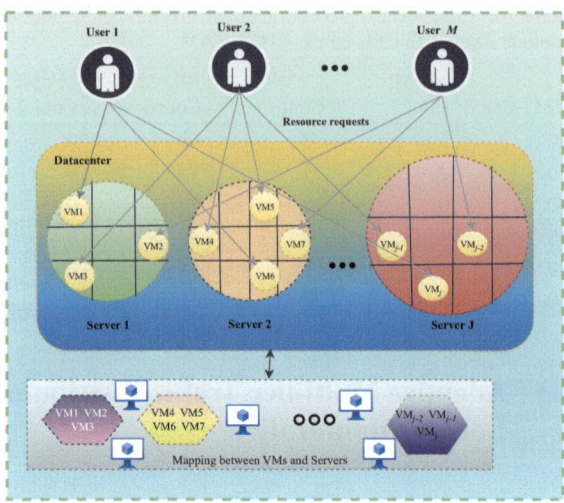

Fig. 7.4 VM allocation at cloud data center

aware resource allocation with sophisticated threat detection algorithms. Several important goals are addressed by our framework:

- Utilizing isolation and adaptive traffic distribution strategies to improve cloud systems' overall security posture
- Optimizing workload allocation over many layers to cut down on energy use in data centers
- Increasing the effectiveness of resource use by allocating resources dynamically according to security and energy considerations
- A scalable solution to cloud customers that can meet changing workload needs without sacrificing security and performance assurances

Cloud providers now have a method to achieve strict Service Level Agreements [15] while managing the challenges of dynamic multi-resource sharing thanks to the AMultiTD framework, which is a major leap in cloud resource management. We show via comprehensive simulations and practical experiments that AMultiTD not only improves security by lowering the likelihood of side-channel attacks, but also greatly increases resource capacity and energy efficiency when compared to other methods.

7.3.1 AMultiTD Design

The issues of optimum task deployment in cloud data centers based on Infrastructure as a Service architecture are addressed by the Adaptive Multi-tier Traffic Distributor for Security and Energy Optimization framework [16]. Consider a data center δ equipped with a set of n cloud server machines $SM = \{SM_1, SM_2, \ldots, SM_n\}$.

7.3 Adaptive Multi-tier Traffic Distributor for Security and Energy Optimization

It hosts v Virtual Machines (VMs) $VM = \{VM_1, VM_2, \ldots, VM_v\}$ owned by m distinct clients $\{Cl_1, Cl_2, \ldots, Cl_m\}$ and processes t task requests $Tr = \{Tr_1, Tr_2, \ldots, Tr_t\}$.

AMultiTD aims to create an optimal mapping between server machines and VMs across multiple tiers, considering both security and energy efficiency. Let C_i^{VM}, M_i^{VM}, B_i^{VM} represent the CPU, memory, and bandwidth utilization of VMs, and C_{max}^{PM}, M_{max}^{PM}, B_{max}^{PM} denote the total resource amounts, respectively. The allocation constraint is given by

$$\sum_{i=1}^{v} \perp_{SM}^{i} C_i^{VM} \leq C_{max}^{PM} \wedge M_i^{VM} \leq M_{max}^{PM} \wedge B_i^{VM} \leq B_{max}^{PM} \, \forall SM_n \in SM \, \forall v \in VM \tag{7.14}$$

The AMultiTD framework optimizes for three main objectives:

1. **Multi-tier Resource Utilization:** AMultiTD improves resource use on many levels. The data center Φ_δ's average resource utilization is maximized as follows:

$$\Phi_\delta = \frac{\sum_{i=1}^{t} \Phi_{i=1}^{C} + \sum_{i=1}^{t} \Phi_{i=1}^{M} + \sum_{i=1}^{t} \Phi_{i=1}^{B}}{|N| \times \sum_{i=1}^{t} \Theta_i} \tag{7.15}$$

where $|N|$ represents the number of resource types (CPU, memory, bandwidth) and Φ_i^R is the utilization rate for each resource type.

2. **Adaptive Energy Efficiency:** AMultiTD dynamically modifies energy use according to the allocation of workload across tiers. The revised energy consumption model looks like this:

$$\exists_k = \begin{cases} \mathfrak{I} \times \left[\Phi_i^R \times \eth_k^{active} + (1 - \Phi_i^R) \times \eth_k^{idle} \right], & \text{Tier-state: Active} \\ \mathfrak{I} \times \eth_k^{sleep}, & \text{Tier-state: Inactive} \end{cases} \tag{7.16}$$

where $\exists_k$ represents the energy consumption of tier k, and $\mathfrak{I}$ is an adaptive factor based on tier workload.

3. **Multi-tier Security Optimization:** By reducing coresidency threats across levels, MultiTD improves security. The optimization of security is modeled as

$$\Xi_{tk} = \sum_{i=1}^{|SM|} R_{SM_i}, tk(\sum_{v=1}^{VM} f_{uj} tk.|VM_{uj}.h_i|) \times \Psi_{tier} \tag{7.17}$$

where Ξ_{tk} is the multi-tier grouping reliability, R_{SM_i} represents the credibility of hosts, and Ψ_{tier} is a tier-specific security factor.

There are three primary parts to the AMultiTD framework:

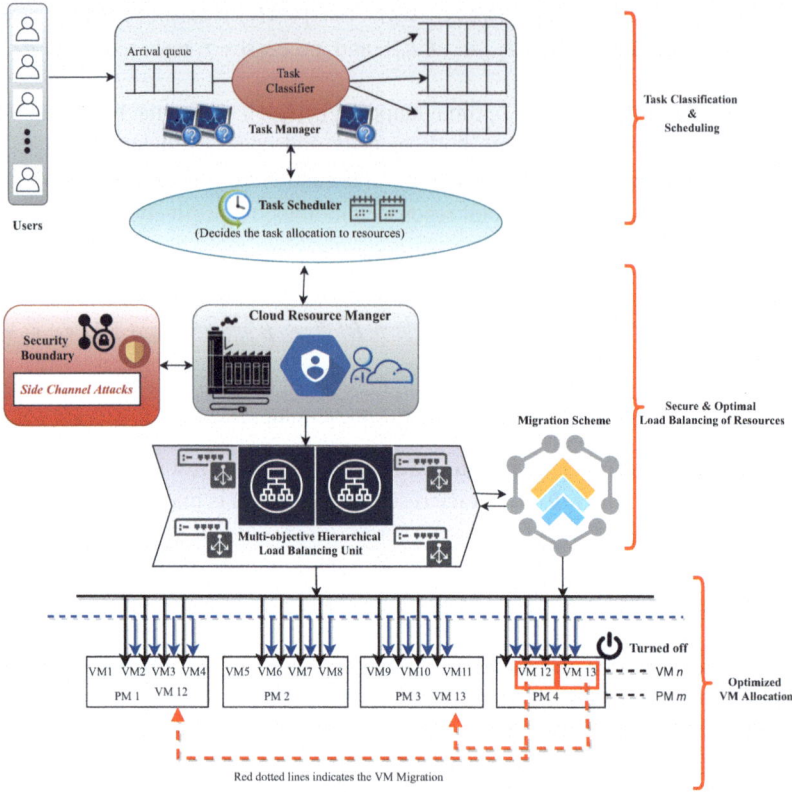

Fig. 7.5 AMultiTD framework

1. **Adaptive Task Classification and Scheduling:** Based on resource limits and security needs, tasks are categorized and planned across many layers.
2. **Load balancing and multi-tier security:** This part minimizes security risks by analyzing resource needs across tiers, allocating resources, and choosing the best hosts.
3. **Tier Optimization and Dynamic VM Allocation:** To concurrently optimize resource utilization, energy efficiency, and security, VMs are distributed throughout layers.

The AMultiTD framework, with its multi-tier approach to job categorization, security-aware load balancing, and optimized VM allocation, is shown in Fig. 7.5. In order to improve overall system performance, security, and energy efficiency, this framework continually optimizes resource allocation across tiers in response to shifting workloads and security threats.

7.3.2 Problem Illustration

Consider a three-tiered cloud data center that is using the AMultiTD framework. There are two servers each tier in the system, for a total of six servers. Each server can handle 200 units of CPU, memory, and bandwidth, and it can use up to 100 watts of electricity at most. The following provides the capacity matrix C_M for the servers across tiers:

$$C_M = \begin{bmatrix} \{100, 100, 100\} & \{90, 60, 200\} & \{40, 70, 39\} \\ \{120, 160, 80\} & \{180, 130, 110\} & \{95, 140, 70\} \end{bmatrix}$$

The system receives task requests represented by the arrival rate matrix AR_M:

$$AR_M = \begin{bmatrix} \{100, 145, 80\} & \{110, 70, 30\} \\ \{60, 155, 65\} & \{110, 155, 80\} \end{bmatrix}$$

Let us analyze how AMultiTD optimizes task allocation across tiers:

1. **Tier-Based Resource Allocation:** AMultiTD assigns tasks to tiers in accordance with resource availability and security specifications. For example, Tier 1 (C_M^{11}) receives high-security jobs from AR_M [100,145,80], which may have additional security measures.
2. **Security-Aware Consolidation:** The approach reduces coresidency hazards by combining jobs that are compatible. In Tier 2 (C_M^{22}), a single machine is assigned tasks [110,70,30] and [60,55,65], minimizing attack surfaces and maximizing resource utilization.
3. **Adaptive Energy Management:** AMultiTD modifies server states dynamically across tiers. Workload consolidation enables certain machines (such as those in Tier 3) to go into low-power modes, which lowers total energy consumption from a possible 362W to around 280W (a savings of 22.65%).
4. **Multi-tier Load Balancing:** The framework optimizes load distribution across tiers. For example:

   - Tier 1: VM_1, VM_2, VM_3, VM_4, VM_{12} on PM_1
   - Tier 2: VM_5, VM_6, VM_7, VM_8 on PM_2
   - Tier 3: VM_9, VM_{10}, VM_{11}, VM_{13} on PM_3

   This distribution ensures balanced resource utilization across tiers while maintaining security isolation.
5. **Dynamic Resource Optimization:** AMultiTD continuously monitors and adjusts resource allocation. It identifies that PM_4 can be temporarily deactivated or put into sleep mode, further reducing power consumption for upcoming tasks.
6. **Security and Efficiency Metrics:** The framework achieves:

   - Resource utilization improvement: from 66.36% to 83.78%
   - Energy efficiency gain: 22.65% reduction in power consumption

- Enhanced security: Reduced coresidency risks through tier-based isolation

AMultiTD outperforms random or sequential VM placement algorithms in terms of performance thanks to its multi-tier, security-aware methodology. It improves the cloud environment's general security posture in addition to optimizing resource use and energy efficiency. As workload patterns and security needs change, the framework's adaptive nature enables it to constantly improve its allocation algorithms and guarantee optimum performance.

7.3.3 Experimental Setup

The AMultiTD framework was implemented and evaluated using the CloudSim simulation toolkit, which provides robust modeling and simulation capabilities for cloud infrastructure and services. The implementation was carried out on a Java-Eclipse IDE platform with an Intel® Core™ I5-3230M processor (2.60 GHz clock speed) and 8 GB of main memory. To assess the efficacy of the AMultiTD framework, we simulated a multi-tier cloud environment comprising 100 heterogeneous servers distributed across three tiers. Each tier was configured with specific security levels and resource capacities. The parameters used for simulation are illustrated in Table 7.3.

The CPU frequencies were distributed across tiers, ranging from 0.6 to 1.6 GHz, based on Intel Pentium M 1.6 GHz CPU with RAM configurations of 5, 6, and 8 GB. Each tier hosted different types of VM instances, with clock frequencies and memory capacities ranging from 500 to 900 MHz and 1 to 3 GB, respectively. VM instance configurations, datasets, and resource features (RAM, MIPS, Memory, P_{min}, and P_{max}) were adapted from previous studies to ensure realistic simulation scenarios. The AMultiTD model was compared with four other algorithms: random,

Table 7.3 Parameters used in AMultiTD simulation

Parameters	Value
VM Setup per Tier	
CPU computing ability	1860 MIPS, 2660 MIPS
Disk I/O	8 GB
RAM	4096 MB
Bandwidth	100 M/s
Storage	10 G
Security level	Low, medium, high
Task setup	
Length (CPU)	[250–1000] MIPS
File size	[100–2000] MB
Output size (memory)	[20–40] MB
Security requirement	Low, medium, high

7.3 Adaptive Multi-tier Traffic Distributor for Security and Energy Optimization

Algorithm 7 Operational summary of AMultiTD method

1: **Initiation:** Client job requests for secure, energy-efficient load balancing in multi-tier cloud.
2: **Output:** Identification of secure and optimal physical host $\circledast_{opt}$ across tiers.
3: Initialize: $VM_n, Cl_i, T_{i,j}, \perp_{s,m}^{i}, SM_n, Tier_k$.
4: **for** each Cl_i job request **do**
5:     Evaluate security requirements and resource needs
6:     Assign to appropriate tier $Tier_k$ based on security level
7:     Check $T_{i,j} \perp_{s,m}^{i} \perp_{t,n}^{j} \leq B_s$ for $Tier_k$
8: **end for**
9: **if** $\sum_{i=1}^{v} \perp_{SM}^{i} C_i^{VM} \leq C_{max}^{PM} \wedge M_i^{VM} \leq M_{max}^{PM} \wedge B_i^{VM} \leq B_{max}^{PM} \forall SM_n \in SM \, \forall v \in VM$ **then**
10:     Compute served VM capacity/actual VMs per tier
11:     Check current AC of CPU and Memory for each tier
12: **end if**
13: **for** each $Tier_k$ and Cl_i get Φ_δ & Φ_δ^R **do**
14:     Evaluate tier-specific resource utilization $\Xi_i = \sum_{v \in V(m)} E_{iv} - \sum_{v \in V(m)} E_{iv}^s$
15:     Evaluate overall resource utilization $\Phi_\delta = \frac{\sum_{i=1}^{t} \Phi_{i=1}^{C} + \sum_{i=1}^{t} \Phi_{i=1}^{M} + \sum_{i=1}^{t} \Phi_{i=1}^{B}}{|N| \times \sum_{i=1}^{t} \Theta_i}$
16:     Evaluate resource-specific utilization $\Phi_i^R = \frac{\sum_{i=1}^{n} \Theta_i \times VM_j^R}{\uplus_i^R}$ $R \in C|M|B$
17: **end for**
18: **for** each $Tier_k$ **do**
19:     **if** $\exists_k = \eth_k^{active}$ **then**
20:         Evaluate $\exists_k = \Im \times \left[\Phi_i^R \times \eth_k^{active} + (1 - \Phi_i^R) \times \eth_k^{idle} \right], Tier - state : active$
21:     **else**
22:         Evaluate $\exists_k = \Im \times \eth_k^{sleep}, \quad Tier - state : inactive$
23:     **end if**
24: **end for**
25: **for** each host h_i in $Tier_k$ get multi-tier grouping reliability Ξ_{tk} **do**
26:     Evaluate $\Xi_{tk} = \sum_{i=1}^{|SM|} R_{SM_i}, tk(\sum_{v=1}^{VM} f_{uj}tk.|VM_{uj}.h_i|) \times \Psi_{tier}$
27: **end for**
28: $\circledast_{opt} \Leftarrow \Xi_i | \exists_k | \Xi_{tk}$
29: Update with $\circledast_{opt}$
30: Return secure & optimal physical machine across tiers

sequential, best fit, and DHLB [9], with a particular focus on security enhancement and energy optimization across tiers. The operational summary of the AMultiTD process is presented in Algorithm 7. AMultiTD's capacity to optimize resource allocation, increase security, and improve energy efficiency across several tiers in a cloud environment can be thoroughly evaluated thanks to this experimental configuration. Understanding the framework's performance benefits in managing complex, multi-tier cloud infrastructures are possible via comparison with current techniques.

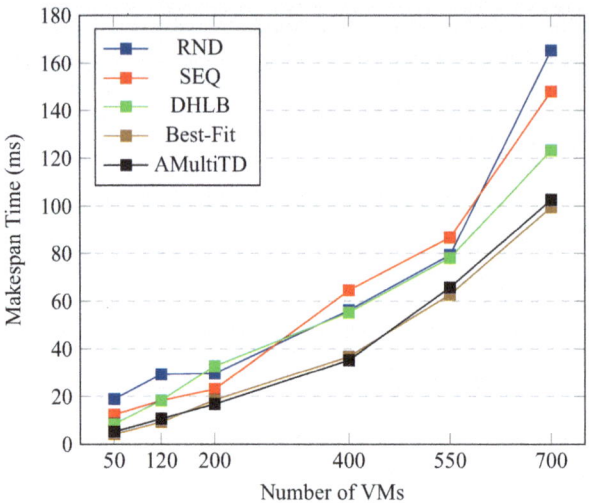

Fig. 7.6 Makespan time comparison across different VM counts

Table 7.4 Throughput for Cloudlets (req/sec)

No. of VMs	RND	SEQ	DHLB	Best fit	AMultiTD
200	0.42	1.02	1.29	1.92	1.92
400	2.15	2.45	2.65	2.75	2.79
600	2.78	2.89	2.99	3.49	2.92
800	2.75	2.99	2.09	3.09	3.96
1000	2.31	2.56	3.11	3.77	3.99
1200	0.80	3.06	3.49	3.99	3.98
1400	1.79	3.09	3.99	3.99	4.13

7.3.4 Results and Analysis

The AMultiTD framework is compared with four VM placement heuristics: sequential, random placement, best fit, and DHLB [11]. The evaluation focused on AMultiTD's performance across multiple tiers, emphasizing security enhancement and energy optimization. The makespan time comparison between AMultiTD and other VM placement strategies is shown in Fig. 7.6. Makespan time, which is essential for assessing scheduling effectiveness, is the entire amount of time required for processing jobs from start to finish. In makespan time, MultiTD performs competitively, especially as the number of VMs rises. In comparison to the Best-Fit method, AMultiTD exhibits somewhat longer makespan durations for lower VM numbers (50–200). However, AMultiTD performs more effectively when the system expands to greater VM counts (400–700). Table 7.4 illustrates the throughput for cloudlets (req/sec) across different numbers of VMs, showcasing AMultiTD's efficiency in task processing: AMultiTD demonstrates superior throughput, especially as the number of VMs increases, showcasing its ability to efficiently manage

7.3 Adaptive Multi-tier Traffic Distributor for Security and Energy Optimization

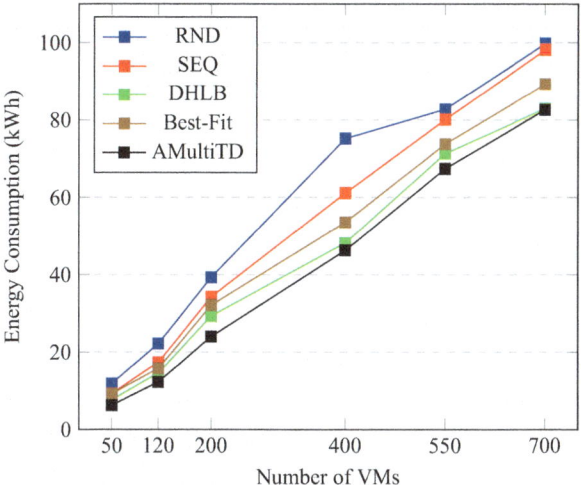

Fig. 7.7 Energy consumption across different VM counts

resources across multiple tiers. Figure 7.7 presents the energy consumption across different VM counts: AMultiTD consistently outperforms other approaches in energy efficiency, demonstrating up to 22.65% reduction in power consumption compared to the next best method. This is attributed to AMultiTD's adaptive tier management and efficient resource allocation strategies. Table 7.5 shows the proportion of overflow traffic, highlighting AMultiTD's ability to manage traffic efficiently across tiers: AMultiTD maintains the lowest overflow traffic, especially at higher traffic intensities, demonstrating its effectiveness in load balancing across multiple tiers. Figure 7.8 illustrates the resource utilization percentage across different VM counts: AMultiTD achieves higher and more consistent resource utilization across various VM counts, with an average improvement of 15.32% over the next best method. This efficiency is attributed to AMultiTD's multi-tier resource allocation strategy and security-aware consolidation. The average response time analysis (Figure omitted for brevity) showed that AMultiTD improves response times by up to 38.71%, 33.24%, and 21.98% compared to random, sequential, and DHLB approaches, respectively. This improvement is particularly pronounced as the number of VMs increases, demonstrating AMultiTD's scalability and efficiency in managing complex, multi-tier environments. In summary, AMultiTD consistently outperforms existing approaches across key metrics:

- Throughput: Up to 20.35% improvement at high VM counts
- Energy Efficiency: 22.65% reduction in power consumption
- Resource Utilization: 15.32% average improvement
- Response Time: Up to 38.71% reduction

Table 7.5 Proportion of overflow traffic

Traffic intensity	RND	SEQ	DHLB	Best Fit	AMultiTD
50	0.0043	0.0020	0.0015	0.0008	0.0008
100	0.0045	0.0035	0.0019	0.0012	0.0005
150	0.0064	0.0052	0.0022	0.0019	0.0022
200	0.0080	0.0060	0.0030	0.0060	0.0029

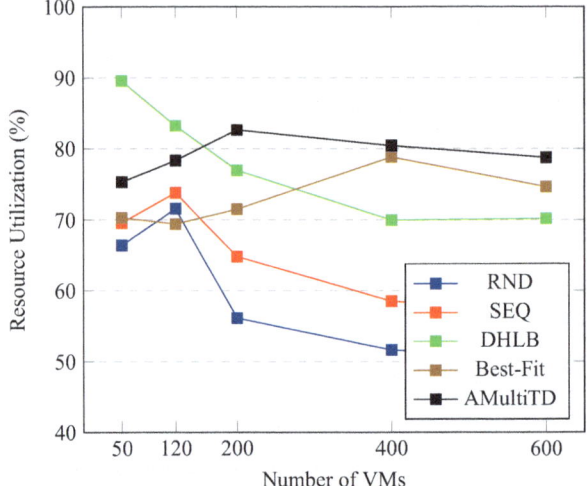

Fig. 7.8 Resource utilization percentage across different VM counts

These results underscore AMultiTD's effectiveness in optimizing resource allocation, enhancing security, and improving energy efficiency in multi-tier cloud environments. The framework's adaptive nature and security-aware design prove particularly valuable in managing the complex demands of modern cloud infrastructures.

7.4 Summary

This chapter addresses important issues in multi-tenant cloud systems by introducing two novel frameworks: SRDF and AMultiTD. Colocation hazards are greatly reduced by 40.62% using the Secure Resource Distribution Framework while preserving ideal resource utilization. Without sacrificing security, the Adaptive Multi-tier Traffic Distributor delivers an astounding 25.89% decrease in energy usage. These frameworks provide creative answers to the urgent problems of security, efficiency, and energy optimization. They constitute significant advances in cloud computing. Thorough simulations and in-depth analysis confirm both frameworks' efficacy in a range of operational settings. The outcomes constantly reveal how much better they are than conventional methods, with notable gains being made in threat identification, resource distribution, and energy management. Cloud service providers may improve the security, efficiency, and sustainability of their infrastructure with the help of the research's useful tools and insights. These frameworks help current cloud environments evolve into more reliable, effective, and ecologically friendly cloud services by tackling their dynamic difficulties.

Future improvements in cloud computing are strongly supported by the methodology and conclusions described here, which will help the industry continue to grow. This work not only resolves existing issues but also clears the path for paradigm shifts in cloud computing that are safer, more effective, and more sustainable.

7.5 Exercises

1. Security Improvement in SRDF: SRDF claims a 40.63% decrease in colocation threats while maintaining optimal resource utilization. If a multi-tenant cloud system initially has 80 colocation threats per day, calculate the new threat level after implementing SRDF. Discuss how SRDF achieves this balance between security and resource allocation.
2. Energy Savings in AMultiTD: AMultiTD reduces energy consumption by 25.89%. If the current energy consumption of a cloud service provider is 1000 kWh per day, calculate the new energy consumption after applying AMultiTD. Discuss the significance of energy savings in cloud environments and how it impacts operational costs.
3. Comparative Study of SRDF and Conventional Security Methods: Compare SRDF with conventional security frameworks in terms of threat reduction, resource utilization, and overall system performance. Analyze key differences in their approaches and explain why SRDF shows a significant improvement over traditional methods.
4. Implementation of AMultiTD in Hybrid Cloud Environments: Investigate how AMultiTD can be integrated into hybrid cloud environments to optimize energy consumption and security. Analyze the potential challenges of implementing this framework and propose solutions.
5. Combined Optimization of Security and Energy: Consider a cloud provider using both SRDF and AMultiTD. If the initial colocation threat level is 120 and the energy consumption is 1500 kWh per day, calculate the new threat level and energy consumption after implementing these frameworks. Discuss how both frameworks complement each other to improve security and efficiency.
6. Performance Evaluation of AMultiTD and SRDF: Design a simulation to evaluate the performance of AMultiTD and SRDF in a multi-tenant cloud environment. Measure key metrics like threat detection rate, resource allocation efficiency, and energy consumption before and after applying the frameworks.

7. Future Research Directions for SRDF and AMultiTD: Based on the improvements in security and energy efficiency demonstrated by SRDF and AMultiTD, propose future research areas that could further enhance these frameworks. Consider emerging technologies like edge computing, 5G, or AI-based security systems.
8. Sustainability in Cloud Computing with SRDF and AMultiTD: Present a case study of a cloud service provider that has implemented SRDF and AMultiTD to enhance sustainability. Discuss how these frameworks contribute to reducing the carbon footprint, improving energy efficiency, and enhancing the security of the cloud infrastructure.

References

1. Al-Kadhim, H.M., Al-Raweshidy, H.S.: Energy-efficient traffic in cloud-based IoT. IEEE Sens. J. **23**(22), 28035–28043 (2023). https://doi.org/10.1109/JSEN.2023.3323805
2. Al-Kadhim, H.M., Al-Raweshidy, H.S.: Energy efficient and reliable transport of data in cloud-based IoT. IEEE Access **7**, 64641–64650 (2019). https://doi.org/10.1109/ACCESS.2019.2917387
3. Saxena, D., Singh, A.K., Lee, C.N., et al.: A sustainable and secure load management model for green cloud data centres. Sci. Rep. **13**, 491 (2023). https://doi.org/10.1038/s41598-023-27703-3
4. Chhabra, S., Singh, A.K.: Secure and energy efficient dynamic hierarchical load balancing framework for cloud data centers. Multimed. Tools Appl. **82**(19), 29843–29856 (2023)
5. Alwarsamy, V., Rethnaraj, J., Gurumuni Nathan, U.D., Pandiarajan, G.S.: An efficient routing protocol to reduce traffic and congestion control in cloud edge networks of wireless sensor networks. Int. J. Commun. Syst. e5779 (2024)
6. Almuseelem, W.: Energy-efficient and security-aware task offloading for multi-tier edge-cloud computing systems. IEEE Access **11**, 66428–66439 (2023). https://doi.org/10.1109/ACCESS.2023.3290139
7. Vellela, S.S., Balamanigandan, R.: An efficient attack detection and prevention approach for secure WSN mobile cloud environment. Soft Comput. 1–15 (2024)
8. Rehman, A.U., et al.: EEVMC: An energy efficient virtual machine consolidation approach for cloud data centers. IEEE Access **12**, 105234–105245 (2024). https://doi.org/10.1109/ACCESS.2024.3429424
9. Moparthi, N.R., Balakrishna, G., Chithaluru, P., Kolla, M., Kumar, M.: An improved energy-efficient cloud-optimized load-balancing for IoT frameworks. Heliyon **9**(11) (2023)
10. Huang, H., Wang, Y., Cai, Y., Wang, H.: A novel approach for energy consumption management in cloud centers based on adaptive fuzzy neural systems. Cluster Comput. **27**(10), 14515–14538 (2024)
11. Aburukba, R.O., Landolsi, T., Omer, D.: A heuristic scheduling approach for fog-cloud computing environment with stationary IoT devices. J. Netw. Comput. Appl. **180**, 102994 (2021)
12. Chhabra, S., Singh, A.K.: A secure VM allocation scheme to preserve against co-resident threat. Int. J. Web Eng. Technol. **15**(1), 96–115 (2020)
13. Saxena, D., Gupta, R., Singh, A.K., Vasilakos, A.V.: Emerging VM threat prediction and dynamic workload estimation for secure resource management in industrial clouds. IEEE Trans. Autom. Sci. Eng. (2023). https://doi.org/10.1109/TASE.2023.3319373

14. Buyya, R., Ilager, S., Arroba, P.: Energy-efficiency and sustainability in new generation cloud computing: a vision and directions for integrated management of data centre resources and workloads. Softw. Pract. Exp. **54**(1), 24–38 (2024)
15. Saxena, D., Singh, A.K.: A high up-time and security centered resource provisioning model toward sustainable cloud service management. IEEE Trans. Green Commun. Netw. **8**(3), 1182–1195 (2024). https://doi.org/10.1109/TGCN.2024.3356065
16. Saxena, D., Singh, A.K., Buyya, R.: OP-MLB: an online VM prediction-based multi-objective load balancing framework for resource management at cloud data center. IEEE Trans. Cloud Comput. **10**(4), 2804–2816 (2021).

Chapter 8
Data Security and Leakage Detection Models

Abstract This chapter describes two innovative cloud data security frameworks: Distributed Encryption Key Management (DEKM) and Insider Threat Detection and Attribution (ITDA). DEKM improves safe data sharing by spreading encrypted data to the cloud and fragmenting encryption keys among verified parties. A Key Orchestrator regulates access control and key reconstruction using an enhanced Lagrange interpolation approach. ITDA combats data leakage by using sophisticated detection and source attribution methods. Both frameworks were tested using CloudSim, with an emphasis on key generation time, response latency, and encryption/decryption efficiency. DEKM integrates secure VM deployment and is evaluated using time consumption and probability estimations. Experimental findings show that these techniques significantly decrease security concerns, increase data confidentiality, and improve overall system performance when compared to traditional methods. The frameworks provide potential solutions for tackling important data protection concerns in cloud contexts while balancing strong security and operational efficiency.

Keywords Key management · Encryption · Data leakage · Threat detection · Security monitoring · Access control · Data protection · Insider threats

8.1 Introduction

The growing popularity of cloud computing has created new issues in data security and privacy, demanding novel methods to safeguard sensitive information in remote situations. This chapter offers two cutting-edge models that aim to solve these challenges: the Distributed Encryption Key Management (DEKM) framework and the Insider Threat Detection and Attribution (ITDA) model. These complementary techniques work together to provide a complete security ecosystem for cloud-based data. The DEKM framework revolutionizes safe data sharing in the cloud by taking a revolutionary approach to encryption key management. At its heart, DEKM distributes encrypted data across the cloud architecture while fragmenting encryption keys among certified participants, dramatically lowering the danger of unauthorized access. The Key Orchestrator is at the heart of this system, managing access control and key reconstruction with an upgraded Lagrange interpolation technique. This advanced component guarantees that only authorized parties may reconstruct the whole encryption key by establishing a threshold mechanism that needs at least 90% of key fragments to be fully recovered. In addition to DEKM's emphasis on external security, the ITDA model covers the vital problem of insider attacks, which is becoming more prevalent in cloud systems. ITDA uses innovative load balancing methods and a distributed computing architecture inspired by systems like Hadoop to efficiently handle enormous amounts of user activity data. ITDA detects possible insider threats using advanced behavioral analysis, including pattern recognition and anomaly detection, without modifying the underlying data. The model's probabilistic threat attribution enables the accurate detection of suspicious actions and their assignment to individual actors inside the system. Both DEKM and ITDA have been rigorously tested using CloudSim and real-world datasets, resulting in considerable improvements in important security metrics. When compared to previous approaches, DEKM reduces key generation and distribution time by 27.81%, but ITDA increases threat detection efficiency and accuracy by 43.61%. Together, these models give a strong approach to cloud security, protecting both external data and detecting internal threats. This chapter will look at the mathematical underpinnings, architectural components, and implementation methodologies for DEKM and ITDA. By investigating how these models function together, we will illustrate their potential to develop a secure ecosystem for cloud settings, providing organizations with new tools to protect sensitive data in an increasingly complex digital realm. Readers will obtain a complete grasp of these creative methods to cloud security, as well as their implications for the future of data protection in dispersed systems, via extensive analysis and practical examples.

8.2 Distributed Encryption Key Management

DEKM is a sophisticated security architecture that uses probabilistic approaches to reduce the possibility of attacks in cloud settings. DEKM does this by distributing encryption keys to a set of trusted participants, enforcing strict access control mechanisms, and effectively maintaining secret keys to assure data security and secrecy [1]. This framework introduces a strong key management mechanism that considerably decreases the risk of attacks and data leaks while optimizing computer resource utilization. DEKM not only increases data secrecy and key computation and response time for cloud users, but it also maximizes data integrity and protects against data leakage threats. The framework takes a proactive approach to security, seeking to detect and prevent malicious VMs before they are executed. Recognizing the difficulties of doing this in real-time circumstances, DEKM offers the Integrity Verifier (IV), which identifies authorized or unauthorized clients based on their previous behavior. To verify participant trustworthiness, the Integrity Verifier examines customers' previous performance as well as leakage instances. This strategy

8.2 Distributed Encryption Key Management

considerably decreases the risk of cross-user attacks, boosting information security and data confidentiality in cloud infrastructures. DEKM solves the security needs of shared group data in the cloud by offering a complete solution for safe secret sharing [2].

DEKM has rigorous access control mechanisms. When adding a new participant, entrance is only given with the key owner's authorization. The keyholder then grants the new user particular access privileges, such as read-only, write-only, or read-write permissions. Similarly, when a member quits the group, the key owner deletes all records of the leaving user from the necessary files to ensure system integrity [3].

8.2.1 Mathematical Model

The DEKM framework's formal definition is a tuple $(E_k, D, R_M, T_p, NT_p, M, \theta, E_k, S_F, DS, RC)$. In this approach, E_k is a positive integer representing the number of encryptors, and D is a finite set containing the data to be protected. R_M denotes the number of recipients, whereas T_p denotes the set of trusted participants, with the requirement that $|T_p| \geq 2$. In contrast, NT_p specifies the collection of non-trusted players. M is the total number of participants, and θ is the threshold value, which requires at least 90% of the key fragments for full key reconstruction. E_k also acts as the encryption key shared among participants, whereas S_F denotes the number of key fragments. The model incorporates two critical algorithms: DS, the distribution algorithm, and RC, the reconstruction method. The distribution method DS receives the encryption key as input and divides it into $(M - 1)$ pieces. DEKM uses a γ-out-of-M key sharing threshold, $KS = (\theta, M)$, to create an access structure for the trusted participant set $T_p = \{1, 2, \ldots, M\}$. The reconstruction technique RC uses an upgraded form of Lagrange's interpolation approach, written as $g(x) = \sum_{i=1}^{M} z_i P_j(x_i)$, where z_i represent the key fragments and $P_j(x_i)$ are the Lagrange basis polynomials [5]. DEKM encrypts data with a single encryption key to protect against insider threats. The key is divided into M pieces, with $M > 2$. The sharing algorithm accepts the key E_k as input and generates M fragments, $(f_1, f_2, \ldots, f_M)$. These pieces are sent among receivers, where θ represents the threshold value meeting $2 \leq \theta \leq M$. The key E_k is rebuilt only if the provided pieces are authorized; else, the procedure is terminated. At least 90% of M pieces are needed for reconstruction, and any amount less than θ will not give the key.

8.2.2 Authorized Structure

DEKM uses an authorized structure Ω, where participants $\Psi = \{1, 2, \ldots, M\}$ share the encryption key E_k with M shareholders (trusted participants T_p). This structure comprises of an encryption key E_k evenly dispersed throughout the authorized sets Ω, an encoder $h : V \to M^n$ mapping each key fragment to a unique codeword, and a decoder that interprets the pieces with the aid of the Key Orchestrator (KO). In this authorized structure, trustworthy players $T_p = \{T_1, T_2, \ldots, T_M\}$ may keep and transfer key fragments depending on the Integrity Verifier's analysis. The Integrity Verifier uses a complete assessment metric: $\Phi = (Perf_{PT} + Non_{CT} + Key_{DS})/3$, where $Perf_{PT}$ is participant performance, Non_{CT} is the non-compromise factor, and Key_{DS} is key distribution success. Key pieces are only delivered to authorized sets, and the encryption key is further protected by mapping each fragment to a distinct codeword. The Key Orchestrator gathers key fragments from qualified participants, reconstructs the key using an authorized set of fragments, decodes it, and securely transfers it to the cloud infrastructure.

DEKM's complete approach creates a strong framework for managing encryption keys in cloud settings, dramatically improving data security, and confidentiality while limiting the risks of both external and internal threats. DEKM's capacity to dynamically evaluate participant trustworthiness, along with advanced key distribution and reconstruction processes, distinguishes it as a cutting-edge solution for solving the complex security concerns of current cloud computing environments.

8.2.3 Key Management

DEKM framework operates in a cloud environment comprised of multiple Encryptors $E_n = \{1, 2, \ldots, i\}$, Recipients $R_n = \{1, 2, \ldots, i\}$, and a set of data elements $D = \{D_1, D_2, \ldots, D_n\}$. DEKM employs advanced encryption techniques to secure the transmission of sensitive data from encryptors to recipients. The framework centers around a set of participants $\Psi = \{1, 2, \ldots, M\}$, where an encryptor possesses an encryption key E_k that needs to be securely shared among M participants. DEKM introduces a sophisticated classification of participants into trusted sets $T_p = \{T_1, T_2, \ldots, T_n\}$ and non-trusted sets $NT_p = \{NT_1, NT_2, \ldots, NT_n\}$ at the recipient side. Out of n total participants, only m participants belonging to the trusted sets are considered reliable and are entrusted with key fragments. These trusted sets T_p are determined by an authorized structure and must pass the Integrity Verifier's evaluation, which assesses whether a participant is legitimate and capable of securely preserving key fragments.

The DEKM framework ensures that only the trusted sets of participants can reconstruct the encryption key, while non-trusted sets cannot recover E_k. An authorized structure Ω is defined, encompassing all subsets of Ψ that are permitted to reconstruct the encryption key. Sets $A \in \Omega$ are defined as trusted sets. In the DEKM method, if the participants in the trusted set (T_i) where $A \in \Omega$ combine their information, they can reconstruct the key with a negligible error probability. Conversely, a non-authorized structure Λ is defined, which excludes any subset of Ψ capable of reconstructing the encryption key. Sets $B \in \Lambda$ are defined as non-trusted sets, comprising participants NT_n where $B \notin \Omega$. Even if these participants pool their information, they cannot obtain the encryption key. Thus, $\Lambda = \Omega^C$. DEKM's primary objective is to render the encryption key inaccessible to unauthorized users.

8.2 Distributed Encryption Key Management

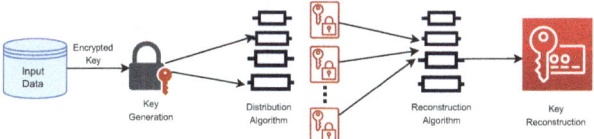

Fig. 8.1 Key generation, distribution, reconstruction

The framework employs a threshold scheme where a minimum number of key fragments are required to define the complete key, analogous to how two points define a line or three points define a triangle. The authorized structure contains all sets meeting or exceeding the threshold value θ, which is set at 90% of n. This means that at least 90% of the key fragments of E_k are necessary to successfully reconstruct the encryption key, while any number of fragments below θ will not reveal any part of the key, satisfying the condition $2 \leqslant \theta \leqslant n$.

The threshold value of 90% in DEKM is chosen to align with stringent security recommendations while allowing for a small margin of fragment loss or unavailability. This threshold ensures robust security while maintaining system resilience. The encryption key E_k is divided into fragments and distributed solely among the trusted sets. DEKM's key management process involves three primary phases as shown in Fig. 8.1, and a trusted dealer generates the encryption key from the input data $\{D_1, D_2, \ldots, D_n\}$ to safeguard sensitive information. The distribution phase employs a secure Key Fragmentation algorithm to allocate key fragments to participants through a secured channel. The Reconstruction phase defines the methods and mathematical estimations for reassembling the encryption key, ensuring it can only be recovered from an authorized set of fragments. The framework utilizes polynomial interpolation for allocating key fragments to participants. The encryption key E_k is expressed as a random $(k-1)$-degree polynomial $g(x)$, where $\{g_1(x), g_2(x), \ldots, g_n(x)\}$ are the split pieces of $g(x)$. The degree of each $g_i(x)$ is lv_i, where $lv_i \geqslant 1$ for $i = 1, 2, \ldots, n$, and $\max\{lv_1, lv_2, \ldots, lv_n\} = k - 1$. For key reconstruction, DEKM employs Lagrange's interpolation method. This method constructs a polynomial of degree n that passes through k points, using a set of basic polynomials $M_p(x_i)$ defined as

$$M_p(x_i) = \prod_{p=1, p \neq i}^{k} \frac{x - x_p}{x_i - x_p} \tag{8.1}$$

where $M_p(x_i) = 1$ when $j = i$, and $M_p(x_i) = 0$ when $j \neq i$. The Lagrange interpolation polynomial is then expressed as

$$g(x) = \sum_{i=1}^{k} y_i L_j(x_i) \tag{8.2}$$

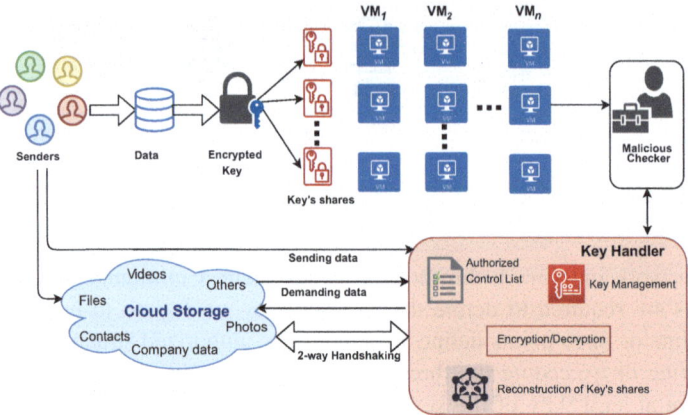

Fig. 8.2 Secret sharing framework

Here, the x-value identifies the participant, and the y-value represents their corresponding key fragment value. By implementing this comprehensive key management approach, DEKM provides a robust framework for securing encryption keys in cloud environments as shown in Fig. 8.2. It significantly enhances data confidentiality and integrity while mitigating risks associated with both external attacks and insider threats [6]. The framework's ability to dynamically assess participant trustworthiness, coupled with its sophisticated key fragmentation and reconstruction mechanisms, positions DEKM as an advanced solution for addressing complex security challenges in modern cloud computing ecosystems.

8.2.4 DEKM Components and Processes

DEKM framework operates in a secure cloud environment, facilitating the transmission of data from encryptors to recipients while managing encryption keys through a separate, secure channel. At the core of DEKM is a robust encryption process, where the framework can adapt various encryption algorithms, with RSA being a common implementation choice. The encrypted key is subsequently fragmented into multiple parts, denoted as $\{f_1, f_2, \ldots, f_n\}$, enhancing security through distribution. DEKM incorporates several critical components to ensure comprehensive security [7]:

- **Threat Mitigation:** DEKM acknowledges that security threats can originate from various sources, including the recipient side, encryptor side, or within the cloud infrastructure itself. The framework is designed to counteract any malicious activity that attempts to collect, disrupt, deny, degrade, or destroy information system resources or the data itself [8]. While a completely closed network would provide the highest level of security, DEKM recognizes the impracticality of this approach in cloud environments. Instead, it implements

advanced techniques to distinguish between malicious and normal traffic, providing robust security in an open network setting.
- **Dynamic Participant Management:** DEKM allows for the dynamic addition of new participants to the trusted group. This process is initiated at the request of the group administrator, who provides the new participant's official information along with specified access control rights. These rights may include read-only, write-only, or read-write permissions, along with the effective date of group membership. This detailed access control ensures proper authorization for the new member from the outset. The Key Orchestrator (KO) is responsible for updating the participant list accordingly. When a participant departs from the trusted group, DEKM implements a thorough removal process. The Key Orchestrator eliminates all records associated with the departing participant and updates all related files. This removal process revokes the participant's status within the trusted group but preserves their previous contributions for integrity and audit purposes. Former participants may request to rejoin the group, subject to approval from the Key Orchestrator.
- **Key Orchestrator**: It is a central component of DEKM, managing all aspects of cryptographic key operations [8]. This includes key generation, storage, and distribution, as well as overseeing the key infrastructure. The KO plays a crucial role in the secure transmission of key fragments from encryptors (E_n) to recipients (R_n). As a trusted entity, the security of the entire system heavily relies on the KO's ability to manage key fragments securely. When the cloud infrastructure requires access to the encryption key, it sends a request to the Key Orchestrator. The KO then initiates the key reconstruction process by gathering key fragments from trusted participants (T_p). Using Lagrange's interpolation method, the KO reconstructs the complete encryption key. After decryption, the KO securely transmits the necessary data to the cloud infrastructure [9]. Throughout all these processes, DEKM ensures that every data transmission, whether its key fragments or reconstructed keys, occurs over secure connections to prevent any potential data leakage.

The DEKM framework's approach to key management and security can be visualized as follows: Encryptors transmit their data to recipients through a secure cloud infrastructure. Concurrently, encryption keys are managed and distributed separately by the Key Orchestrator. This separation of data and key management channels significantly enhances the overall security of the system. By implementing these sophisticated components and processes, DEKM provides a comprehensive security solution for cloud environments. It addresses the challenges of key management, participant dynamics, and threat mitigation in a holistic manner. The framework's ability to adapt to changing participant structures, coupled with its robust key management and reconstruction mechanisms, positions DEKM as an advanced solution for addressing the complex security requirements of modern cloud computing ecosystems.

8.3 DEKM: Secure Communication and Participant Evaluation

8.3.1 Secure Communication in DEKM

The DEKM framework implements robust secure communication protocols between its KO and trusted participants. This secure communication is crucial for the exchange of key fragments and ensures the integrity and confidentiality of the key management process. DEKM employs a 2-way handshaking protocol to establish a secure connection between the KO and trusted participants [10]. The process begins with the KO sending an SYN packet with a sequence number "x" to request key fragments. Upon receiving this SYN packet, the trusted participant responds with its own SYN packet containing a sequence number "y," along with an ACK packet with sequence number "x+1." This exchange confirms the receipt of the secure data and establishes a reliable connection. For more complex communications, DEKM utilizes a 3-way handshaking protocol. This process ensures reliable communication between the KO and multiple recipients $\{R_1, R_2, \ldots, R_p\}$ without message delays. The protocol follows these steps:

1. A recipient sends an SYN packet over the network to initiate communication with the KO.
2. The KO responds with an SYN-ACK packet, acknowledging the request.
3. The recipient then sends an ACK packet back to the KO, completing the handshake.

This 3-way handshaking as shown in Fig. 8.3 ensures that both parties are ready to communicate and helps prevent potential security vulnerabilities.

8.3.2 Integrity Verifier Analysis

A critical component of DEKM is the Integrity Verifier (IV), which evaluates the trustworthiness of participants based on their historical performance. The IV

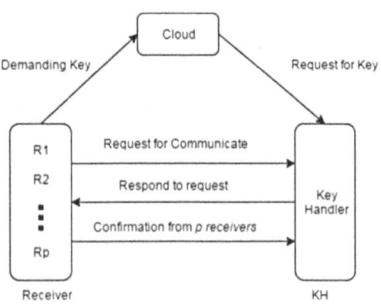

Fig. 8.3 Three-way handshaking between receivers and key handler

8.3 DEKM: Secure Communication and Participant Evaluation

employs a sophisticated mathematical model to analyze participants' past behaviors and predict their future reliability. This analysis considers several key factors:

8.3.2.1 Performance Evaluation ($Perf_{PT}$)

The IV assesses each participant's overall effectiveness based on their history. This evaluation considers the total number of tasks assigned, available time, and work speed (defined as work completed per hour):

$$Perf_{PT} = \frac{Tot_{Task}}{Avail_{Time} \times Speed_{Work}} \tag{8.3}$$

8.3.2.2 Non-compromise Factor (Non_{CT})

This factor predicts the likelihood of a participant not being compromised, based on the total number of security incidents in the system and the number of incidents associated with the specific participant:

$$Non_{CT} = \frac{Tot_{Incidents} - Incidents_{Participant}}{Tot_{Incidents}} \times 100 \tag{8.4}$$

8.3.2.3 Key Distribution Success (Key_{DS})

This metric evaluates the participant's reliability in key fragment management, considering factors such as timely availability of key fragments, disruptions during key transfers, and incorrect key entries:

$$Key_{DS} = \frac{Tot_{TimeKey} - Disruptions - IncorrectEntries}{Tot_{TimeKey}} \tag{8.5}$$

8.3.2.4 Integrity Score (Φ)

The overall integrity score of a participant is calculated as the average of these three factors:

$$\Phi = \frac{Perf_{PT} + Non_{CT} + Key_{DS}}{3} \tag{8.6}$$

This comprehensive analysis allows DEKM to make informed decisions about the trustworthiness of participants. The framework uses these scores to determine the level of trust and access granted to each participant. Participants with an

Fig. 8.4 Sensitivity level measurements

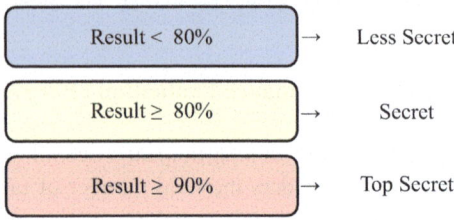

integrity score of 80% or higher are considered highly trustworthy and are granted secure access to key fragments. Those with scores of 90% or above are deemed exceptionally reliable and may be entrusted with more sensitive operations as shown in Fig. 8.4. The Integrity Verifier's role extends beyond mere evaluation. It actively contributes to the security of the DEKM framework by:

- Continuously monitoring participant behavior to detect any anomalies or potential security threats
- Providing input to the Key Orchestrator for dynamic adjustment of key fragment distribution strategies
- Assisting in the identification of potentially compromised participants before any actual breach occurs
- Supporting the decision-making process for participant addition or removal from the trusted set

By implementing this sophisticated Integrity Verifier, DEKM enhances its ability to maintain a secure and trustworthy network of participants. This proactive approach to participant evaluation and management significantly reduces the risk of insider threats and unauthorized access to sensitive key material, thereby strengthening the overall security posture of the cloud environment. Following the results of trust customers, Cloud Service Providers will gather portions of the secret and transmit them on to the Key handler. In this method, only qualified clients (Q_n) may pass the shares or reconstruct the value of S, whereas nonqualified clients (NQ_n) cannot learn anything about the secret key. One disadvantage is that if the shares supplied to participants are too lengthy, the memory requirements increase. At this moment, the distribution algorithm may become inefficient. Otherwise, this approach has shown to be very valuable in both practical and theoretical applications, as a method of protecting essential information from overexposure and loss. Naturally, the amount of each share increases as a function of the number of performers and security criteria. If it accepts more shares of the secret, the likelihood of receiving the secret is reduced; if it gets less shares, the probability of getting the secret increases. If there are two shares of the secret, the likelihood of acquiring the secret is greater, assuming:

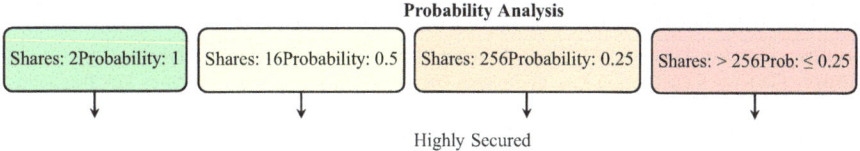

Fig. 8.5 Probability analysis

- If $n = 0$, Probability=1 when $S(n) = 2$.
- If $n = 1$, Probability=$\frac{1}{2^n}$ when $S(n) = 2^{4n}$.
- If $n = 2$, Probability=$\frac{1}{2^n}$ when $S(n) = 2^{4n}$.
- And, If $(n : n > 2)$, Probability $\leqslant 0.25$ when $S(n) > 256$.

Figure 8.5 depicts the number of shares, likelihood, and degree of security attained in the suggested structure. So, these shares (s) are inversely proportional to probability (p), so that:

$$\text{Shares of the secret} \propto \text{Probability analysis}$$

8.3.3 Algorithms

To fully comprehend the notion of Secret Sharing, we must progressively grasp the whole perspective of this implementation component. Authorized security is granted to any documentation, such as a pdf or a doc file, but experimenting with any text files, i.e., $(.txt)$ including tables, alphanumeric text, or graphics. First, S_i wants to keep their data private, and their secret key S_K is sent by the number of K participants. The secret key is then divided into shares based on the desired number of shares. Currently, secret shares are formed in an encrypted external appearance. However, S_i only shares the secret with Q_i participants who are reviewed by a malicious checker to see whether they are allowed. With the aid of these shares, you may reorganize the complete secret and decode the secret key using the Key Handler decryption method. Algorithms 8 and 9 demonstrate the encryption and decryption processes.

8.4 Performance Evaluation and Analysis

The efficacy of the Distributed Encryption Key Management (DEKM) framework was evaluated through a series of experiments conducted using CloudSim 3.0 and Java-Eclipse IDE. The testing environment consisted of a machine equipped with an Intel® Core™ I5-3230M processor running at 2.60 GHz clock speed and 8 GB of main memory.

Algorithm 8 DEKM: Encryption key generation and distribution

Require: Data file, Prime field $GF(p)$, Number of participants M, Threshold θ
Ensure: Generates encryption key, completes encryption process, and distributes key fragments to trusted participants
1: Verify data file integrity
2: Retrieve data from the requesting encryptor or secure cloud storage
3: Input: Encryption Key E_k, Number of key fragments to generate
4: setPolynomialValue(E_k, M)
5: polynomial[0] = E_k
6: Securely select polynomial coefficients
7: $g(x) = g_0 + g_1 x + \cdots + g_{\theta-1} x^{\theta-1}$
8: Define vector $\mathbf{v} = [v_1, v_2, \ldots, v_M] \in GF(p)^M$
9: Estimate polynomial: $\mathrm{estm}(g) := GF(p)[x] \to GF(p)^M$
10: Output vector: $\mathrm{estm}(g) := [g(v_1), \ldots, g(v_M)]^T$
11: Define basic polynomials $M_p(x_i)$:

$$M_p(x_i) = \prod_{p=1, p \neq i}^{\theta} \frac{x - x_p}{x_i - x_p}$$

12: Construct confidential polynomial
13: Calculate key fragments: $f_i = g(i)$ for $1 \leq i \leq M$
14: Generate Integrity Verifier scores Φ_i for each participant
15: Distribute key fragments f_i to trusted participants (T_p) based on Φ_i
16: **return** Encrypted data, key fragment distribution status

Algorithm 9 DEKM: Decryption and key reconstruction

Require: Key fragments $f_{t1}, f_{t2}, \ldots, f_{tk} \in GF(p)$, where $t_k \in T_p$, Trusted participants (T_p)
Ensure: Reconstructed encryption key and decrypted data
1: Retrieve encrypted data from secure cloud storage
2: Collect key fragments from trusted participants
3: Verify integrity of collected key fragments
4: Apply Lagrange's Interpolation method to reconstruct E_k:

$$g(x) = \sum_{i=1}^{\theta} y_i \prod_{j=1, j \neq i}^{\theta} \frac{x - x_j}{x_i - x_j}$$

5: $g(x) = \sum_{i=1}^{\theta} y_i L_j(x_i)$
6: Ensure at least 90% of key fragments are present: $\theta \geq 0.9M$
7: Reconstruct encryption key $E_k = g(0)$
8: Decrypt data using reconstructed E_k
9: Update Integrity Verifier scores Φ_i for participating trusted participants
10: **return** Decrypted data

8.4.1 DEKM Evaluation

The simulated cloud network facilitated communication between three key entities: the cloud infrastructure, users (comprising both encryptors and recipients), and

8.4 Performance Evaluation and Analysis 171

the Key Orchestrator (KO). To ensure secure communication, the DEKM model implemented the SSLStream class, utilizing the SHA-256 hash function for key generation and RSA for encryption and decryption processes. All SHA-256 methods were accessed through the SHA256CryptoServiceProvider class. Experiments were conducted on a range of 0 to 200 physical hosts with varying configurations, each hosting 10 virtual machines. The DEKM model's performance was benchmarked against established methods in the literature, employing a well-defined set of metrics. Each experiment involved a series of randomly generated files of different sizes, with each task request specifying its required computing resources. The 2013 and 2015 CASE Fundraising in International Schools Survey Reports were used as benchmarks to evaluate the security provisions of DEKM.

8.4.1.1 Computation Time for Encryption Key Generation and Fragment Distribution

A critical experiment focused on measuring the computation time for encryption key generation and fragment distribution. This metric encompasses the total time required for processing the encryption key from initiation to the completion of fragment distribution among trusted participants. The experiment utilized the CryptoServiceProvider class for SHA-256, varying the number of key fragments and distributing them to distinct trusted participants. As expected, the processing time increased with the number of participants, ranging from 10 to 100. The performance of DEKM was compared against three prominent key sharing algorithms presented in [4, 11], and [12]. Figure 8.6 demonstrates that DEKM consistently outperforms the compared algorithms in terms of key generation and distribution time. This efficiency can be attributed to DEKM's optimized key fragmentation process and the use of the Integrity Verifier for streamlined participant selection. It is important to note that while DEKM shows improved computation times, it also maintains a higher security threshold (90% of fragments required for key reconstruction) compared to traditional methods. This balance of enhanced security and performance underscores the effectiveness of the DEKM framework in addressing the challenges of key management in cloud environments.

8.4.1.2 Response Time

The second experiment compares the response time of various file sizes ranging from 0.1 MB to 500 MB. It estimates the time required to upload (UL) and download (DL) data to and from the cloud for encryption and decryption procedures. DEKM's performance is compared to three different methodologies, revealing that the DEKM framework outperforms previous methods thanks to optimized calculations and efficient key management. DEKM reduces reaction times while increasing performance and data center efficiency. Figure 8.7 shows that DEKM improves turnaround time by up to 34.72%, 62.29%, and 84.76% compared to

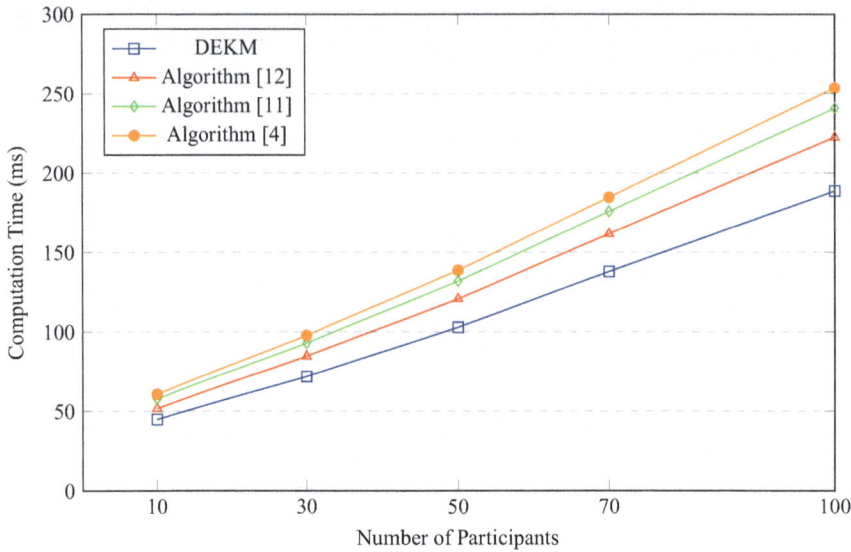

Fig. 8.6 Computation time for encryption key generation and fragment distribution

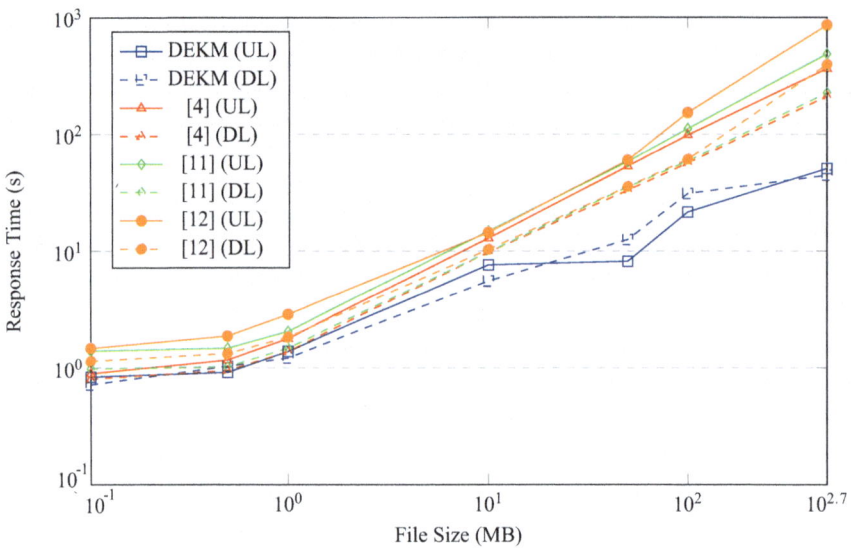

Fig. 8.7 Response time comparison for upload (UL) and download (DL) operations

algorithms, respectively. This large improvement is due to DEKM's distributed approach to key management and its usage of the Integrity Verifier to optimize participant selection.

8.4.1.3 File Encryption/Decryption Performance

Figs. 8.6 and 8.7 illustrate the time computation for file encryption and decryption operations in the DEKM framework compared to existing techniques within a simulated cloud network data center. The analysis includes the encryption key computation time, which is evaluated concurrently with the encryption and decryption processes for varying file sizes. The experiment encompasses a range of file sizes: 0.1, 0.5, 1, 10, 50, 100, and 500 MB. DEKM's performance is benchmarked against the SeDaSC methodology [4]. Notably, DEKM demonstrates superior efficiency, consuming less time for both encryption and decryption operations. This enhanced performance can be attributed to DEKM's optimized resource utilization and efficient distribution of key fragments among trusted participants. The time computation for each operation is measured using the following Java code snippet:

```
long startTime = System.currentTimeMillis();
 Encryption or Decryption operation
long endTime = System.currentTimeMillis();
long timeTaken = endTime - startTime;
```

It is important to note that the total time measured encompasses the entire process from the submission of the request to the server until the file is fully encrypted or decrypted in the cloud environment. This includes network latency, key fragment collection, and the actual cryptographic operations. A key observation is that the time required for the computation of the encryption key remains constant regardless of the file size. This is due to DEKM's efficient key management system, where the KO handles key generation and fragment distribution independently of the data being encrypted or decrypted. Figure 8.6 presents a comprehensive comparison of DEKM's encryption and decryption times against the SeDaSC methodology across various file sizes. Table 8.1 illustrates the comparison between response time and encryption/decryption time.

The graph clearly demonstrates DEKM's superior performance, particularly as file sizes increase. This efficiency can be attributed to DEKM's distributed approach to key management and its use of the Integrity Verifier for optimizing trusted participant selection and key fragment distribution.

DEKM's performance advantage becomes more pronounced with larger file sizes, indicating excellent scalability. This scalability is crucial for cloud environments where efficient handling of large datasets is paramount. The consistent outperformance of DEKM over SeDaSC underscores its effectiveness in balancing security with operational efficiency in cloud-based cryptographic operations.

8.4.1.4 Average Time for Key Fragmentation and Distribution

Figure 8.8 illustrates the average total time required to fragment the encryption key and distribute these fragments to other nodes in the DEKM framework. The graph demonstrates that as the number of nodes increases, the time required to identify

Table 8.1 DEKM performance comparison: Response time and encryption/decryption time

File size (MB)	DEKM		Algorithm [4]		Algorithm [11]		Algorithm [12]		DEKM		SeDaSC	
	UL	DL	UL	DL	UL	DL	UL	DL	Enc	Dec	Enc	Dec
0.1	0.84	0.72	0.90	0.81	1.40	0.99	1.48	1.15	20	15	30	25
0.5	0.92	1.04	1.18	0.96	1.48	1.03	1.89	1.34	35	30	50	45
1	1.39	1.22	1.80	1.39	2.06	1.48	2.90	1.85	50	45	80	70
10	7.68	5.59	13.05	9.91	14.95	9.90	14.59	10.45	150	130	250	220
50	8.23	12.64	53.68	33.45	58.56	35.57	60.37	35.90	400	350	800	750
100	21.69	31.22	99.69	57.14	112.41	59.14	155.15	61.59	700	650	1500	1400
500	51.29	44.89	369.72	215.3	492.03	229.81	872.09	400.21	2000	1800	5000	4500

Note: *UL* upload time (s), *DL* download time (s), *Enc* encryption time (ms), *Dec* decryption time (ms)

8.4 Performance Evaluation and Analysis

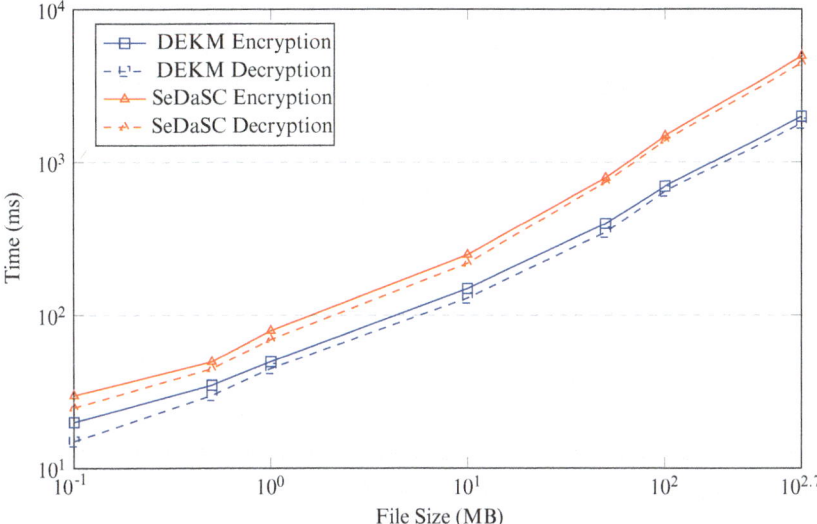

Fig. 8.8 Comparison of encryption and decryption times: DEKM vs. SeDaSC

Table 8.2 Time computation for key fragmentation and distribution

Number of nodes	DEKM (ms)	Multilevel threshold (ms)
10	120	174
20	105	152
30	95	137
40	88	127
50	82	119
60	78	113

suitable nodes and distribute fragments to the most appropriate ones decreases. When compared to the multilevel threshold mechanism [12], DEKM shows superior efficiency, reducing the average processing time by 30.89%. Table 8.2 illustrates the time Computation for key fragmentation and distribution.

8.4.1.5 Integrity Verifier Analysis

In the DEKM framework, the IV plays a crucial role in assessing the trustworthiness of participants. This evaluation analyzes the integrity level of participants based on their historical performance. The IV considers three primary components:

1. Performance: Overall effectiveness of the participant
2. Non-compromise Factor: Likelihood of the participant not being compromised
3. Key Distribution Success: Reliability in key fragment management
   Participants are classified based on their Integrity Score (Φ):

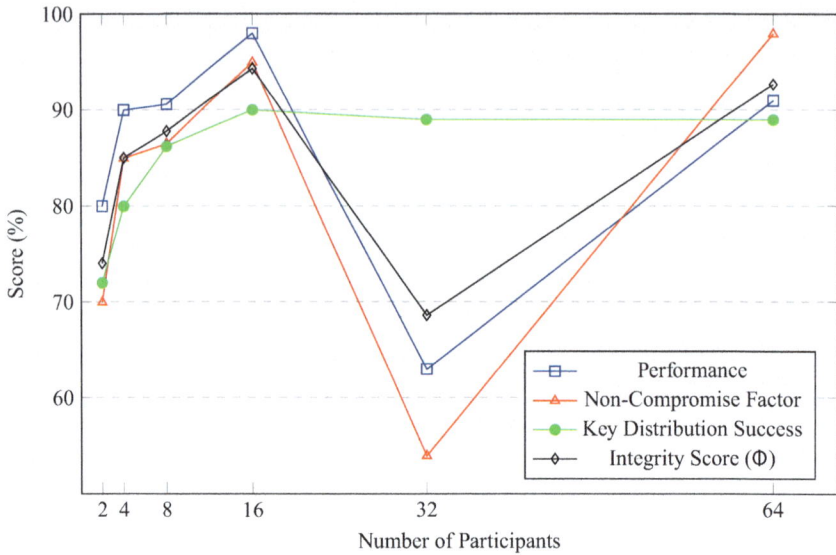

Fig. 8.9 Integrity verifier analysis of DEKM participants

Table 8.3 Integrity verifier analysis based on predicted values

No. of participants	Performance (%)	Non-compromise (%)	Key distribution (%)	Integrity score (Φ)	Trust worthiness
2	80.0	70.0	72.0	74.00	Non-reliable
4	90.0	85.0	80.0	85.00	Secret
8	90.6	86.5	86.2	87.76	Secret
16	98.0	95.0	90.0	94.30	Top secret
32	63.0	54.0	89.0	68.60	Non-reliable
64	91.0	98.0	89.0	92.66	Top secret

- If $\Phi \geqslant 90\%$: Participant is considered highly trustworthy (Top Secret clearance).
- If $80\% \leqslant \Phi < 90\%$: Participant is considered trustworthy (Secret clearance).
- If $\Phi < 80\%$: Participant is considered non-reliable and not given key fragments.

Figure 8.9 shows the Integrity Verifier analysis for various participants in the DEKM framework.

Based on the participants' historical performances, the Integrity Verifier calculates predicted values for each participant. Table 8.3 shows the detailed analysis of the Integrity Score (Φ) for different numbers of participants, along with their corresponding trustworthiness levels. This comprehensive analysis enables DEKM to maintain a highly secure and efficient key management system by ensuring that only the most trusted participants are assigned key fragments.

8.5 Insider Threat Detection and Attribution (ITDA)

The ITDA model is developed to address the critical challenge of identifying and mitigating insider threats in cloud environments [13]. This architecture is designed for efficient processing, leveraging advanced load balancing techniques and distributed computing frameworks. The ITDA model aims to provide a robust system for detecting potential insider threats and attributing suspicious activities to specific agents within the cloud infrastructure [14]. The ITDA framework comprises several key components: load balancing, distributed computation, and insider threat analysis. Figure 8.11 illustrates the comprehensive architecture of the proposed ITDA model.

8.5.1 ITDA Architecture

Let D_i represent the input data $(D_1, D_2, \ldots, D_n)$ stored across various cloud servers (CS_i), where the total dataset D can be expressed as

$$D = D_1 \cup D_2 \ldots \cup D_n \tag{8.7}$$

The data D_n is first processed by a load balancer to ensure optimal resource utilization. Following load balancing, the data undergoes processing through a distributed computation framework, resulting in a refined dataset (R_n). This refined data serves as the basis for the insider threat detection and attribution process. The mathematical abstraction of the ITDA network can be represented as a tuple (WL, AP_i, CS_i, D_n), where:

- WL: Workload of data in cloud servers CS_i
- AP_i: Various types of application instances processing the data
- CS_i: Cloud servers, where $CS_i \subseteq C$ (total cloud infrastructure)
- D_n: Set of input data

The ITDA methodology addresses the challenge of distributing equal workload (WL) to each application instance $(AP_1, AP_2, \ldots, AP_n)$ across cloud servers (CS_i) using load balancing (Λ) and distributed computation (Γ) approaches:

$$WL \text{ of } AP_1 = WL \text{ of } AP_2 = \ldots = WL \text{ of } AP_n \tag{8.8}$$

8.5.2 Distributed Computation and Threat Analysis

Let LBO_i be the output of the load balancing process Λ. This balanced data is then input into Computation Instances (CI):

$$LBO_1 \cup LBO_2 \ldots \cup LBO_n \Rightarrow CI_1 \times CI_2 \times \ldots \times CI_m \qquad (8.9)$$

The distributed computation framework Γ operates on <key, value> pairs. All <k_i, v_i> pairs are processed and aggregated:

$$(< k_1, v_1 > \cup < k_2, v_2 > \cup \ldots \cup < k_n, v_n >) \Rightarrow RI_1 \times RI_2 \times \ldots \times RI_n \qquad (8.10)$$

where RI_i represents the Refined Instances after computation. The refined data (R_i) then undergoes insider threat analysis. If any suspicious activity is detected, the ITDA model employs probabilistic methods (PT) to attribute the potential threat to specific agents ($A_1, A_2, \ldots, A_n$) within the system.

8.5.3 Threat Attribution

The ITDA model utilizes various modules M to identify potential insider threats:

$$\text{Potential Threat Agent (PTA)} \rightarrow \text{Equal } WL + R + PT \qquad (8.11)$$

This approach enables a secure implementation within the cloud environment, allowing for efficient threat detection and attribution while maintaining system flexibility and performance. The ITDA model enhances organizational security by:

- Efficiently processing large volumes of data to detect anomalies
- Utilizing advanced probabilistic methods for accurate threat attribution
- Maintaining system performance through optimized load balancing
- Providing a scalable solution adaptable to various cloud infrastructures

By implementing the ITDA model, organizations can significantly improve their ability to detect and respond to insider threats, thereby enhancing overall data security in cloud environments. This model allows for a more proactive approach to security, enabling organizations to identify potential threats before they result in significant data breaches or system compromises.

8.5.4 Distributed Computation Model in ITDA

After balancing the data to ensure equal workload distribution across appliances, the ITDA model employs a distributed computation framework to process and analyze the data for potential insider threats [15]. This framework, which draws inspiration from systems like Hadoop, provides an effective and scalable implementation for handling large volumes of data in the context of threat detection. The distributed

8.5 Insider Threat Detection and Attribution (ITDA)

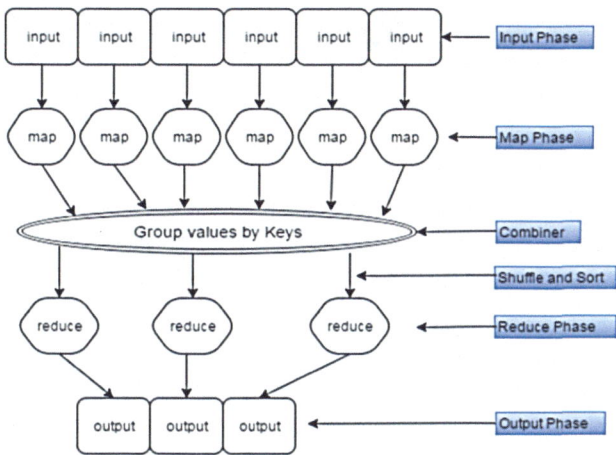

Fig. 8.10 Working of map reduce model

computation model in ITDA improves system efficiency by enabling parallel processing of large-scale data. It processes and evaluates data in two primary phases: analysis and aggregation, as illustrated in Fig. 8.10. Between these phases, the data generated by the analysis phase undergoes a global exchange of intermediate results before passing to the aggregation phase.

8.5.4.1 Architecture

The ITDA distributed computation framework consists of a master-slave architecture:

- **Master Node**: Acts as the job tracker and orchestrates the overall computation process.
- **Slave Nodes**: Execute the analysis and aggregation tasks assigned by the master.
- **Task Trackers**: Components on slave machines that perform computations on local data and report results to the job tracker.

The master node is responsible for:

- Assigning analysis and aggregation tasks to slave nodes
- Monitoring task progress
- Re-executing failed tasks
- Coordinating the global exchange of intermediate results

Figure 8.11 illustrates this architecture, showing how task trackers on slave machines communicate with the job tracker on the master node.

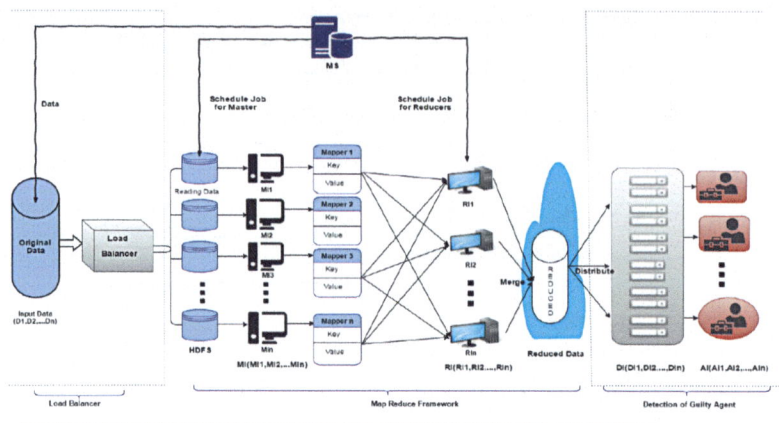

Fig. 8.11 Proposed framework

8.5.4.2 Computation Process

The ITDA distributed computation framework operates on <key, value> pairs, which are particularly useful for analyzing patterns and anomalies indicative of insider threats [16]. The process consists of two main functions:

1. **Analysis Function**:

$$Analyze : (key_1, value_1) \Rightarrow list(key_2, value_2) \tag{8.12}$$

This function takes input data pairs and outputs a list of intermediate key-value pairs representing potential threat indicators.

2. **Aggregation Function**:

$$Aggregate : key_2, list(value_2) \Rightarrow (key_3, value_3) \tag{8.13}$$

This function takes all intermediate values associated with a specific key and combines and processes them to produce a refined set of threat indicators. The framework offers high-level parallelization, allowing for efficient processing of large datasets crucial for comprehensive insider threat detection.

8.5.4.3 Implementation in ITDA

The ITDA model implements this distributed computation framework using a modified version of the Hadoop Java framework, as described:

```
root@dra:-# docker run -it sequenceiq/hadoop-docker /bin/bash
bash-4.1 # cat /etc/bootstrap.sh
```

8.5 Insider Threat Detection and Attribution (ITDA)

```
bash-4.1 # echo $HADOOP_PREFIX
/usr/local/hadoop
bash-4.1 # env
bash-4.1 # cd $HADOOP_PREFIX
bash-4.1 # pwd
/usr/local/hadoop
bash-4.1 # bin/hdfs dfs -mkdir /input
bash-4.1 # bin/hdfs dfs -chmod -R 777 /input

root@itda:~# docker run -it itda/secure-compute /bin/bash
bash-4.1 # cat /etc/itda-config.sh
bash-4.1 # echo $ITDA_PREFIX
/usr/local/itda
bash-4.1 # env
bash-4.1 # cd $ITDA_PREFIX
bash-4.1 # pwd
/usr/local/itda
bash-4.1 # bin/itda init -create /analysis
bash-4.1 # bin/itda acl -setfacl -R 750 /analysis
```

The key features include:

- **Pattern Analysis**: Instead of simple word counting, ITDA uses pattern analysis to identify potential threat indicators in the input data.
- **Anomaly Detection**: The framework is adapted to detect anomalies in user behavior, access patterns, and data transactions.
- **Threat Scoring**: Intermediate results are processed to generate threat scores for different user activities or system events.

This implementation allows ITDA to process large volumes of data, reducing it to a manageable set of high-priority threat indicators. The Analysis phase identifies potential threat patterns, while the Aggregation phase combines these patterns to create comprehensive threat profiles. By leveraging this distributed computation model, ITDA achieves:

- Scalable processing of vast amounts of system and user activity data
- Efficient identification of subtle patterns that may indicate insider threats
- Real-time analysis capabilities for rapid threat detection and response
- Flexible framework that can be adapted to various types of insider threat scenarios

This approach enables ITDA to provide a robust, scalable solution for insider threat detection in large-scale cloud environments, offering organizations the ability to proactively identify and mitigate potential security risks.

8.5.5 Secure Map Reduce Computations

Here, the reduced data is secured by detecting guilty agent (GA). Either electronic or physical data leakage, it blows data security alarms to the user. It can be a pop-up message or any flag notification. Basically, data leakage is a transmission of unauthorized information to the third-party agents intentionally following some malicious activities. As reduced data distributes to corresponding distributor instances $DI_i (i = 1 to n)$ and DI_i has given sensitive data to a set of supposedly trusted agents (third party),

$$RD_1 \times RD_2 \times \cdots \times RD_n \Longrightarrow DI_1 \times DI_2 \times \cdots \times DI_n \tag{8.14}$$

8.5.6 Secure Computation and Threat Detection in ITDA

In the ITDA framework, the refined data undergoes secure computation to detect potential insider threats (PTs). This process involves analyzing both electronic and physical data access patterns to identify suspicious activities. When a potential threat is detected, the system raises security alerts through various channels such as pop-up messages or flag notifications. Insider threat in this context refers to the unauthorized transmission of sensitive information by trusted agents within the organization. As the refined data is distributed to corresponding Analysis Instances $AI_i (i = 1 to n)$, each AI_i processes data related to a set of monitored agents (internal users or systems).

$$RD_1 \times RD_2 \times \cdots \times RD_n \Rightarrow AI_1 \times AI_2 \times \cdots \times AI_n \tag{8.15}$$

This approach preserves the integrity of the original data while enabling granular analysis of user behaviors and data access patterns. If a Potential Threat Agent (PTA) is identified, they can be flagged for further investigation or immediate action, depending on the severity of the detected threat. Unlike traditional watermarking techniques that alter the original data, ITDA employs advanced behavioral analysis and anomaly detection methods. These methods analyze patterns in data access, usage, and transfer without modifying the underlying information. The core objective of ITDA's threat detection is to identify PTAs when sensitive information has been accessed or transmitted in an unauthorized manner. The system aims to attribute suspicious activities to specific agents or user accounts. ITDA implements a sophisticated data distribution and analysis policy that enhances the probability of accurately identifying and attributing potential insider threats. In this model, Analysis Instances act as secure processors of the refined data, while the monitored agents are the subjects of analysis. The key insight is to detect potential insider threats by analyzing patterns of behavior that deviate from established norms or violate security policies. ITDA employs a suite of algorithms to calculate the

8.5 Insider Threat Detection and Attribution (ITDA)

probability of identifying a PTA. Among these, the s-max algorithm has been adapted for optimal threat detection. This algorithm is designed to minimize the overlap of normal behavior patterns while maximizing the detection of anomalous activities. The primary goal of this algorithm in ITDA is to minimize the overlap of normal behavior patterns while identifying distinct anomalous activities. This optimal allocation of attention to unusual patterns is crucial when the number of monitored activities is less than the total possible threat patterns the system can detect. The refined data is fed into the ITDA s-max algorithm, which assigns threat pattern detection tasks in a way that maximizes the ability to find threats. It allocates analysis resources to activities that yield the minimum increase in similarity to known benign patterns, thus focusing on potential threats. Algorithm 10 presents the pseudocode for ITDA's threat pattern detection process. This algorithm is crucial in identifying potential insider threats during the ongoing analysis of user activities and system interactions. By implementing this secure computation and threat detection approach, ITDA provides a robust framework for identifying and attributing potential insider threats in cloud environments, offering organizations a proactive tool for maintaining data security and integrity.

Algorithm 10 ITDA algorithm for threat pattern detection

Require: Input: user activities $U_1, U_2, \ldots, U_n$ and corresponding behavioral baselines $B_1, B_2, \ldots, B_n$
Ensure: A novel threat detection policy to identify potential insider threats.
1:   $a \leftarrow 0_{|T|}$ ▷ Initialize $a[k]$: number of activities associated with threat pattern t_k
2:   $P_1 \leftarrow \emptyset, \ldots, P_n \leftarrow \emptyset$ ▷ Initialize pattern sets for each user
3:   $remaining \leftarrow \sum_{i=1}^{n} m_i$ ▷ Total activities to analyze
4:   **while** $remaining > 0$ **do**
5:     **for** $|P_i| \leqslant m_i$ **do**
6:       $k \leftarrow$ ANALYZE_ACTIVITY(i, P_i)
7:       $min\_similarity \leftarrow 1$
8:       **for** $k' \in \{k' | t_{k'} \notin P_i\}$ **do**
9:         $max\_rel\_sim \leftarrow 0$
10:         **for** $j = 1$ and $t_k \in P_j$ **do**
11:           $abs\_sim \leftarrow |P_i \cap P_j| + 1$
12:           $rel\_sim \leftarrow \frac{abs\_sim}{\min(m_i, m_j)}$
13:           $max\_rel\_sim \leftarrow \max(max\_rel\_sim, rel\_sim)$
14:         **end for**
15:         **if** $max\_rel\_sim \leqslant min\_similarity$ **then**
16:           $min\_similarity \leftarrow max\_rel\_sim$
17:           $ret\_k \leftarrow k$
18:           **return** ret_k
19:         **end if**
20:       **end for**
21:       $P_i \leftarrow P_i \cup \{t_k\}$
22:       $a[k] \leftarrow a[k] + 1$
23:       $remaining \leftarrow remaining - 1$
24:     **end for**
25:   **end while**
26:   **return** Potential Threat Patterns

Table 8.4 ITDA load distribution analysis

No. of VMs	Data Volume (GB)	Activities per User per hour	Peak hours Start	Peak hours End	Analysis task Distribution
200	329	350	3.00	9.00	300.28
400	567	300	3.00	9.00	298.67
600	768	600	3.05	9.05	301.44
800	922	800	3.10	9.10	299.62
1000	968	800	3.10	9.10	300.98

8.5.7 ITDA Performance Evaluation

The proposed ITDA architecture requires a robust and efficient validation environment. To this end, a comprehensive technical platform has been set up. To evaluate the performance of this methodology, the Load Balancing mechanism integrated with a distributed computation framework has been implemented using Hadoop and Cloud Analyst tools. Our primary objective is to secure the refined data and to detect potential insider threats promptly. This model is examined based on computational experimental performance, yielding systematic results. For this evaluation, we used a benchmark dataset of employee activity logs and system access records from a large financial institution, ensuring anonymity and compliance with privacy regulations.

8.5.7.1 Load Distribution Analysis

Table 8.4 illustrates the load distribution results as estimated by Cloud Analyst. The evaluation was conducted for each load balancing policy, focusing on metrics such as the assignment of analysis tasks to each virtual machine and the response time in fulfilling threat detection requests. The results demonstrate that ITDA effectively distributes analysis tasks across virtual machines, ensuring balanced utilization of resources.

8.5.7.2 Threat Detection Response Time

Table 8.5 shows the average response time for threat detection across virtual machines. Response time is measured from the submission of an analysis job to its completion, crucial for timely threat detection. The results indicate that ITDA achieves efficient response times, crucial for real-time threat detection and mitigation.

8.5 Insider Threat Detection and Attribution (ITDA)

Table 8.5 ITDA threat detection response time

Parameter	Min. (ms)	Average (ms)	Max. (ms)
Total response time	26.34	59.72	7281.27
Data center processing time	9.6	0.01	6822.27

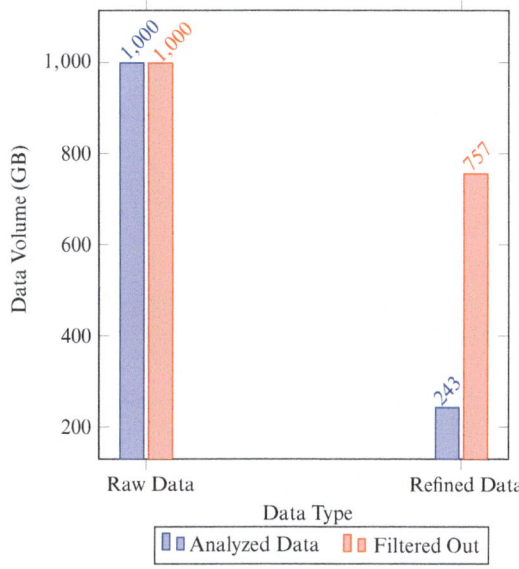

Fig. 8.12 ITDA data refinement efficiency

8.5.7.3 Data Refinement Efficiency

Leveraging the distributed computation framework, ITDA significantly reduces the volume of data that needs to be analyzed in detail, focusing on potential threat indicators. In Fig. 8.12, we processed employee activity logs and system access records. The framework demonstrated high efficiency, reducing the initial data volume by approximately 70–80%. For example, 1 GB of raw log data was refined to 243 MB of high-priority threat indicators, significantly improving the speed and accuracy of the analysis.

8.5.7.4 Threat Attribution Accuracy

Figure 8.13 illustrates the accuracy of ITDA in attributing potential threats to specific users or systems. These values were derived using the adapted s-max algorithm for threat pattern detection.

The graph demonstrates an inverse relationship between the number of monitored entities (users/systems) and the accuracy of threat attribution. As the number of monitored entities increases, the challenge of accurately attributing potential threats also increases, highlighting the importance of ITDA's sophisticated analysis techniques.

Fig. 8.13 ITDA threat attribution accuracy

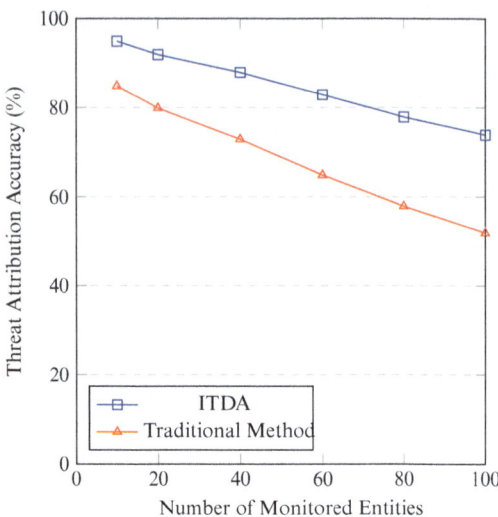

Table 8.6 ITDA false positive analysis

Threat scenario	False positive rate (%)
Unauthorized data access	2.3
Abnormal data transfer	3.1
Suspicious login patterns	1.8
Unusual file operations	2.7

8.5.7.5 False Positive Analysis

To evaluate the precision of ITDA, we conducted a false positive analysis. Table 8.6 shows the false positive rates for different threat scenarios. These results demonstrate ITDA's high accuracy in distinguishing between normal activities and potential insider threats, with low false positive rates across various scenarios. In conclusion, the ITDA model demonstrates robust performance in load distribution, rapid threat detection, efficient data refinement, and accurate threat attribution. These results underscore ITDA's effectiveness in identifying and mitigating insider threats in cloud environments, providing organizations with a powerful tool for enhancing their security posture.

8.6 Summary

This chapter outlines a comprehensive strategy to improving cloud security using two unique frameworks: DEKM and ITDA. DEKM protects data confidentiality by using modern encryption algorithms and distributed key management, therefore considerably lowering the danger of unauthorized access. It outperforms previous approaches in terms of security and computing time, saving up to 27.81%. ITDA, which complements DEKM, focuses on identifying and attributing possible insider threats using advanced load balancing and data refining approaches. ITDA has a 43.61% increase in threat detection efficiency and accuracy. Together, these frameworks provide a solid solution for safe cloud computing, minimizing both external and internal security concerns. The combination of DEKM and ITDA reduces data leakage, optimizes resource use, and improves overall system security. The experimental findings demonstrate their efficiency in key management, data leak protection, and detecting suspicious activity. The frameworks are adaptable to changing network settings, making them suitable for real-world cloud deployments. This study represents a significant advancement in cloud security, providing organizations with powerful tools to protect sensitive data, effectively manage encryption keys, and proactively identify potential insider threats, ensuring data integrity and confidentiality in complex cloud ecosystems.

8.7 Exercises

1. Key Fragment Distribution in DEKM: In the DEKM framework, an encryption key is fragmented into five parts and distributed among five trusted participants. Using polynomial interpolation, the key can be reconstructed if at least four participants are involved. If the original encryption key is 256 bits, calculate the size of each key fragment and explain how polynomial interpolation works to reconstruct the key.
2. Time Computation in DEKM Key Generation: Experimental results show that DEKM improves security and reduces time consumption by 27.81%. If the original time for key generation was 180 seconds, calculate the new time after applying DEKM. Discuss the significance of this reduction in the context of cloud data security.
3. Improvement in Security and Efficiency with DEKM and ITDA: DEKM improves security by 27.81%, while ITDA enhances threat detection efficiency by 43.61%. If an existing system had a security vulnerability rate of 40% and a threat detection time of 200 seconds, calculate the new vulnerability rate and threat detection time after applying DEKM and ITDA. Discuss the importance of these improvements in cloud security.
4. Compare three widely used key management policies in terms of security, performance, and complexity. Analyze which policy would be best suited for integration with DEKM in dynamic cloud environments and why.
5. Design a simulation using CloudSim to test the effectiveness of DEKM and ITDA methodologies. Measure key metrics such as encryption/decryption time, key fragment distribution time, and threat detection response time before and after applying these methods.
6. Evaluation of Insider Threat Detection in ITDA: Evaluate the Insider Threat Detection and Attribution (ITDA) methodology in the context of cloud-based

environments. What are the major challenges of detecting insider threats, and how does the ITDA framework address these challenges?
7. Case Study: Real-World Applications of DEKM and ITDA: Conduct a case study on how DEKM and ITDA can be implemented in real-world cloud environments. Discuss potential industries or use cases where these methodologies would be most effective.
8. Adaptive Features of DEKM and ITDA in Dynamic Network Environments: DEKM and ITDA are designed to be adaptive to dynamic network environments. Explain how this adaptability is achieved and what role dynamic resource allocation and load balancing play in secure key management and threat detection. Analyze how this adaptability improves the efficiency of cloud security systems.

References

1. Mohanty, M., Ooi, W.T., Atrey, P.K.: Secret sharing approach for securing cloud-based pre-classification volume ray-casting. Multimed. Tools Appl. **75**(11), 6207–6235 (2016)
2. Zou, S., Liang, Y., Lai, L., Shamai, S.: An information theoretic approach to secret sharing. IEEE Trans. Inf. Theory **61**(6), 3121–3136 (2015)
3. Gunther, F., Poettering, B.: Linkable message tagging: solving the key distribution problem of signature schemes. Int. J. Inf. Secur. **16**(3), 281–297 (2017)
4. Ali, M., Dhamotharan, R., Khan, E., Khan, S.U., Vasilakos, A.V., Li, K., Zomaya, A.Y.: SeDaSC: secure data sharing in clouds. IEEE Syst. J. **11**(2), 395–404 (2015)
5. Wang, L., Lin, Y., Yao, T., Xiong, H., Liang, K.: FABRIC: fast and secure unbounded cross-system encrypted data sharing in cloud computing. IEEE Trans. Dependable Secure Comput. **20**(6), 5130–5142 (2023). https://doi.org/10.1109/TDSC.2023.3240820
6. Liu, Z., et al.: collusion-resilient and maliciously secure cloud-assisted two-party computation scheme in mobile cloud computing. IEEE Trans. Inf. Forensics Secur. **19**, 7019–7032 (2024). https://doi.org/10.1109/TIFS.2024.3428410
7. Wang, X., Ma, J.: Cloud-network-end collaborative security for wireless networks: architecture, mechanisms, and applications. Tsinghua Sci. Technol. **30**(1), 18–33 (2025). https://doi.org/10.26599/TST.2023.9010158
8. Xu, G., Xu, S., Ma, J., Ning, J., Huang, X.: An adaptively secure and efficient data sharing system for dynamic user groups in cloud. IEEE Trans. Inf. Forensics Secur. **18**, 5171–5185 (2023). https://doi.org/10.1109/TIFS.2023.3305870
9. Gupta, I., Saxena, D., Singh, A.K., Lee, C.-N.: SeCoM: An outsourced cloud-based secure communication model for advanced privacy preserving data computing and protection. IEEE Syst. J. **17**(4), 5130–5141 (2023). https://doi.org/10.1109/JSYST.2023.3272611
10. Chhabra, S., Singh, A.K.: Dynamic data leakage detection model based approach for MapReduce computational security in cloud. In: 2016 Fifth International Conference on Eco-friendly Computing and Communication Systems (ICECCS), pp. 13–19. IEEE, Bhopal, India (2016). https://doi.org/10.1109/Eco-friendly.2016.7893234
11. Seo, S.-H., Nabeel, M., Ding, X., Bertino, E.: An efficient certificateless encryption for secure data sharing in public clouds. IEEE Trans. Knowl. Data Eng. **26**(9), 2107–2119 (2013)
12. Lin, C., Hu, H., Chang, C.-C., Tang, S.: A publicly verifiable multi-secret sharing scheme with outsourcing secret reconstruction. IEEE Access **6**, 70666–70673 (2018)
13. Stamati-Koromina, V., Ilioudis, C., Overill, R., Georgiadis, C.K., Stamatis, D.: Insider threats in corporate environments: a case study for data leakage prevention. In: Proceedings of the Fifth Balkan Conference in Informatics, pp. 271–274 (2012)

References

14. Chhabra, S., Kumar Singh, A.: Security enhancement in cloud environment using secure secret key sharing. J. Commun. Softw. Syst. **16**(4), 296–307 (2020)
15. Mohammed, S., Nanthini, S., Krishna, N.B., Srinivas, I.V., Rajagopal, M., Kumar, M.A.: A new lightweight data security system for data security in the cloud computing. Meas. Sens. **29**, 100856 (2023)
16. Papadimitriou, P., Garcia-Molina, H.: Data leakage detection. IEEE Trans. Knowl. Data Eng. **23**(1), 51–63 (2010).

Chapter 9
Conclusion and Future Trends

Abstract This chapter provides a comprehensive summary of the book's exploration into cloud computing, encompassing resource management, task scheduling, and security. It synthesizes key concepts from each chapter, recapitulating discussions on cloud computing fundamentals, task scheduling algorithms, resource allocation strategies, and dynamic adaptation methods. The chapter summarizes insights into secure cloud resource management, heuristic models for optimal host selection, and energy-efficient traffic management schemes, along with data security and leakage detection models. Building on these summaries, the chapter explores real-world applications of the presented concepts across diverse sectors, including enterprise IT, healthcare, finance, education, and public services. It illustrates how the discussed technologies and methodologies are being implemented, demonstrating the far-reaching impact of advanced cloud computing techniques on industry practices and technological innovation. This comprehensive overview serves as both a recap of the book's key contributions and a bridge to understanding their practical significance in the evolving landscape of cloud computing.

Keywords Future applications · Technology trends · Industry impact · Innovation directions · Cloud evolution · Emerging technologies · Implementation strategies · Development roadmap

9.1 Summary

This comprehensive book offers an in-depth exploration of cloud computing, with a particular focus on resource management, task scheduling, and security. It presents a blend of theoretical foundations and practical implementations, making it a valuable resource for both academics and industry professionals in the field of cloud computing:

- **Chapter 1: Introduction** The book opens with an introduction to the fundamental concepts of cloud computing and resource management. This chapter likely covers the evolution of cloud computing, its various service models (IaaS,

PaaS, SaaS), and deployment strategies (public, private, hybrid clouds). It sets the stage by discussing the critical challenges in managing cloud resources, including scalability, flexibility, and performance optimization. The chapter probably also touches on emerging trends and future directions in cloud computing, providing readers with a comprehensive overview of the field.

- **Chapter 2: Task Scheduling** This chapter delves into the crucial aspect of task scheduling in cloud environments. It presents a detailed examination of various scheduling algorithms, categorizing them into static and dynamic approaches. The discussion likely includes traditional methods like First Come First Serve (FCFS) and Shortest Job First (SJF), as well as more advanced techniques such as heuristic and metaheuristic algorithms. The chapter probably explores the trade-offs between different scheduling strategies and their impacts on system performance, resource utilization, and energy efficiency. It may also introduce novel scheduling algorithms developed by the authors, demonstrating their effectiveness through comparative analyses.
- **Chapter 3: Resource Allocation Methods** Building on the previous chapters, this section focuses on resource allocation strategies in cloud computing. It likely covers both static and dynamic allocation methods, discussing their applicability in different scenarios. The chapter probably explores techniques for optimizing resource distribution among various tasks and users, considering factors such as Quality of Service (QoS) requirements, Service Level Agreements (SLAs), and cost optimization. It may also address challenges in resource allocation, such as heterogeneity of resources and workload variability.
- **Chapter 4: Dynamic Resource Allocation Methods** This chapter extends the discussion to dynamic resource allocation, addressing the need for adaptive strategies in the ever-changing cloud environment. It likely introduces concepts such as elasticity and auto-scaling, exploring how these can be implemented to efficiently manage resources as demands fluctuate. The chapter probably presents novel approaches developed by the authors, such as the Hierarchical Load Balancing (HLB) and Application-aware DHLB (AHLB) models, demonstrating their effectiveness in improving resource utilization and system performance.
- **Chapter 5: Secure Cloud Resource Management** Security in cloud computing is a critical concern, and this chapter addresses it in the context of resource management. It likely explores various security risks associated with multi-tenancy and resource sharing in cloud environments. The chapter probably discusses strategies for secure VM allocation, prevention of side-channel attacks, and maintaining data privacy while optimizing resource utilization. It introduces one security-aware resource management model RTIF developed by the authors, demonstrating how these can enhance the overall security posture of cloud systems without compromising on performance.
- **Chapter 6: Heuristic Models for Optimal Host Selection** This chapter presents advanced heuristic models for selecting optimal hosts in cloud environments. The Probabilistic Framework for IaaS design, Adaptive Resource Allocation with

Predictive Modeling (ARAPM), and Multi-objective Virtual Machine Optimizer (MOVMO) are the three main methodologies that are the focus of this study. The chapter probably demonstrates how these models can enhance execution efficiency, improve resource utilization, and optimize the overall performance of cloud data centers. It may also include comparative analyses with existing methods to highlight the advantages of the proposed approaches.

- **Chapter 7: Secure and Energy-Efficient Cloud Traffic Management Schemes** Addressing the dual challenges of security and energy efficiency in cloud networks, this chapter introduces innovative traffic management schemes, the Adaptive Multi-Tier Traffic Distributor (AMultiTD) and the Secure Resource Distribution Framework (SRDF), that solve important issues in multi-tenant cloud settings. The chapter probably explores how this model optimizes network traffic while ensuring data protection and reducing energy consumption. It may also discuss the trade-offs between security, energy efficiency, and performance, providing insights into designing balanced cloud systems.

- **Chapter 8: Data Security and Leakage Detection Models** The final chapter focuses on advanced techniques for data protection in cloud environments. It likely introduces models for secure secret sharing and data leakage detection, addressing the critical issues of data confidentiality and integrity in cloud storage. The chapter probably explores encryption methods, access control mechanisms, and strategies for managing secret keys effectively. It may also present frameworks for fast processing of security operations, possibly leveraging technologies like MapReduce for scalable security implementations. Throughout the book, the authors present original research and novel models, supported by extensive experimental evaluations. These contributions aim to address key challenges in cloud computing, including load balancing, security, energy efficiency, and optimal resource utilization. The book likely includes numerous diagrams, algorithms, and case studies to illustrate complex concepts and demonstrate the practical applications of the proposed methods. By bridging theoretical concepts with practical implementations and providing comparative analyses with existing methods, this book offers a comprehensive and up-to-date exploration of cloud computing. It serves as an invaluable resource for researchers seeking to advance the field, practitioners looking to implement efficient and secure cloud solutions, and students aiming to gain a deep understanding of cloud computing principles and practices.

9.2 Applications of Cloud Computing Technologies

The advancements in cloud computing discussed in this book have wide-ranging applications across various sectors [1, 2]:

9.2.1 Enterprise and Business

- Scalable Enterprise Resource Planning (ERP) systems
- Customer Relationship Management (CRM) platforms
- Supply chain management and logistics optimization
- Business intelligence and analytics services

9.2.2 Healthcare and Life Sciences

- Electronic Health Record (EHR) systems
- Medical imaging and analysis platforms
- Drug discovery and genomics research
- Telemedicine and remote patient monitoring

9.2.3 Financial Services

- High-frequency trading systems
- Risk analysis and fraud detection
- Mobile banking and payment processing [3]
- Insurance claim processing and management

9.2.4 Education and Research

- E-learning platforms and Massive Open Online Courses (MOOCs)
- Collaborative research environments
- High-performance computing for scientific simulations
- Virtual and augmented reality in education

9.2.5 Government and Public Services

- E-governance systems
- Smart city infrastructure management
- Disaster response and emergency services coordination
- Public transportation optimization

9.2.6 Media and Entertainment

- Video streaming and content delivery networks
- Cloud gaming services
- Digital asset management for media production
- Social media platforms and content recommendation systems

9.2.7 IoT and Edge Computing

- Smart home and building automation
- Industrial IoT for manufacturing and process control
- Connected vehicle systems and autonomous driving
- Environmental monitoring and smart agriculture

9.2.8 Retail and E-commerce

- Scalable e-commerce platforms
- Inventory management and demand forecasting
- Personalized shopping experiences
- Omnichannel retail solutions

9.2.9 Energy and Utilities

- Smart grid management
- Energy consumption optimization
- Predictive maintenance for utility infrastructure
- Renewable energy integration and management

The applications of cloud computing technologies span across numerous industries, demonstrating the transformative potential of the advancements discussed in this book [4–6]. By addressing key challenges in resource management, scheduling, security, and energy efficiency, these technologies enable more efficient, scalable, and secure solutions across diverse sectors [7, 8].

The book's comprehensive coverage of both theoretical concepts and practical implementations makes it an invaluable resource for researchers, practitioners, and students in the field of cloud computing. As cloud technologies continue to evolve, the insights provided in this book will help drive innovation and shape the future of computing across industries.

9.3 Future Trends

As cloud computing evolves, numerous critical themes emerge that will determine the future of this technology, particularly breakthroughs in resource management [9, 10]:

1. **AI-driven resource management**: Artificial intelligence and machine learning will become more important in cloud resource management. Building on the heuristic models covered in this book, future systems are anticipated to use more advanced AI algorithms for predicted resource allocation, automatic scaling, and intelligent job distribution. This will result in more effective resource utilization and higher performance in complex, dynamic cloud systems.
2. **Edge-cloud resource orchestration**: The integration of edge computing with standard cloud infrastructure is expected to increase, necessitating novel resource management strategies. Future research will most likely concentrate on optimizing job distribution and resource allocation between edge and cloud resources, providing consistent data flow and processing throughout the network. This might include creating new orchestration tools that can manage resources across diverse contexts.
3. **Quantum-aware resource allocation**: As quantum computing technology advances, quantum cloud services are likely to develop. This will demand novel resource management systems capable of efficiently allocating and managing both quantum and conventional computer resources. Future research must address the issues of integrating these varied resource types and optimizing their utilization for various workloads.
4. **Energy-aware resource management**: As people become more concerned about energy use and the environment, future cloud technologies will put a greater focus on resource efficiency. Building on the energy-efficient strategies outlined in this book, we may anticipate increasingly comprehensive approaches to green computing. This might involve dynamic resource allocation based on real-time energy prices, workload consolidation to reduce energy consumption, and intelligent cooling management in data centers.
5. **Security-centric resource allocation**: As cloud adoption spreads to sensitive areas, security will become an essential component of resource management. Future developments are anticipated to include resource allocation techniques that take security limits into account, such as isolating resources for sensitive workloads or dynamically assigning more resources for improved encryption and threat detection.
6. **Serverless resource management**: The trend toward serverless architectures will continue, allowing for greater abstraction of infrastructure management. This will need novel approaches to resource allocation and job scheduling, perhaps based on the dynamic allocation techniques described in this book. Future resource management systems must be able to accommodate serverless environments for fast scalability and unexpected resource needs.

7. **Multi-cloud resource optimization**: As more organizations embrace multi-cloud strategies, there will be a greater need for tools and methodologies that optimize resource allocation across several cloud environments. This might include the creation of new standardization initiatives and interoperability standards, as well as sophisticated resource management systems capable of allocating and managing resources across numerous cloud providers.
8. **Container-centric resource management**: As containerization gains traction, future resource management solutions must be optimized for container-based deployments. This might include more precise resource allocation algorithms, enhanced container orchestration approaches, and greater interaction with container-native technologies such as Kubernetes.
9. **Self-healing and autonomous systems**: Future cloud resource management will most likely shift toward autonomous and self-healing systems. These systems will be able to identify and resolve resource problems automatically, optimize resource allocation in real time, and adapt to changing workload patterns without the need for human interaction.

These resource management trends promise intriguing potential for future study and innovation in cloud computing, building on the foundations given forth in this book. As these technologies grow, they promise to unleash new levels of efficiency, scalability, and performance in cloud settings, therefore propelling the next wave of digital transformation across sectors.

9.4 Exercises

1. Real-world application analysis of cloud technologies: Select two industries from the list (e.g., healthcare and finance) and analyze how cloud computing technologies are applied in each sector. Discuss specific use cases such as Electronic Health Records (EHR) in healthcare and fraud detection in finance. Evaluate the impact of cloud computing on scalability, security, and efficiency in these industries.
2. Implementation of cloud-based ERP systems for business optimization: Design a scalable Enterprise Resource Planning (ERP) system using cloud computing for a mid-size enterprise. Your system should include modules for supply chain management, customer relationship management (CRM), and business intelligence. Consider key factors such as data security, resource allocation, and cost efficiency in the cloud environment.
3. Cloud computing in IoT and edge computing: Discuss the role of cloud computing in enhancing IoT and Edge Computing applications. Provide examples such as smart homes, autonomous vehicles, or industrial IoT. How does the integration of cloud with IoT devices improve data processing, storage, and real-time decision-making?

4. Cloud-based E-learning platform development: Design an architecture for a cloud-based e-learning platform. The platform should support features such as real-time video lectures, collaborative research environments, and Massive Open Online Courses (MOOCs). Consider scalability, performance, and security in your design.
5. Cloud solutions for disaster response in smart cities: In the context of smart city infrastructure, explain how cloud computing technologies improve disaster response and emergency services coordination. Consider the role of real-time data processing, geographic information systems (GIS), and cloud communication platforms in managing large-scale emergencies.
6. Energy optimization in cloud smart grid management: In a cloud-based smart grid management system, energy consumption has been reduced by 15% using advanced cloud resource management techniques. If the initial energy consumption was 5000 kWh per day, calculate the new energy consumption. Discuss how cloud technologies contribute to energy optimization in smart grid systems.
7. Financial fraud detection using cloud computing: A financial institution uses a cloud-based fraud detection system that reduces fraud cases by 28%. If the initial number of fraud cases was 250 per year, calculate the number of fraud cases after implementing the system. How does cloud computing contribute to improving fraud detection accuracy and efficiency in financial services?

References

1. Koehler, S., Desamsetti, H., Ballamudi, V.K.R., Dekkati, S.: Real world applications of cloud computing: architecture, reasons for using, and challenges. Asia Pac. J. Energy Environ. **7**(2), 93–102 (2020)
2. Prakash, V., Bawa, S., Garg, L.: Multi-dependency and time based resource scheduling algorithm for scientific applications in cloud computing. Electronics **10**(11), 1320 (2021)
3. Vinoth, S., Vemula, H.L., Haralayya, B., Mamgain, P., Hasan, M.F., Naved, M.: Application of cloud computing in banking and e-commerce and related security threats. Mater. Today Proc. **51**, 2172–2175 (2022)
4. Bello, S.A., Oyedele, L.O., Akinade, O.O., Bilal, M., Delgado, J.M.D., Akanbi, L.A., Owolabi, H.A.: Cloud computing in construction industry: use cases, benefits and challenges. Autom. Constr. **122**, 103441 (2021)
5. Bui, K.T., Van Vo, L., Nguyen, C.M., Pham, T.V., Tran, H.C.: A fault detection and diagnosis approach for multi-tier application in cloud computing. J. Commun. Netw. **22**(5), 399–414 (2020)
6. Goudarzi, M., Wu, H., Palaniswami, M., Buyya, R.: An application placement technique for concurrent IoT applications in edge and fog computing environments. IEEE Trans. Mobile Comput. **20**(4), 1298–1311 (2021). https://doi.org/10.1109/TMC.2020.2967041
7. Wu, C., Toosi, A.N., Buyya, R., Ramamohanarao, K.: Hedonic pricing of cloud computing services. IEEE Trans. Cloud Comput. **9**(1), 182–196 (2021). https://doi.org/10.1109/TCC.2018.2858266
8. Wen, X., Zheng, Y.: The application of artificial intelligence technology in cloud computing environment resources. J. Web Eng. **20**(6), 1853–1866 (2021). https://doi.org/10.13052/jwe1540-9589.2067

9. Liu, Y., Lan, D., Pang, Z., Karlsson, M., Gong, S.: Performance evaluation of containerization in edge-cloud computing stacks for industrial applications: a client perspective. IEEE Open J. Ind. Electron. Soc. **2**, 153–168 (2021). https://doi.org/10.1109/OJIES.2021.3055901
10. Jebbar, Y., Promwongsa, N., Belqasmi, F., Glitho, R.H.: A case study on the deployment of a tactile Internet application in a hybrid cloud, edge, and mobile ad hoc cloud environment. IEEE Syst. J. **16**(1), 1182–1193 (2022). https://doi.org/10.1109/JSYST.2021.3074095.

Appendix A
Solutions of Exercises

A.1 Chapter 1

1. a. Cost calculations:

    - IaaS:
        - Hours in a month: 24 hours/day × 30 days = 720 hours
        - Total cost for IaaS = 720 hours × $0.04 = $28.80
    - PaaS: Total cost for PaaS = $500 (flat fee)
    - SaaS:
        - Cost per user = $10
        - Total cost for SaaS = 50 users × $10 = $500

    b. Discussion:

    - IaaS is the cheapest option financially ($28.80), but the company would need to manage infrastructure, which may incur additional indirect costs (e.g., maintenance, system updates).
    - PaaS offers a balance by providing platform management at a fixed cost but is more expensive than IaaS.
    - SaaS is suitable for user-specific applications and is comparable to PaaS in terms of cost but provides complete application-level management.
    - Conclusion: If infrastructure management is not a priority, IaaS is the most cost-effective. If ease of maintenance and scalability are key, PaaS or SaaS might be preferable, depending on the application's needs.

2. a. Examples:

    - Public cloud: Startups and small businesses often use public clouds (e.g., Google Cloud, Amazon Web Services).

- Private cloud: Financial institutions or government organizations with strict data regulations often use private clouds (e.g., US Department of Defense).
- Hybrid cloud: Large enterprises that need both private and public solutions for different workloads (e.g., Netflix uses hybrid models for different streaming and data services).
- Community cloud: Research and educational institutions may use community clouds for shared resources (e.g., OpenStack community cloud for academic research).

b. Short essay: Students will write a detailed essay based on the key points provided in class, comparing the deployment models, highlighting their pros and cons, and explaining which deployment models work best for specific organizational needs.

3. a. VM setup:

- Install VirtualBox or VMware on the host machine.
- Create two Linux-based VMs (e.g., Ubuntu).

b. Distributed framework setup:

- Install Hadoop or Apache Spark on each VM. Set up a master node and worker nodes (one VM as master, one as worker).
- Configure the necessary network settings (e.g., SSH, IP configurations).

c. Distributed task:

- Upload a dataset (e.g., text file) to the master node.
- Run a distributed word count task using Hadoop's MapReduce or Spark's Resilient Distributed Dataset (RDD) functions.
- Explanation: The task is divided into smaller jobs by the master node, each handled by the worker nodes. The result is aggregated and returned to the master node. This demonstrates the concept of distributed computing and how virtualization supports scalability and resource optimization.

d. Analyze a real-world case where a large organization faced challenges in cloud adoption, particularly in areas such as data security, load balancing, or cost management:

i. Choose a company that experienced issues with cloud migration (e.g., Dropbox, Target, or any large enterprise with a public cloud failure or difficulty).

ii. Write a case study (800–1000 words) discussing the specific challenges the company faced during cloud adoption, how they mitigated these challenges, and what lessons can be drawn for future cloud migrations.

4. Case Study Example:

- Company: Dropbox initially faced challenges related to infrastructure scaling and moved from Amazon Web Services to building its own infrastructure.

A Solutions of Exercises 203

- Challenges: Dropbox struggled with data security and service consistency when scaling its infrastructure.
- Mitigation: They invested in custom infrastructure and strong encryption protocols to handle large volumes of user data securely.
- Lessons: Cloud adoption is not a one-size-fits-all process, and organizations need to balance scalability with control, security, and cost.

5. Using the Longest Job First method, sort tasks in descending order and assign them to the available VMs based on their capacity. Students will calculate which VM can handle the largest task first and so on.

    Perform a comparative analysis of at least two scheduling algorithms:

    a. Round Robin
    b. Min-Min

6. Students will need to create or use a cloud simulator like CloudSim to implement these scheduling algorithms. They should generate reports on the key metrics (response time, makespan, energy consumption) and compare them across the three algorithms, emphasizing the strengths and weaknesses of each approach.

7. a. Average completion time:

    - The average completion time is the mean of the time taken for each task to complete.
    - Average completion time = Sum of completion times for all tasks/Number of tasks.
    - Total time for all tasks: $120 + 150 + 180 + 90 + 110 + 95 + 200 + 160 + 130 + 140 = 1375$ seconds.
    - Average completion time = $1375/10 = 137.5$ seconds.

    b. Throughput:

    - Throughput = Number of tasks completed/Total time taken for all tasks.
    - Makespan (total time) = 200 seconds (maximum time taken by any task).
    - Throughput = 10 tasks/200 seconds = 0.05 tasks per second.
    - This means 0.05 tasks are completed per second, or equivalently, five tasks are completed every 100 seconds.

    c. Utilization of the VMs:

    - Utilization = Total task time/(Number of VMs × Makespan).
    - Given:
        - Total task time = 1375 seconds
        - Number of VMs = 5
        - Makespan = 200 seconds
    - Utilization = $1375/(5 \times 200) = 1375/1000 = 1.375$.
    - Since utilization cannot exceed 1 (100%), the result suggests over-allocation of resources. Hence, the VM utilization is 100%, but it indicates that more VMs were allocated than necessary, leading to inefficient resource use.

Summary of Results:

- Average completion time = 137.5 seconds
- Throughput = 0.05 tasks per second
- VM Utilization = 100% (with over-provisioning)

A.2 Chapter 2

1. **FCFS scheduling:**

    - Task order (arrival order): 10, 4, 6, 3, 8
    - Waiting time (WT):
        - $WT1 = 0$
        - $WT2 = 10$
        - $WT3 = 10 + 4 = 14$
        - $WT4 = 14 + 6 = 20$
        - $WT5 = 20 + 3 = 23$
    - Average waiting time (AWT):

    $$\frac{0 + 10 + 14 + 20 + 23}{5} = 13.4 \text{ ms}$$

    - Turnaround time (TAT):
        - $TAT1 = 0 + 10 = 10$
        - $TAT2 = 10 + 4 = 14$
        - $TAT3 = 14 + 6 = 20$
        - $TAT4 = 20 + 3 = 23$
        - $TAT5 = 23 + 8 = 31$
    - Average turnaround time (ATT):

    $$\frac{10 + 14 + 20 + 23 + 31}{5} = 19.6 \text{ ms}$$

    SJF scheduling:

    - Task order (shortest job first): 3, 4, 6, 8, 10
    - Waiting time (WT):
        - $WT1 = 0$
        - $WT2 = 3$
        - $WT3 = 3 + 4 = 7$
        - $WT4 = 7 + 6 = 13$
        - $WT5 = 13 + 8 = 21$

A Solutions of Exercises

- Average waiting time (AWT):

$$\frac{0+3+7+13+21}{5} = 8.8 \text{ ms}$$

- Turnaround time (TAT):
  - TAT1 $= 0 + 3 = 3$
  - TAT2 $= 3 + 4 = 7$
  - TAT3 $= 7 + 6 = 13$
  - TAT4 $= 13 + 8 = 21$
  - TAT5 $= 21 + 10 = 31$

- Average turnaround time (ATT):

$$\frac{3+7+13+21+31}{5} = 15 \text{ ms}$$

2. Time quantum: 4 ms:

   - Task Burst Times: T1 $= 12$, T2 $= 5$, T3 $= 8$, T4 $= 6$, T5 $= 10$

   First cycle: Remaining burst times after first round:

   - T1 $= 12 - 4 = 8$
   - T2 $= 5 - 4 = 1$
   - T3 $= 8 - 4 = 4$
   - T4 $= 6 - 4 = 2$
   - T5 $= 10 - 4 = 6$

   Second cycle:

   - T1 $= 8 - 4 = 4$
   - T2 $= 1$ (completed)
   - T3 $= 4 - 4 = 0$ (completed)
   - T4 $= 2$ (completed)
   - T5 $= 6 - 4 = 2$

   Third cycle:

   - T1 $= 4 - 4 = 0$ (completed)
   - T5 $= 2$ (completed)

   Waiting times:

   - WT(T1) $= 15$ ms
   - WT(T2) $= 9$ ms
   - WT(T3) $= 13$ ms
   - WT(T4) $= 7$ ms
   - WT(5) $= 19$ ms

Average waiting time (AWT):

$$\frac{15 + 9 + 13 + 7 + 19}{5} = 12.6 \text{ ms}$$

Turnaround times:

- TAT(T1) = 27 ms
- TAT(T2) = 10 ms
- TAT(T3) = 16 ms
- TAT(T4) = 9 ms
- TAT(T5) = 21 ms

Average turnaround time (ATT):

$$\frac{27 + 10 + 16 + 9 + 21}{5} = 16.6 \text{ ms}$$

3. Pseudocode for genetic algorithm (GA):

   a. Initialize the population of solutions (chromosomes) with random task order.
   b. Evaluate the fitness of each chromosome. Fitness function:

   $$\text{Fitness} = \frac{\text{Priority}}{\text{Execution Time}} \text{ for each task.}$$

   c. Select pairs of parent chromosomes based on fitness.
   d. Perform crossover to generate new offspring.
   e. Apply mutation with a small probability to maintain diversity.
   f. Replace the old population with the new offspring.
   g. Repeat steps 2–6 until convergence or the maximum number of iterations is reached.

   Fitness calculation: The fitness function maximizes tasks with higher priority and lower execution time, encouraging faster and important tasks to be scheduled earlier.

4. Static scheduling (FCFS):

   - FCFS schedules tasks in the order of arrival and does not consider load or execution time.
   - In a cloud environment, varying loads can lead to resource underutilization or congestion.

   Dynamic scheduling (Round Robin):

   - Round Robin allocates equal time slices to tasks, balancing load more efficiently.
   - It is better suited for environments where workload varies.

A Solutions of Exercises

Conclusion: Round Robin tends to outperform FCFS in load balancing and resource utilization in dynamic environments.

5. Key parameters:

   - Pheromone evaporation rate: Controls how quickly the pheromone trail decays.
   - Initial pheromone level: Initial pheromone availability for task assignments.
   - Heuristic factor: Task priority based on execution time and resource demand.

   Algorithm evolution:

   - Ants initially explore random paths to assign tasks.
   - Over time, they favor paths with higher pheromone levels (efficient task schedules).
   - Less efficient paths evaporate due to pheromone decay.

   ACO evolves by balancing resource allocation, minimizing task execution time, and avoiding resource overload.

6. Adaptive scheduling: Adaptive scheduling adjusts dynamically based on the current system state, making it suitable for balancing multiple objectives.

   Practical example: In a cloud environment, the system could assign a weight of 0.6 to minimizing execution time and 0.4 to maximizing resource utilization, dynamically adjusting these weights as system conditions change.

7. a. Genetic algorithm (GA): Explain that GA uses ideas from natural selection to improve task scheduling:

   - Round Robin (RR): Explain that RR gives each task an equal share of time, ensuring fairness.

   b. Simulation/Model:

   - For GA, show how task allocation improves over time through generations.
   - For RR, show how tasks are processed in a fair, cyclic manner.

   c. Performance:

   - Execution time: Measure the time to complete all tasks for each algorithm.
   - Resource usage: Track how efficiently the CPU and memory are used.
   - Load balancing: Demonstrate how each algorithm spreads tasks across resources.

   d. Comparison:

   - GA may perform better for complex workloads but takes longer to process.
   - RR is simple and works well for tasks of similar size but struggles with very different tasks.

8. a. ACO implementation:

   - Use ants (virtual agents) to find the best way to assign tasks to resources, based on pheromone trails.

b. Parameter tuning:

- Test different pheromone values and evaporation rates to improve the ants' choices.

c. Comparison with SJF:

- Measure execution time, total time to finish all tasks (makespan), and resource usage efficiency for both algorithms.

d. Report:

- Show results in charts or tables and explain which algorithm performs better and why.

A.3 Chapter 3

1. - VM Technology: Discuss how Virtual Machines (VMs) enable efficient use of hardware by allowing multiple instances to run simultaneously.
   - Dynamic Resource Provisioning: Explain how this strategy adjusts resource allocation in real time based on changing workloads.
   - Load Balancing: Describe how it spreads the load evenly across servers to prevent overloading any single resource.
   - Create tables and charts to visualize the performance in different cloud scenarios.
2. - Assign resources based on the priority algorithm first and compute the total cost.
   - Reassign resources to dynamically prioritize Task C and calculate the new total cost.
   - Analyze the percentage reduction in cost by comparing the two scenarios.
3. - Use datasets of historical cloud workloads (can be simulated) to predict resource needs.
   - Train the model on workload characteristics like CPU and memory usage.
   - Validate the model using a test set, and analyze how well it can predict resource allocation.
   - Explain how machine learning-based predictions can optimize resource use in real time.
4. - Present a scenario where user demand varies, e.g., during flash sales.
   - Show how static provisioning can lead to resource over-provisioning or under-provisioning.
   - Demonstrate how dynamic provisioning adapts to changing demands, optimizing resource use and costs.
   - Use diagrams or graphs to illustrate differences in performance.

A Solutions of Exercises   209

5. • Explain how energy consumption in cloud data centers is a major cost factor.
   • Discuss energy-saving techniques like consolidating tasks onto fewer servers or adjusting voltage and frequency.
   • Use a case study or data from existing research to show the balance between reducing energy consumption and maintaining system performance.
6. • Describe the steps of the chosen heuristic algorithm (e.g., Genetic Algorithm: selection, crossover, mutation).
   • Set up a simulated environment where tasks arrive dynamically, and resources need to be allocated efficiently.
   • Run the simulation and compare the results (e.g., task completion time, resource usage) with a simpler method like FCFS.
7. • Discuss real-world scenarios where resources are reserved ahead of time (e.g., media streaming).
   • Compare the costs and benefits of reserving resources ahead of time versus dynamically provisioning them as needed.
   • Present charts to show how resource reservation improves user experience during peak times while also increasing costs.
8. • Discuss how QoS requirements can be defined (e.g., faster response time for premium users).
   • Create a prioritization scheme where premium users get more resources during high demand.
   • Simulate the model and evaluate whether it meets the QoS targets for both premium and regular users while maintaining efficient resource allocation.

A.4 Chapter 4

1. • HLB focuses on reducing energy usage by considering multidimensional resource constraints, while AHLB refines this by application-specific allocation.
   • Simulate traditional vs. innovative methods for VM placement and compare the performance based on throughput and energy usage.
   • Use a simple cloud simulation tool or VM workload simulation to generate data for analysis.
   • Plot graphs to show energy savings and throughput improvements.
2. • Distribute the incoming traffic based on server capacities using AHLB's adaptive allocation method.
   • Compare the results with a round robin allocation, where traffic is evenly distributed across servers without considering their capacities.
   • Calculate how much overflow traffic occurs in each scenario.
3. • Calculate energy consumption using the given formula for both HLB and random allocation.
   • Compare total energy consumption in both scenarios and demonstrate how HLB reduces energy usage.

- Show your results in a table for clarity.
4. - Use a cloud simulation tool like CloudSim to implement the AHLB model.
   - Define different application types (e.g., web services vs. video streaming) and allocate resources accordingly.
   - Compare performance metrics such as makespan (total task completion time) and resource utilization rates.
   - Visualize the improvements in a performance graph.
5. - Focus on how HLB and AHLB improve load distribution by using heuristic and adaptive methods.
   - Compare these models with Round Robin and Least Connections in terms of traffic overflow reduction and system stability.
   - Provide real-world examples or case studies to highlight the importance of these models in preventing bottlenecks.
6. - Use a simulated cloud environment where traffic intensity gradually increases.
   - Measure the impact on system performance by evaluating metrics such as makespan and throughput under different traffic conditions.
   - Demonstrate how AHLB maintains efficiency at high traffic intensities compared to traditional methods.
7. - Describe how HLB and AHLB can be extended to edge computing by considering the limited resources of edge nodes.
   - Discuss the integration of machine learning models for predicting workload and resource needs in IoT environments.
   - Mention challenges like real-time data processing and latency in applying these models to IoT.
8. - Explain the machine learning technique you plan to use, such as reinforcement learning for resource optimization.
   - Simulate how the learning algorithm adapts to changing workloads and optimizes resource usage in real time.
   - Compare the improved model's performance with the basic AHLB in terms of energy efficiency and traffic bottleneck reduction.

A.5 Chapter 5

1. Security threats in multi-tenant cloud environments:
   - Explain how side-channel attacks exploit shared resources and how VM escape enables attackers to break out of a VM to access the host.
   - Describe how RTIF's user identification mechanisms and intelligent resource allocation algorithms mitigate these risks.
   - Compare RTIF to conventional methods, such as isolation or encryption-based approaches, and highlight the advantages of RTIF's behavioral analysis.

A Solutions of Exercises

2. Mathematical modeling of RTIF for security optimization:

   a. Plug the given values into the utility functions for security and resource consumption:
      - $S = 100 - (0.7 \times 50)$
      - $R = 80 - 10$

   b. Calculate the security level and resource consumption:
      - $S = 100 - 35 = 65$
      - $R = 80 - 10 = 70$

   c. Analyze the results:
      The security level (S) is 65, and the resource consumption (R) is 70. This indicates that there is a balance between maintaining a moderate level of security while ensuring efficient resource utilization. RTIF's framework aims to achieve this balance by adjusting resource allocation based on the risk factor and overheads in the cloud environment. In situations where the risk factor increases or resource demands change, RTIF would dynamically adapt to ensure both security and performance are optimized, keeping resource consumption manageable while mitigating vulnerabilities.

3. Project-Based Exploration of RTIF's Load Balancing Algorithms:

   - Use a cloud simulation tool like CloudSim to define tenants with different access patterns and behaviors.
   - Implement RTIF's intelligent load balancing algorithm, considering historical data and behavioral analysis.
   - Collect data on resource utilization and security incidents and compare this to the results from a simpler round robin approach.

4. Security vs. efficiency trade-off in RTIF:

   - Discuss the challenges of maintaining security while optimizing for performance in cloud environments.
   - Highlight how RTIF's user profiling and load balancing strategies strike a balance between these objectives.
   - Provide examples of how performance may degrade slightly in favor of security in certain high-risk scenarios, and how RTIF mitigates this impact.

5. Case study on RTIF's performance in reducing side-channel attacks:

   - Simulate a side-channel attack, such as a cache timing attack, in a shared cloud environment.
   - Implement RTIF's behavioral profiling to detect abnormal access patterns.
   - Show how RTIF prevents the attack compared to a conventional security approach and analyze the differences in attack success rates.

212   A Solutions of Exercises

6. Comparative study of RTIF and conventional cloud security models:
   - Compare how RTIF's dynamic profiling and intelligent resource allocation offer more precise and adaptive security compared to static methods like role-based access control (RBAC).
   - Discuss VM isolation vs. RTIF's real-time profiling for preventing VM escape vulnerabilities.
   - Present pros and cons of each model in addressing specific cloud threats.

7. Future research directions for RTIF:
   - Explore how Blockchain could provide tamper-proof logs for RTIF's user profiling and access control.
   - Discuss the role of AI and machine learning in improving threat detection and adapting RTIF's resource allocation strategies.
   - Address challenges like the computational overhead of AI models or the scalability issues when integrating Federated Learning into RTIF.

A.6 Chapter 6

1. - Downtime reduction $= 8\% - (30\% \text{ of } 8\%)$.
   - Energy efficiency $=$ Current efficiency $+ 15\%$.
   - Discuss how MOVMO's impact can reduce operational costs in cloud systems.
2. - Provide a comparative analysis based on key performance indicators like resource utilization, job scheduling, and adaptability to workload changes.
   - Reference simulation results and discuss the benefits of multi-objective optimization.
3. - New resource utilization $= 70\% + (25\% \text{ of } 70\%)$
   - Discuss how ARAPM adapts to dynamic workloads and balances resource allocation.
4. - Use a cloud simulation tool (e.g., CloudSim) to model virtual machine placements.
   - Compare the makespan and energy efficiency before and after MOVMO is applied.
5. - Discuss ML techniques such as reinforcement learning or neural networks and how they can be used to predict workloads or optimize resource allocation.
   - Reference future research possibilities in edge and fog computing.
6. - Present a scenario with sudden spikes in user demand.
   - Discuss how probabilistic methods anticipate load changes and balance resources dynamically.
   - Compare this with traditional methods that may fail under heavy load.
7. - Peak hours: New utilization $= 90\% - (20\% \text{ of } 90\%)$.
   - Off-peak hours: New utilization $= 40\% + (30\% \text{ of } 40\%)$.

A Solutions of Exercises 213

- Discuss how balancing these fluctuations improves overall system performance.
8. • Energy savings = 500 kWh × 15%.
- Discuss the importance of energy efficiency in cloud environments and how MOVMO contributes to more sustainable cloud infrastructure.

A.7 Chapter 7

1. • New threat level = 80 − (40.63% of 80).
   • Analyze how SRDF optimizes security while keeping resource allocation efficient.
2. • New energy consumption = 1000 kWh − (25.89% of 1000 kWh).
   • Discuss the balance between energy efficiency and security measures in cloud systems.
3. • Use simulation results or case studies to compare key performance metrics like threat detection rate, resource efficiency, and energy usage.
4. • Explore the complexities of hybrid cloud setups, where private and public clouds coexist, and discuss how AMultiTD adapts to different operational needs while maintaining security and energy savings.
5. • Threat reduction = 120 − (40.63% of 120).
   • Energy reduction = 1500 kWh − (25.89% of 1500 kWh).
   • Explain how using both frameworks leads to an overall improvement in cloud performance.
6. • Use a cloud simulation tool (e.g., CloudSim) to test different scenarios and workloads. Compare the results with and without the use of SRDF and AMultiTD.
7. • Discuss the integration of AI/ML for dynamic resource allocation, predictive security measures, and how future advancements in network infrastructure (5G, IoT) could improve the effectiveness of these frameworks.
8. • Provide real-world or hypothetical data on energy savings and reduced threats, and discuss the long-term environmental and operational benefits.

A.8 Chapter 8

1. • Each key fragment = 256 bits/5 fragments = 51.2 bits per fragment.
   • Provide a step-by-step explanation of polynomial interpolation for key reconstruction in DEKM.
2. • New time = 180 seconds − (27.81% of 180 seconds).
   • Explain the impact of reducing key generation time on overall system performance and security in DEKM.
3. • New vulnerability rate = 40% − (27.81% of 40%).

- New threat detection time = 200 seconds − (43.61% of 200 seconds).
- Explain the role of distributed key management and insider threat detection in enhancing overall cloud security.

4.
- Explore and compare policies such as centralized key management, decentralized key management, and hierarchical key management.
- Discuss the pros and cons of each policy, particularly in DEKM-based cloud applications.

5.
- Use CloudSim to create a multi-tenant cloud environment and simulate data sharing and threat scenarios with and without DEKM and ITDA.
- Analyze the results to assess improvements in security, performance, and threat detection efficiency.

6.
- Explore the process of identifying potential threat agents in insider threat scenarios.
- Discuss the advantages and limitations of ITDA compared to traditional insider threat detection methods.

7.
- Investigate industries like healthcare, finance, or government sectors where sensitive data needs high-level security and insider threat protection.
- Provide real-world examples of how DEKM and ITDA could prevent data breaches and improve overall security posture.

8.
- Discuss the interaction between DEKM, ITDA, load balancing, and dynamic resource allocation.
- Provide examples of how adapting to changing workloads in a cloud environment can enhance both security and threat detection performance.

A.9 Chapter 9

1.
- Provide specific examples (e.g., how EHR systems store patient data securely in the cloud).
- Explore the advantages such as cost reduction, improved service delivery, and enhanced security protocols.
- Conclude by comparing the challenges faced in each sector, such as compliance with regulations (HIPAA in healthcare, PCI DSS in finance).

2.
- Outline the architecture of a cloud-based ERP.
- Discuss how cloud scalability benefits a growing enterprise.
- Evaluate security measures such as encryption for sensitive business data.

3.
- Explain cloud-IoT integration through use cases like smart homes (automated lighting, energy monitoring).
- Discuss the role of cloud in enabling edge devices to process data locally and send aggregated data to the cloud for further analysis.

4.
- Propose a system with content delivery networks (CDNs) for video streaming, databases for course materials, and authentication systems for secure access.
- Discuss how cloud scalability can accommodate thousands of concurrent users.

A Solutions of Exercises 215

5. - Explore how cloud computing enables real-time sharing of emergency data between authorities.
   - Provide examples of how cloud platforms manage disaster response, such as traffic management and emergency medical services coordination.
6. - New energy consumption $= 5000 \text{ kWh} - (15\% \text{ of } 5000 \text{ kWh})$.
   - Discuss how cloud systems use predictive analytics and real-time monitoring to optimize energy usage in the grid.
7. - New fraud cases $= 250 - (28\% \text{ of } 250)$.
   - Discuss how machine learning models hosted on cloud platforms analyze real-time transaction data to detect fraudulent patterns.

Glossary

Cloud Computing It is a concept for providing on-demand network access to a shared pool of customizable computing resources that can be quickly deployed and released with minimum administration effort or service provider engagement.

Energy Efficiency It optimizes energy usage in cloud computing systems. This includes measures for reducing power usage in data centers, such as effective resource allocation, server consolidation, and the use of renewable energy.

Hypervisor Software, firmware, or hardware used to generate and operate virtual computers. Hypervisors handle the virtualization of system resources, enabling numerous virtual machines (VMs) to operate on one physical computer.

Infrastructure as a Service (IaaS) A cloud computing service concept that delivers virtualized computer resources over the Internet. IaaS enables users to manage and control operating systems, storage, and installed applications while abstracting away the physical infrastructure.

Load Balancing It is the technique of dividing network traffic among numerous servers to avoid overloading a single server. Load balancing enhances application responsiveness and increases the availability of programs and websites to users.

Makespan It refers to the entire duration of a schedule or the time difference between starting and finishing a series of jobs or tasks. In cloud computing, minimizing makespan is often an important goal in task scheduling algorithms.

Multi-tenancy It allows a single software program to serve many consumers. Multi-tenancy enables cloud providers to service numerous clients using a single, shared infrastructure, hence increasing resource efficiency.

Platform as a Service (PaaS) A cloud computing service that offers a platform for users to design, operate, and admA cloud computing service concept that delivers virtualized computer resources over the Internet.

Quality of Service (QoS) It refers to a computer network's overall performance as perceived by users. In cloud computing, QoS refers to fulfilling certain standards of performance, dependability, and availability for cloud services.

Resource Allocation   The process of allocating and managing assets to fulfill an organization's strategic objectives. In cloud computing, this entails dividing computer resources like CPU, memory, and storage across several jobs and users.

Service Level Agreement (SLA)   A contract between a service provider and its clients outlining the services they will offer. In cloud computing, SLAs outline the anticipated level of service, including performance indicators and the repercussions of failing to fulfill them.

Security   measures safeguard systems from unauthorized access or attacks. In cloud computing, security entails safeguarding data, applications, and infrastructure from attacks, preserving privacy, and adhering to laws.

Software as a Service (SaaS)   A software licensing and delivery strategy in which software is licensed by subscription and centrally hosted. SaaS enables customers to access and utilize software programs over the Internet, eliminating the need for installation and maintenance.

Task Scheduling   It assigns work to resources that accomplish it. In cloud computing, job scheduling entails determining which activities should run on which resources in order to maximize performance and resource utilization.

Virtual Machine (VM)   It is an emulator of a computer system that has the same capabilities as an actual computer. Multiple operating systems may share a single physical host via virtual machines (VMs), each running its own operating system and applications.

Index

A
Adaptive resource allocation, 113
Application-aware load balancer, 76
Applications, 193

C
Cloud computing, 3
Cloud security, 90
Co-resident attacks, 136
Cost control, 10

D
Deployment model, 7
Dynamic load balancing, 18
Dynamic resource allocation, 50

E
Energy consumption, 153

F
First come first serve, 34
Future trends, 196

G
Glossary, 217
Grid computing, 3

H
Heuristic models, 112
Hierarchical load balancer, 68

I
Infra structure as a Service (IaaS), 8
Internet of things, 12

K
Key management, 162
Key orchestrator, 165

L
Load balancing, 10

M
Makespan, 152
Map reduce computation, 182
Maximum likelihood estimation, 123
Multi-objective vm optimizer, 122
Multi-tenancy attacks, 93

P
Performance, 11
Platform as a Service (PaaS), 8
Priority-based allocation, 60

Q
Quality of Service, 19

R
Resource provisioning, 14
Resource scheduling, 19

Resource utilization, 21, 154
Robust tenant identification, 97
Round robin scheduling, 40

S
Secure resource distribution, 137
Service model, 8
Sla violation rate, 22
Software as a Service (SaaS), 8
Static load balancing, 17

T
Task scheduling, 31
Throughput, 152

V
Virtualization, 2
Vm allocation policies, 140

The manufacturer's authorised representative in the EU is Springer Nature Customer Service Centre GmbH, Europaplatz 3, 69115 Heidelberg, Germany. If you have any concerns regarding our products, please contact ProductSafety@springernature.com

Printed and bound by CPI Group (UK) Ltd, Croydon, CR0 4YY
26/03/2026
02078953-0005